Media Writing

Also by the authors and published by Palgrave Macmillan

Craig Batty and Zara Waldeback, **WRITING FOR THE SCREEN: Creative and Critical Approaches**

Sandra Cain, **KEY CONCEPTS IN PUBLIC RELATIONS**

Media Writing

A Practical Introduction

Craig Batty
and
Sandra Cain

First published 2010 by
PALGRAVE MACMILLAN

Palgrave Macmillan in the UK is an imprint of Macmillan Publishers Limited, registered in England, company number 785998, of Houndmills, Basingstoke, Hampshire RG21 6XS.

Palgrave Macmillan in the US is a division of St Martin's Press LLC, 175 Fifth Avenue, New York, NY 10010.

Palgrave Macmillan is the global academic imprint of the above companies and has companies and representatives throughout the world.

Palgrave® and Macmillan® are registered trademarks in the United States, the United Kingdom, Europe and other countries

ISBN 978–0–230–21876–5

This book is printed on paper suitable for recycling and made from fully managed and sustained forest sources. Logging, pulping and manufacturing processes are expected to conform to the environmental regulations of the country of origin.

A catalogue record for this book is available from the British Library.

A catalog record for this book is available from the Library of Congress.

10   9   8   7   6   5   4   3   2   1
19   18   17   16   15   14   13   12   11   10

Printed in China

Contents

Acknowledgements

The authors would like to thank students and colleagues at both the University of Portsmouth and Southampton Solent University for their support and inspiration. They would like to thank their families and friends for their continued patience, belief and love. The authors would also like to offer special thanks to Amanda Greenwood for her research on newspaper writing, and Suzannah Burywood, Emily Salz and Beverley Tarquini at Palgrave Macmillan.

The authors and publishers would like to thank the following for kind permission to reproduce copyright material: the author and the University of Illinois Press for the use of Shannon and Weaver's 'Schematic diagram of a general communication system' from *The Mathematical Theory of Communication*, copyright © 1949, 1998 by the Board of Trustees of the University of Illinois; Elsevier for the use of the 'WHAT model' from Boyd *et al.*, *Broadcast Journalism*, copyright © 2008; Faber & Faber and FSG Books for the use of an excerpt from the screenplay *Almost Famous*. Every effort has been made to contact all the copyright-holders, but if any have been inadvertently omitted the publishers will be pleased to make the necessary arrangement at the earliest opportunity.

Introduction:
What is Media Writing?

This book is driven primarily by two key factors. Firstly, there has been a notable rise in the number of programmes based on media writing offered at university level, both in the UK and abroad. Many universities are now able to deliver programmes which combine a range of media and professional writing activities, and as such there is a need to write a book which caters for students of such programmes. Secondly, and moreover, is the desire to bring together a range of media writing forms which not only have their specific and distinct styles and practicalities, but which are seen to share crucial common features. Most media writing books on the current market tend to focus upon either one specific form of writing (journalism, public relations, screenwriting) or a group of seemingly related forms of writing (writing for print, writing for the Web). By bringing together a range of media writing forms in one book, the intention here is not merely to offer a broader scope than other books but to suggest that media writing can be understood as a discipline which boasts huge potential for crossover and the transferability of skills. In short, rather than a single-minded view of one or two forms of media writing, we are offering an exploration of a range of media writing practices which emanate from a set of flexible tools – tools of writing for any form of media.

In this way, 'media writing' can be understood as a concept, an umbrella term under which various forms of writing for media exist. As such, understanding how the concept of media writing operates and the generic traits that the forms of writing share will enable you, not only as a student but a future media writing practitioner, to develop a solid base of knowledge and skills useful across a range of writing practices. In other words, rather than solely developing an understanding of one or two forms of media

1

writing (PR and advertising, for example), examining what media writing actually *is* will give you the capability of writing across the range of forms available. After all, the writing industry is an ever-changing one and so being able to adapt to new and advanced forms, or just alternate between existing ones, is an extremely valuable aptitude.

To begin with this premise, we would like to offer some initial ideas towards an understanding of media writing as a *concept*, and the importance of studying the subject in such a way:

- It develops an understanding of the role of **communication** in the world, and how communicators (media writers) go about exchanging messages.
- It creates an awareness of the role of **story** with **purpose**: the need to 'say something' or have an argument that will affect the audience in some way.
- It identifies the need to carefully **shape** and **plot** writing in such a way that will be accessible to audiences and successfully relay the message (purpose).
- It defines the need for **persuasion** and **conviction**, the means by which the writer successfully exchanges the purpose of the written artefact.
- It encourages the notion of appropriate audience **address**, something crucial to any form of writing.

With this book, we aim to outline some of the key theories, principles and practical tools to aid your development as a media writer across a range of popular media writing forms. Each chapter will guide you through the main underpinning ideas and practices of that form, giving you the opportunity to experiment with writing processes and consider case studies to enhance your understanding of them. Although each chapter will focus upon a different form of media writing, we encourage you to make connections between the forms and understand how they share a common skill set (as highlighted above). To reiterate, one of the driving forces of this book is to bring together a range of writing forms and practices which, although they may appear different on the surface, share many key elements at their heart. Therefore, allowing connections to emerge between the various forms will undoubtedly foster a greater mastery of practice and hopefully develop better opportunities of securing work in the media writing industry. After all, today's market requires writers who are equipped with transferable skills and who are able to work flexibly across forms.

Task I.1

Choose the form of media writing that appeals to you most. Using the above list, make some brief notes about how this form embodies the ideas presented. You may find that at this stage your understanding is unclear; this is all right, but see how far you can get for now.

Media writing as communication

To give a broader context to the understanding of media writing, it is useful to look at some ideas from communication studies; after all, media writing is concerned with written (and complementary visual) ways of communicating messages. From news stories to advice columns, film scripts to radio advertisements, messages are exchanged via persuasive techniques to capture audiences who are willing to receive them. A media writer's job, therefore, is to understand this and act upon it, to send out written messages to 'attract and have an effect on large audiences' (Marsen, 2006: 9). This quotation reinforces what we outlined above: that all forms of media writing need a *purpose*. As we will detail in the following chapters, no matter which form of writing you are working in, it is imperative to know the intended outcome. This varies of course, from persuading an audience to buy a new product, to uncovering a truth with an investigative newspaper article, to using the power of character and dialogue to make an audience laugh. Whatever the form of writing in question, and however that form is constructed, the key concept is that it must have a purpose; once this is known, the media writer can begin to communicate this to the audience.

In her book on communication studies, Sky Marsen (ibid.: 3) provides some useful definitions of what communication actually is. Our aim in listing these below is to examine them and understand how they can be translated for writers, highlighting common themes which can be elaborated upon specifically for the act of media writing. These definitions of communication are, in her own words (and with references supplied by her):

- 'Social interaction through messages' (Fiske, 1990: 2).
- 'A process in which participants share information with one another in order to reach a mutual understanding' (Rogers, 1995: 35).
- 'An activity in which symbolic content is not merely transmitted from one source to another, but exchanged between human agents, who interact within a shared situational and/or discursive context' (Price, 1997: 5).
- 'A process whereby people in groups, using tools provided by their culture, create collective representations of reality' (Trenholm, 1993: 31).
- 'A process in which there is some predictable relation between the message transmitted and the message received' (Garber, 2003: 2).

These definitions share some common ground, namely a focus upon the exchanging of information and messages, the tools used to achieve this, and the way that audiences receive such information. As such, we can extract the core elements from these definitions and argue that the central theme to emanate from them is:

> **people use tools in order to relay messages to a given audience, the ideal result being that the messages are understood and interpreted as intended.**

This reinforces the above notions of **story, purpose, shape, plot, address, persuasion** and **conviction**: communication is about telling a story with a purpose, using the tools of shape, plot and address to persuade the audience that the story is correct (conviction). From these initial ideas, then, we can begin to broaden our knowledge of media writing as a concept and, as proposed, reinforce the notion that it has an inherent level of transferability.

Telling stories

Above all, we want to argue that the primary function of all writing is to tell a story with a purpose. In media writing, the meaning of 'story' is broad: it can be any kind of story, not merely an obvious one of fiction. There is a clear sense of story in a personal documentary (one's own story), in print or broadcast news (someone else's story), and even in advertising (the story of a product), and so we can see all these forms of media writing (and more) as a specific form of story-telling. Watson suggests that 'by our stories, as it were, shall we be known; and sometimes such stories have the power of myths to leave all facts – and often reality – behind' (1998: 130). This is a clear indication that, in whatever form we are writing, we are telling a story: ours, yours, theirs, someone's, something's. The interesting second part to Watson's quotation suggests that it is the underlying meaning that connects with us, the audience; the fact of the matter may exist (news story, historical fact, product feature), but it is the way which we interpret this into and onto ourselves that strikes the true chord. 'Story is both the oldest and the most universal form of interactive expression' (ibid.: 131), therefore it is story that enables the connection between the writing and its audience, between intention and interpretation. When telling such a story, the media writer has to make a series of decisions about what lies at the heart of the writing. For example, it is important to consider: what does an audience want to know? Furthermore, what does an audience *need* to know? In advertising, for example, the audience may want to know that a car can reach a top speed of a hundred and fifty miles per hour; however, the advertiser may think it more important to tell them that the car is ten miles per hour faster than the previous model. In a magazine feature, the reader may want to know what happened to a mother once her son was taken into care; the publisher may think it cannier to tell the reader how this tragically affected her emotional state. Whatever the decision about the underlying story, the writer must be aware of what it is so that he or she can then start telling the story in a suitable way, utilizing the tools of writing available to that specific form. Subsequently, although the way in which the narrative is put together is important, the actual story being conveyed is what drives the writer and the writing. As Watson concurs, 'story-within-discourse is essentially a conveyor of value, articulating meaning symbolically' (ibid.: 133); the story is thus the value of media writing, and the audience is expected to absorb this.

To highlight the importance of story value, here are some examples of media writing where the central purpose is to tell the audience a story about something which, ideally, they will understand, believe and perhaps act upon:

Undercover documentary

Stories in undercover documentaries are often used to make an audience angry, perhaps by showing the injustice of someone's actions. For example, the narrative could follow a 'cowboy builder' who is swindling elderly people out of their money, or a crooked bank manager who is selling customers worthless investment policies. The key idea here is that the audience is told a story of other people's misfortunes, where the intention is to reveal these 'criminal' people, make sure they are punished for their crimes, and make the audience aware of potential dirty deeds that they may come across.

Radio advertisement

Let us say that an advertisement is for a new soft drink: the story told, probably in the form of a voiceover narrator and perhaps some fictional characters, is one that will make the drink sound appealing and worth buying. The advertisement may allude to the value of buying the drink (what it will give to its consumers), and may even profess how it is better than other drinks on the market. The story here is of the product (the soft drink), selling its features and benefits with the intention of listeners agreeing that it sounds good and then going out to buy it.

Magazine travel feature

The writer in this case is telling the reader a story about a place. The feature article written will undoubtedly give positive information about the place, covering topics such as weather, hotels, facilities and places of interest to visit. Sometimes the writer may give the sense of being on a journey through the place, making the readers feel as if they are actually there, experiencing the same pleasures. The intention with such writing is that readers may feel the urge to go to the same place, signalling a demand that the story should probably be one of escapism: it should appeal to the reader's imagination and senses.

Campaign website

Websites can be a quick, cheap and effective way of telling a story that has a strong intention. Created by someone with a particular belief or viewpoint, the story in this case is of the cause being campaigned for. It will usually include background information of the cause, case studies to highlight the problem (perhaps using interviews) and, crucially, ways of solving the issue being faced. The intention is that those reading the website will agree with what is being suggested, and as a result will want to act upon the issue by joining the campaign.

Task 1.2

Choose any form of media writing. Read or view the material presented, and ask yourself the following: What is the story being told? Why is the story being told? Who is it being told by? What are the intended outcomes? Assessing this story intention, does it appear to be successful upon first reading?

Using narratives

Stories do not just tell themselves; they need a structure which contains the meaning of the story and, using the tools available, tells it to the audience. In other words, a story is only tellable if the person telling it uses a narrative. For the media writer, the use of narrative is central to the 'success' of the writing, the narrative here alluding to the writing's shape, structure and use of writerly technique. What we have to remember in all forms of media writing is that although the narrative may have different nuances, it still embodies the core need to tell a story with a purpose. Narrative thus acts as a way of framing or 'dressing up' a story in a form that suits its audience, using recognizable techniques (such as plot, character and language) to convince and persuade them to 'accept' the story. As Fulton *et al.* assert:

> In a world dominated by print and electronic media, our sense of reality is increasingly structured by a narrative. Feature films and documentaries tell us stories about ourselves and the world we live in. Television speaks back to us and offers us 'reality' in the form of hyperbole parody. Print journalism turns daily life into a story. Advertisements narrativise our fantasies and desires. (2005: 1)

This reminds us that narrative is central to everything we do in life, and because media writing features in all aspects of most people's lives, narrative has to be understood thoroughly before it can be applied in practice. Watson and Hill argue that the study of narrative is central to any form of communication, writing that questions of 'how [narratives] are put together, what their functions are and what uses are made of them by those who read, listen to or watch stories' (2007: 184) must be considered. In this sense, narrative in media writing is concerned with how the writing is structured, what purpose it possesses and how an audience will thus experience it.

Hence the study of media writing narratives has two fundamental elements to it: what is the narrative technique being used and what does it seek to do? Or, what writerly techniques does the writer employ in the writing and what is trying to be achieved by using them? Once more we are brought back to the notion of story and the idea of narrative as a mode of storytelling. If narrative as 'story mode has the power to bring about a sense of shared experience and of shared values' (ibid.), then the media writer uses the best narrative possible in order to capture the audience and make the story believable/accepted/felt. So, whether using characters and visual symbolism in film to tell the protagonist's story, or spoken facts and a jingle in a TV advertisement to tell the product's story, narrative is employed to achieve the desired audience effect. As an example, Watson discusses the use of narrative in news production. He writes: 'the more we examine news production the more it resembles the process which produces fiction; that is, the creative process' (1998: 131). Here Watson posits that print and broadcast news is not actually a form of writing that merely draws together known facts; rather, it creatively organizes the facts of an issue, event, person, etc. and offers an interpretation of them. In other words, a narrative is created using the 'real' facts, and the audience is told a story rather than merely given information. This of course brings to the fore notions of objectivity and subjectivity: can news be objective if it is someone's story? Is storytelling itself dictated by subjectivity? Although here we do not intend to explore such ideological concerns, the fact remains that in news, as in any form of media writing, a narrative *must* be constructed in order to tell the story effectively.

Fulton *et al.* take a pretty dim view of media's use of narrative. They argue that narrative is nothing more than a form of representation which can be seen as a way of manipulating audiences into believing stories, purely for commercial reasons: 'the economic function of the media, to generate profit, undermines the idea of narrative as some kind of innate or universal structure common to all humanity. Narrative in the media becomes simply a way of selling something' (2005: 3). Although we would argue that this is not so cut-and-dried, and in fact audience experience of media can be personally fulfilling and rewarding, the idea of media narratives 'selling something' is useful for consideration. As we have already discussed, the purpose of media writing is to tell a story with a purpose, and although that purpose may not always be to sell something in financial terms, the purpose is always to sell an idea or an ideal.

Task 1.3

Take a newspaper and read one of its main stories. What do you think the article is trying to 'sell'? Is it a point of view, or a truth, or an ideal? Look at the way the article is constructed and try to work out why the writer has written the article in that way. Are there any noticeable techniques?

If story, purpose and narrative bind all forms of media writing together, then it is in the specific narrative deployment that each form takes its own shape and direction. These specific shapes and directions will be explored thoroughly in the main chapters of this book, but for now it is useful to give an indication of some of them.

Once more, although every form of media writing approaches narrative technique in a specific way, they all sit together under a wider umbrella of common narrative techniques.

- **Plot**. This is the way in which the story is shaped or structured. In a film or TV drama, structure usually adheres to a common 'model' where the plot has a familiar, mainstream pattern. Feature articles, press releases and advertisements, for example, similarly conform to a tried-and-tested structure. Whatever the form, audiences usually expect the writing to be shaped in a particular way so that it can be understood. Some writers experiment and 'defy the rules', but for now it is most useful to think in traditional terms.
- **Character/subject**. In fictional media writing this means the person(s) created to tell the story: protagonist, antagonist, etc. In factual forms, such as documentary or broadcast news, characters become subjects. Subjects are those the story is about: who is featured, who is being interviewed, who is the expert giving advice? Sometimes the writer has a presence in the writing, such as a narrator (documentary, feature article). This too is character, where the writer as first-person character guides the audience through the narrative.
- **Language and voice**. If there is a narrator or announcer in the writing, then this literally means the language and voice that he or she is using. There may be a specific tone to try and catch the audience's attention (seductive), or it may be that the wording is employed for a particular effect (humorous, silly, authoritative). What is important with language and voice is its effective use to connect with the audience, make them want to continue reading or listening to the story, and persuade them to accept what is being told.
- **Address**. Linked closely to language and voice, address is the overall tone and style that an audience is 'spoken to' by the writing. The underlying tone is that of persuasion, but usually this is not so evident on the surface. For example, the tone may be humorous but with a hidden, darker message. Style is the way in which this tone is presented, through writerly techniques. Examples include: as a truthful, 'authority figure' in news reporting; as a

friendly, sister-like advisor in women's magazines; as a seductive temptress in television advertising.

- **Layout**. In print forms of media writing, layout is integral to how the story is shaped and presented to the reader. Newspapers are divided into columns for easy reading and have attractive front covers which are designed to appeal to the reader's eye and also give a glimpse of what will be featured inside. Magazines are similar, with glossy, colourful covers featuring eye-catching words (Scandal! Shock! Sex!) and images (celebrities, tragedies). Articles often integrate images which help to narrate, if not dramatize, the story.

- **Imagery**. Images can say more than words; but often it is the connection between image and text that bears real significance. In advertising, key words are used alongside images to reinforce something important about the product or service. Images tell stories in thematic, metaphorical ways too, such as film's use of *mise en scène* (visual arrangement of a scene) to denote character, theme, mood and genre. In this way, we can think about images as having their own language, speaking to an audience on a different level, yet one complementary to the written word.

Task I.4

Go back to the newspaper story from the above task and reconsider it in light of the narrative techniques outlined above. Can you identify some or all of the techniques? How effective are they?

Persuading and convincing

The narrative techniques outlined above serve the core purpose of persuading. The story in the writing has a purpose, and an audience needs to be convinced of this by the writer's use of persuasive techniques. As Berger outlines in his discussion of magazine advertisements' use of rhetoric (persuasion), the techniques deployed 'are stimuli designed to evoke appropriate responses' (1998: 68) in the reader, and meaning 'is what a [reader], listener or viewer gets *out* of his experience with the communicator's stimulus' (Schwartz, cited in Berger, ibid.). Narrative techniques, then, are stimuli positioned within the text in order to create the desired effect: an appreciation of the story being told, and an agreement of or an action derived from the writing's purpose.

Conviction of meaning (purpose) is thus key to all forms of media writing. Sometimes an idea may be flawed or not properly considered, but if it is convincing and shows promise, then it may be accepted in principle. As with creative writing, a lot of time is spent in developing and drafting media writing artefacts, so even in the early stages of production it is vital that conviction prevails. It may seem obvious, but if someone commissioning work is not convinced by your ideas, then it is unlikely that your work will be commissioned. Persuasion, conviction and rhetoric thus become strong currency in the world of media writing, constantly building upon ideas and concepts to drive towards the perfectly finished product. It is, then, the job of the media writer to ensure that the best possible use is made of all relevant narrative techniques, during all stages of development; after all, an argument with no holes to prise open is an argument hard to disagree with.

Writers write!

Just like creative writers, media writers must practise their writing skills in order to improve technique. The end result of a media writing project (a PR package, a news programme) may be different from that of a creative writing project (a collection of poems, a novel), but the process is not always so different. Screenwriters, journalists, publicists and copywriters must *all* develop their craft through constant writing practice, whether that be working on numerous small-scale projects in the first instance or undertaking regular writing exercises to keep the writerly brain going. In fact, we would urge all media writers habitually to engage in writing of some sort, because good writing often comes from much writing. As an example, even before the first draft of a media writing project is formulated, engaging with writing of some sort (free-writing, letter writing, blogging, poetry) will focus the brain's attention on structure, style and language, and will prise open the writer's creativity. From this, the media writer can then use the experience of writing openly and creatively in order to focus upon the project in hand, perhaps now being able to find the right structure, style, detail, angle, etc. Most creative writing textbooks have a raft of useful exercises in them, so this may be a good place to start.

Research for media writers

Although, then, media writing can involve creativity and creative thinking, it is essential that the media writer possesses strong research skills. University study certainly facilitates the development of research skills, where students in any subject develop a range of transferable skills such as: sourcing relevant materials (books, journal articles, websites, people); using databases; filtering information; bringing facts, figures and viewpoints together to make a coherent argument; and problem solving. There are various ways in which such research skills feed directly into the practice of media writing. For example:

> the extent to which we feel ourselves to be part of an audience depends on whether or not we feel addressed by a media text. Does it speak to us directly? Does it use a language we recognise as ours? Do we feel included in the world view and attitudes articulated by the text? (Fulton *et al.*, 2005: 5)

Here we are reminded that research into audience is absolutely crucial. If you wish to capture, entertain or fascinate your audience, then you have to make sure that you absolutely understand your audience in order to achieve this. As Berger notes, 'you should write with a sense of obligation to your readers' (1998: 134). Writers, therefore, cannot second guess their audience and hope that the writing will appeal; they must know the audience, research other writing in the field targeted at that audience, and perhaps even undertake primary research (interviews, focus groups) to understand the audience more fully and the kind of writing that would appeal to them. After all, 'in order to get people to read something you have written, you must take pains to attract their attention, gain their interest, and make it easy (and desirable) for them to continue reading' (ibid.: 123). Audience research is just one crucial area that a media writer needs to research; others can be summarized as:

- Depending on the form of writing, **facts and figures** may have to be researched. In writing derived from actual truth (news, documentary, public relations), facts and figures must be accurate and easily proven. If anything untrue is stated as truth, then the writer (and employer) is culpable. Written apologies may have to be produced, at least; at worst, legal proceedings may be taken. Even in fictional forms which draw from but do not rely upon facts and figures, keeping as near to the truth as possible will result in a more ethical, honest and trusted piece of writing.

- As such, relevant **legalities** may have to be researched by the writer. In news writing especially, writers must ensure that they do not say anything that could be construed as illegal. There are numerous books on law for journalism, for example, which are not only useful for writers working in that form, but essential.

- Writers really need to undertake research into their intended **publication** or **broadcast medium**, and the industry **market** more generally. For example, an aspiring television scriptwriter should research broadcasters and independent production companies who may be interested in their type of work. Similarly a magazine feature writer must research the magazine market and identify possible outlets for his or her work, considering the type of work they commission and their house style. It is vitally important that writing is pitched to the right people; so research of this nature will save valuable time and effort in avoiding rejections. Books such as the annual *Writers' and Artists' Yearbook* and *The Writer's Handbook* are an invaluable source for this kind of information.

- The **institutions** publishing and producing written work are also useful to research. In this sense, writers can find out what is currently happening in their particular field and how their writing may change according to this. Examples include: new chief executives or directors with new agendas for a company's future; new laws or policies that may affect content; changes to procedures for applying for funding; mergers with other companies which may affect publication or production processes.

- The **craft** of writing is something any aspiring writer must research; and, not only in the early stages of a writing career, but throughout. New discoveries about writing practice and form are always emerging, so it is vital for a writer to be aware of the latest developments. With this, it is also important to research a variety of craft methodologies, eventually finding one or two that are personally the most effective. This way, working with a range of craft approaches may result in a fresher and somewhat original way of working.

- As part of craft research, it is useful to research **other writers** and the approaches that they take. Whether through reading interviews or attending workshops and masterclasses, other writers' perspectives offer valuable personal insights, hints and tips, and often a sense of inspiration.
- **Wider contexts** of writing, such as cultural positioning, audience reception and social constraints, offer a level of research which can actually have a startling impact upon writing. Rather than seeing such research as 'academic' and merely 'theoretical', writers should embrace opportunities for investigating wider ideas and contexts in which media writing is positioned. According to John Fowles, writers are a combination of the 'wild man' and the 'academic': 'the wild man gathers details of the story via associations, via the imagination and through the fickle rambling process of trying to form a narrative of events. The academic tends to the pruning of what is produced, but also gathers other forms of knowledge, the elements that lie outside the writer's direct knowledge' (cited by Neale, 2006: 65). Together, wild man and academic form the fabric of a successful writer.

As can be seen, media writers must be extremely perceptive to information relevant to their work, and actively seek to find solutions to potential problems. Rather than viewing research as dry, boring or even detached from the writing process, we would like to argue that it is actually enriching and can be very fruitful. In some cases, research is absolutely vital; in others, it adds a valuable dimension to the work, and can even spark fresher, more original ideas.

Using this book

The remainder of this book is now dedicated to an exploration of seven key forms of media writing: Print Journalism: Newspapers;

Print Journalism: Magazines; Broadcast Journalism; Public Relations and Media Relations; Copywriting and Advertising; Screenwriting: Fiction; and Screenwriting: Fact. Each chapter will introduce some of the key theories and concepts supporting the practice of writing in these forms, using a range of practical tools and applied case studies to offer a grounded, contemporary understanding. The chapters will begin by outlining a set of 'learning outcomes' for each area of study, which are intended to set out key goals to be reached by working through the material provided. The positioning of creative and critical tasks throughout the chapters is intended to encourage independent learning and reflection, and guidance on careers features at the end of each chapter to highlight some of the job opportunities that are available and possible ways of achieving them. These seven chapters are then followed by a conclusion which reconsiders the impact that digital technology has had upon media writing. Although the practicalities of writing digitally are embedded into the seven chapters, we purposefully want to use the conclusion to reflect more philosophically upon some of the changes that have taken place, and are still taking place, within the sphere of media writing. It is difficult to call this the 'future' of media writing because the future is happening right now; however, a conclusion that speculates upon the impact of digital technology is necessary to highlight both the changes themselves and their respective contextual debates.

We really hope that you enjoy working through this book and find it useful in your aim of working as a media writer. If there is one final thing we would encourage, it is this: be open minded to all forms of media writing and consider the transferability of skills. Writing is a very popular and thus very competitive industry, and we all have to start somewhere.

Print Journalism: Newspapers

News stories are about people and situations; they tell us what happened to someone, where, when, how and why; they have a particular angle and are driven by topicality; they use short, simple sentences, written in the active voice, and are embedded with facts, statistics and quotations; overall, news stories relate to us emotionally because they comment upon the world that we are living in. This first chapter will thus guide readers through the practices and processes undertaken by a journalist aspiring to write for a newspaper that seeks to epitomize truth, balance and moral integrity. It will chart the 'journey' of a newspaper journalist, from a consideration of the qualities required to 'succeed', to the actual hands-on procedures for sourcing, researching and writing the news story.

By the end of this chapter, you should be able to:

- Understand the role of a journalist, and what qualities are usually desired.
- Recognize ethical considerations of newspaper journalism and begin to apply them to a proposed news story.
- Evaluate the importance that news values play in constructing a news story.
- Recognize the uses and limitations of the different ways that news stories are sourced.
- Understand how news stories are structured and apply to them the appropriate newspaper language.
- Demonstrate a familiarity with other types of newspaper writing, such as the feature, review and personal column.

The newspaper landscape

There are numerous types of newspaper in circulation across the globe, each having their own distinctive style and purpose. In Britain, Harris and Sparks broadly classify these as: 'tabloid dailies for readers who want to be entertained as well as informed; quality dailies with a mostly better-educated, often professional readership; specialist papers such as the *Financial Times*; town evening papers serving big conurbations; county weeklies spreading across counties' (1997: 4). Here we are presented with a range of newspapers that are published concurrently (daily or weekly), each one vying for the reader's attention. Sparks reminds us that 'newspapers in Britain are first and foremost businesses ... They exist to make money, just as any other business does' (1999: 46), and as such this is why newspaper 'branding' is important: a way of knowing what kind of information will be presented in a newspaper before it is even purchased. If we consider national daily newspapers, there are obvious brands available, normally associated with the level of 'quality' on offer to readers. We would, for example, expect to associate *The Times*, *Daily Telegraph*, *the Guardian*, *the Independent* and *Financial Times* with the 'quality market'; the *Daily Mail* and *Daily Express* with the 'mid market'; and *The Sun*, *Daily Mirror* and *The Star* with the 'popular market'. Internationally, the quality market would include *The Wall Street Journal*, *The Australian* and *Le Monde*; the mid market *USA Today* and *Chicago Sun-Times*; and the popular market *New York Post*, *Herald Sun* and *Bild*. Although it may seem obvious that newspapers should be suitably branded in order to appeal to their target readership, it should never be underestimated, especially for a journalist wishing to write for one. Newspapers offer a sense of 'togetherness' and kinship with regards to a given news story, and so it is crucial that the content and style of the writing offers this to readers. For Sparks, 'it is quite understandable that most people would prefer to read about things that matter to them and which they might influence, rather than the arcane of power over which they have no real power' (1999: 54). In other words, readers of a newspaper have to feel that they share the views being presented on the page, and that those views empower them, not disempower them.

In one way, the newspaper market could be viewed as overly saturated with titles; in another way, this could be viewed as useful because it allows a freedom of choice and a range of 'voices' to be heard. In such a highly populated newspaper market, then, it is important that journalists know what the newspaper(s) they write for is about (attitude, point of view), the style and form that it takes (voice, approach), and who it is aimed at (readership). In crude terms, 'newspapers must pander to the needs and expectations of readers' who become loyal to them and 'understand the languages and read "their" newspaper expecting to agree with its comments and opinions' (Pape and Featherstone, 2005: 50).

Task 1.1

Choose three newspapers from those listed above and identify the 'brand' that they offer. Who is expected to read this newspaper? How is this obvious from the style of writing? What attitudes and points of view are presented? How is this obvious from the content?

According to Randall:

> A newspaper's role is to find out fresh information on matters of public interest and to relay it as quickly and as accurately as possible to readers in an honest and balanced way. That's it. It may do lots of other things, like telling them what it thinks about the latest movies, how to plant potatoes, what kind of day Taureans might have or why the government should resign. But without fresh information it will be merely a commentary on things already known. Interesting, perhaps, stimulating even; but comment is not news. Information is. (2000: 22)

This is a useful summary to remind us that newspapers are exactly that: sheets of paper that contain *news*; and news is *new* information, not a regurgitation of old information. To this end, the content of a newspaper should be surprising and dramatic (Harris and Sparks, 1997: 3), pulling readers into a discussion of something they do not yet know about; it is like the divulging of a secret, or in the case of tabloid newspapers, salacious gossip. News, according to Roshco, is a consequence of the human desire 'to know the state of the surrounding social and physical environment. "What's the news?" is a concise way of asking either two questions: "What has happened that I didn't anticipate?" or "What is likely to happen that I haven't anticipated?"' (1999: 33). Usually in newspapers, a central subject or 'character' is the agent through which we learn about our social and physical environment; a story told about how a human being is embroiled in or affected by the situation, or a story told through the eyes of someone involved. According to Harris and Sparks, readers of newspapers 'identify with people in trouble: they are intrigued by those involved in controversy, with people at the centre of great events' (1997: 5). This places importance upon the role of a subject in a news story and how readers need *someone* rather than *something* to connect with in order to make the world intelligible.

The basic fabric of all news stories is answering a series of questions: who, what, where, when, why and how? Such questions reinforce a desire in the reader to know things; to find out things about the world in the quickest way possible. A news story will thus present: 'who has the story happened to? What has happened to them? The best stories will also tell the reader where it happened, why it happened, when it happened and how it happened' (Pape and Featherstone, 2005: 21). It is interesting to consider why we thrive on news stories. Why do we want or need to know what is going on in the world? How does it affect us, personally? Specifically for the writer, why do we want to tell people what is going on in the world? How does it make us feel that our stories are being read by others? Whatever the answers to these questions, one fact remains: our culture thrives on telling stories, and in the specific case of newspapers these stories have a massive impact upon how we live our lives:

> How we dress for work, sometimes the route we take to work, what we plan to do this weekend, our general feelings of well-being or insecurity, the focus of our attention toward the world beyond immediate experience, and our concerns about the issues of the day all are influenced by daily news. (McCombs, 1998: 25)

The role of the journalist

'People use the news to help them make up their minds so they can function as informed citizens' (Burns, 2002: 50), and as such the role of the journalist in society is extremely important. Journalists are not just writers who create stories that they hope are read and enjoyed by people; they are writers whose words and opinions on a subject matter can dictate how people think and feel, ultimately shaping the way that the world moves forward. According to Bromley, journalists have commonly seen themselves as 'narrators, social observers and authors of the "first draft of history"' (1994: 39), which undoubtedly makes the role of a journalist more than a mere mortal. Fletcher cites a 2003 YouGov poll which considered how people view journalists:

> The survey of around 2,000 people discovered that broadsheet journalists were among the most trusted of all members of the population. Reporters from ITV, Channel 4 News and the BBC were ranked closely together, sandwiched between local police officers on the beat and head teachers in state schools. They were ahead of vicars and priests. (2005: 12)

This tells us not only that some newspaper journalists are deemed 'the purveyors of truth' but that the general public actually turns to the work of journalists in order to glean an accurate view of the world. This raises the notion that a journalist must consider the relationship that exists between being ethical, authentic and responsible, with that of being business-minded and somewhat 'ruthless'. In fact, Burns notes that a challenge for the modern journalist is 'to find a way to negotiate the often-competing professional, commercial and ethical considerations involved in finding and presenting news … It is a complex business – trying to please your editor, your employer, yourself, and the whole audience' (2002: 7). A fuller discussion of ethics will follow below, but for now it is important to consider that issues of censorship (self- and external) are integral to the role of a 'good' journalist.

Above all, the role of a journalist is to question: to question the world and to question people's actions in the world. By doing so, according to Randall (2000: 3), he or she will:

- Discover and publish information that replaces rumour and speculation.
- Resist or evade government controls.

- Inform, and so empower, voters.
- Subvert those whose authority relies on a lack of public information.
- Scrutinize the action and inaction of governments, elected representatives and public services.
- Scrutinize businesses, their treatment of workers and customers, and the quality of their products.
- Comfort the afflicted and afflict the comfortable, providing a voice for those who cannot normally be heard in public.
- Hold up a mirror to society, reflecting its virtues and vices and also debunking its cherished myths.
- Ensure that justice is done, is seen to be done and investigations carried out where this is not so.
- Promote the free exchange of ideas, especially providing a platform for those with philosophies alternative to prevailing ones.

As can be seen from this list, a journalist functions on many levels, but all of them aiming to provide fact and a sense of truth, disempower those who abuse their power, and help the 'common man' to assert his voice. News stories that take these facets into account can always strive to be a pure reflection of the day's events, but of course they can never be one hundred percent so because the stories are constructions made by the journalist. When researching a story 'there are usually several contending voices, each claiming to have expert knowledge and providing conflicting accounts ... The journalist plays a key role in disentangling these claims and simplifying complex ideas for the "lay" public' (Anderson, 1997: 57). The journalist can thus be understood as a mediator, negotiating between different sources of information and then offering what he or she believes to be a 'real' account. McCombs offers the analogy of an onion to allude to such a process: 'the core of the onion, the daily news report, is surrounded and shaped by several layers of influence. At the outer layer are the news makers and events, including the pseudo-events arranged for news coverage that provide much of the grist for daily news' (1998: 33).

Finally here, let us outline the various roles of the newspaper journalist. Many journalists will, during their career, work across a range of levels, perhaps starting as an in-house general reporter, then specializing in a particular area (crime, politics, entertainment, etc.), and progressing through the ranks up to editor. The following list offered by Pape and Featherstone (2005: 2–7) summarizes these roles:

- **Editor:** the one who has overall control of the newspaper. They will decide upon content, style and tone.
- **Deputy editor:** one grade below the editor, but may share many of the same day-to-day duties and responsibilities.
- **Assistant editor:** may perhaps look after supplements or a particular department.
- **News editor:** in charge of handling all news stories, and may also control the news desk where story ideas come in.
- **Subeditors:** their remit includes making sure that all copy is accurate and matches the house style, and controlling the overall page layout.
- **Reporters:** journalists who find and write stories, often travelling around to find information. They can be employed either in-house or freelance.
- **Specialists:** journalists who specialize in a particular area of reporting, or who are attached to an on-going event (war, business, politics, etc.).
- **Advertising sales staff:** not a journalism job as such, but one undertaken by many graduates as a first step into the industry. The role involves selling advertising space to customers, creating revenue for the newspaper.

What makes a good journalist?

A journalist must have an extremely strong sense of story. That is to say, he or she must be able to see an underlying meaning to a given situation, and know instinctively how this will relate to the emotions of a reader. Whether the corruption lurking beneath a publicly funded organization, the sad truth about a celebrity's demise into ruin, or the sheer gusto and might of a dying mother, finding the emotional heart to a story 'is what makes journalism such a rewarding profession – in reporting what is important and newsworthy, journalists have an opportunity to draw to the public attention matters that might otherwise be ignored' (Pape and Featherstone, 2005: 17).

As already highlighted, there can be a fine line between objectivity and subjectivity, truth and entertainment, and so it is the journalist's remit to handle a given story in such a way that it is honest with facts yet at the same time appealing to the reader's curiosity. In short, the journalist must consider how *newsworthy* a story is; what value does it possess, and is it something readers want or need to hear about?

Bearing this in mind, it is useful to summarize some key 'qualities' of a good journalist. The following list, provided by Randall (2000: 4–9), should work to illuminate whether journalism is really the career path wanting to be followed:

- Keen news sense.
- Passion for precision.
- Never make assumptions.
- Never be afraid to look stupid.
- Be suspicious of all sources.
- Leave your prejudices at home.
- Realize you are part of a process.
- Empathy with readers.
- The will to win.
- Sense of urgency.
- Individuality.
- Determination.
- A bit of cheek.

As well as these interior qualities, it is worth also considering some exterior qualities essential to journalism. As we all know, journalism is a fast-paced, highly pressured and often 'cut-throat' environment, and as such a journalist must always be capable of meeting the specific requirements of the industry. Clayton characterizes such exterior qualities as 'the professional approach', which are defined as: reliability; producing consistently high-standard work; achieving deadlines; always arriving punctually for appointments; checking that all facts are correct, including places, times, dates and the spelling of names; writing work to specified word lengths and presenting it in the most easily and quickly assimilated manner (2000: 9). Fletcher quotes Sarah Sands, then the Deputy Editor and Saturday Editor of the *Daily Telegraph*, who gives a list of what to do and what not to do when working in the industry (2005: 72). This is an invaluable resource for the media writer wishing to enter journalism: hints and tips coming straight from the editor's mouth:

What to do:
- Cockiness.
- Offer to do anything – run errands, get tea, stand on doorsteps, night or Sunday shifts.
- Generosity – credit contribution from others.
- Drink with colleagues (but don't get a reputation!).
- Always look alert and ready.
- Avoid becoming aggrieved when colleagues seem to be getting further than you.
- Work harder.
- Develop resilience and treat every setback as a springboard.
- Humour.
- Use the gloominess of old timers to emphasize your own cheerfulness.

What not to do:
- Too much cockiness.
- Moaning.
- Negativity.
- Looking for reasons why stories can't work rather than reasons why they can.
- Getting yourself on the press junket to Barbados.

Task 1.2

Look at all of the qualities listed above and write down which ones you feel describe you. Look at the ones that do not describe you, and consider whether these would have a negative impact upon your potential as a journalist.

Ethics

As briefly highlighted above, ethics form a crucial part of a journalist's working life. A common debate related to this is the dichotomy between serving 'the public interest' and serving 'what the public is interested in'. For example, the public might be interested in the sexual exploits of an MP, but do they have a right to know them? Similarly, the public might not be wholly interested in what bank bosses are being paid in bonuses, but should they indeed know about this? Burns highlights this notion of 'in the public interest' by telling us that 'it is served by telling an audience things they need, or have a right to know. As part of deciding whether something is in the public interest, you must decide if telling the story could harm anyone, and if this harm is justified' (2002: 54). For Clayton: 'remember, you are a camera. Go and observe. Report the facts as you see – no more. Never overestimate the readers' knowledge, never underestimate their intellect. Give the general public the truth and let their integrity do the rest' (2000: 24). What remains an integral facet to the working journalist, then, is a full consideration of truth and integrity to readers. Of course, journalists will always have a point of view towards a news story, but if they allow this to take over the facts in hand and become too personally involved, they will produce nothing but propaganda. As McCombs reminds us:

> After all, it is not the goal of professional journalists to persuade anybody about anything. The canons of objectivity, which have dominated professional journalistic practice and thought for generations, explicitly disavow any effort at persuasion. This is not to say that the news stories of the day are not exactly that, new *stories*. They are indeed! And like all stories, they structure experience for us, filtering out many of the complexities of the environment and offering a polished, perhaps even literary, version in which a few objects and selected attributes are high-lighted. (1998: 26)

The ethically ideal model of truth, balance and integrity is evident from the much-used metaphor of mining: 'journalists *dug* for the facts (often described as *nuggets* of information) which lay hidden until they brought them into *light*. Regardless of the consequences, the journalist's prime duty was discovery and revelation. This placed a premium on accuracy, as inaccurate information was effectively of no public use' (Bromley, 1994: 101). So, rather than purposely aiming to promote their agendas in everything they write, journalists should work independently of themselves, of their own views, beliefs, experiences and any 'unprofessional' links with third-party organizations. This relates closely to the idea that the media should act as the Fourth Estate: it should 'reflect public interest and not be aligned to government or powerful social groups. According to this view the media operate relatively independently and are not, in any major sense, mouthpieces of the state' (Anderson, 1997: 46). Although, as will be discussed later, it is sometimes difficult to escape the notion of subjectivity and personal agenda, this idea of newspapers being part of the Fourth Estate should be duly considered by anyone wishing to enter the print journalism industry.

With this in mind, the following ethical guidelines are offered by Randall (2000: 134–8) to all practising and would-be journalists:

- Journalists should serve only their papers and their readers.
- Every story should be an honest search for the truth.
- No inducements to publish should be accepted.
- Journalists should not allow advertisers to influence, directly or indirectly, the paper's editorial content.
- Do not use your position to threaten or gain advantage.
- Do not promise to suppress stories for friendship or favours.
- Do not invent or improve information.
- You should not benefit personally from information you acquire.

As well as ethical considerations, legalities affect journalists (indeed, all media writers), which are complex and constantly changing. In magazines and newspapers, the work of staff writers is checked for libel by media lawyers; the work of freelancers, however, can slip through the net, resulting in lengthy, embarrassing and costly court trials. All media writers should have access to an up-to-date copy of Welsh et al.'s *McNae's Essential Law for Journalists* and Tom Crone's *Law and the Media*, as well as reading the Codes of Practice from the National Union of Journalists (NUJ) and the Press Complaints Commission (PCC).

Copyright

Copyright is a set of exclusive rights which regulate the use of a particular creative work or expression of an idea or information. It exists in a wide range of creative, intellectual or artistic forms. Copyright law only covers the form in which ideas have been manifested; it does not protect the actual idea, concept, fact, style or technique which may have been represented by copyrighted work. In the European Union, and similarly in most other countries, copyright lasts for the lifetime of the author plus seventy years from his or her death. If the work is to be published posthumously, it lasts for seventy years from the end of the year of publication. Infringement of such copyright means to include a 'substantial' quotation from another person's work in a feature article or book without first seeking permission. The crux of the problem here is the word 'substantial' as this is open to interpretation. Consequently, the notions of 'fair dealing' and 'distinctive' have been put in place to counteract the problem. As a rough guide, a writer can quote three hundred words without having to seek permission from the original source, as long as full credit is given. Unfortunately, quoting a few lines of a poem or a script can be considered infringement of copyright because of the distinctive nature of the poem or the script as a whole. 'Fair dealing' is where more than three hundred words have been quoted, and acknowledged, where:

> the defence of fair dealing acknowledges the wider interest of freedom of speech by allowing considerable latitude in the use of copyright material for certain worthy purposes. The CPDA [the Copyright, Designs and Patents Act 1988 as amended by the Copyright Regulations 1995] limits these purposes to news reporting, criticism and review, and research and private study. (Crone, 2002: 98)

Libel

In law, defamation is the communication of a statement which makes a false claim, expressly stated or implied to be factual, which may harm the reputation of an individual, business, product, group, government or nation. Libel is a harmful statement in a fixed medium, such as writing, pictures, signs or electronic broadcasts, including CDs, DVDs and blogging. If a statement is considered derogatory, there are still some circumstances in which it may be allowed, such as proving it to be the 'truth'. Proving adverse public character statements to be true is the best defence against prosecution for libel. 'Absolute privilege' means that a statement cannot be sued as defamatory, even if it were made maliciously: such as applies, for example, to evidence given in court. 'Qualified privilege' may be used as defence by a journalist who believes information, for example local government documents, to be in the public interest. The Human Rights Act of October 2000 suggests a move in theory towards greater freedom of expression in the media; but all media writers need to set this against the right of privacy. The balance between the two is still being struck in the British courts.

The two most important safeguards a writer can take to avoid libel are to check all sources to make sure they are absolute and correct, and to check all interviewees' quotations for defamation. Failure to do so may result in objections made to the PCC, an independent, self-regulatory body which deals with complaints about the editorial content of newspapers and magazines. The PCC seeks to maintain high professional standards of journalism, such as the avoidance of harassment and media intrusion, by providing high-quality training for journalists and editors. Sample areas of high consideration include accuracy, the opportunity to reply, privacy, discrimination and confidentiality of sources.

Although such legalities are set standards that cannot be compromised, the ideal of ethical morality is arguably more fluid. The notion of newsworthiness in a story in some ways undermines ethics, because what might be 'worthy' for one might be 'wrong' for another. As Keeble outlines, although many journalists are profoundly concerned about ethical issues and determined to improve standards, 'the dominant attitude in the mainstream press prioritises "getting the story" and the demands of a deadline above all else' (1994: 21). This tells us two things. Firstly, the imposition of a deadline means that occasionally not every detail has time to be thoroughly researched or approved by the relevant people. Secondly, a priority to 'get the story' assumes that a journalist may do everything in his or her power to make the scenario being investigated interesting, ultimately meaning that truths may be altered or painted in a different shade to reality. It is here that the idea of *news values* becomes significant.

News values

Editors may use the findings of market research to establish a profile of their audience's interests, so that their newspaper can reflect the 'right' perspective on the world. More often though, the editors rely on their own feelings about what readers want. This often comes down to professional judgement based on 'My reader is like me, therefore what I like, my reader likes'. The problematic part of this approach is that it tends to focus only on voices from the mainstream – the dominant ideology – and ignores alternative points of view. This can create a distorted view of society. (Burns, 2002: 110–11)

Burns's statement tells us that above all a newspaper editor is interested in what his or her readers will think of the stories presented and, of course, how this will affect continuing sales of the newspaper. Due to these commercial considerations, those working in newspaper journalism apply news values to anything they wish to write about. In short, a news value advises a journalist whether his or her story is worth running or not: will anyone be interested? Many stories do have news values of some sort embedded within them, and the task is to unearth these so that a reader will want to engage with the story. Judging the news values of a story, or its *newsworthiness*, is perhaps one of the most important processes undertaken by a journalist. Quite simply, a lack of news value may mean that a story is not worth pursuing. After all, who wants to read a story that has no appeal or emotional titillation?

Perhaps the most obvious example of a story loaded with news value is 'the scoop'. Found predominantly in tabloid newspapers, especially *The Sun*, *News of the World* and *Daily Mirror*, a scoop is a big, exclusive story that readers will only find in that particular newspaper at that time. Often concerned with sex, sleaze and scandal, a scoop 'exemplifies the value to a news medium of maximising immediacy ... it maximises both recency and immediacy because the event is not revealed to the press until news of it is published. The fact of the publication becomes the news' (Roshco, 1999: 35). This is a prime example of how news values are embedded into journalism, primarily because the exclusivity of the story makes for an attention-grabbing front page that is sure to increase sales. Literally a 'hold the front page' story, a scoop promises its readers that what they are about to read will be shocking, startling and somewhat unbelievable.

News values, then, are a primary consideration of journalists. Although discussions of news values appear in critical, theoretical texts (mostly referencing the well-known model offered by Galtung and Ruge, 1965), they are also a useful reference for those interested in practice. News values offer 'benchmarks' for what makes a 'good' story, and although they can be seen as ideologically constructed and potentially damaging to discussions of ethics, there is no escaping that they exist and that they have meaning. If a journalist is working freelance, for example, he or she will undoubtedly want to pitch stories that have the best chance of being commissioned; in other words, stories that possess the best news value. Pape and Featherstone cite Harcup and O'Neill's news values (2005: 21) as useful indications of what makes a newspaper story 'good'. We have elaborated upon these and offer them as such:

- **The power elite:** powerful individuals who we want to read about, both positively (family life, achievements) and negatively (secrets, scandals).
- **Celebrity:** we are seemingly obsessed with stars and celebrities, and constantly want to know what they are doing, what they are wearing, where they are eating, who they are dating, etc.
- **Entertainment:** stories about human interest, 'caught off-guard' photographs, an unfolding drama, animals or sex, for example.
- **Surprise:** something that we really did not expect, either positive (reduction in mortgage rates, pregnancy of a celebrity) or negative (the collapse of a well-known retailer, death).
- **Bad news:** conflict or tragedy, usually with an element of 'it could have happened to you' attached.
- **Good news:** mountain rescues or medical cures, for example.

- **Magnitude:** stories significant in terms of the number of people involved, or their potential impact upon a large number of people (us).
- **Relevance:** stories about issues or groups perceived as relevant to the readership (we know them, we remember them, etc.).
- **Follow-ups:** used on previous major stories, namely those that have gripped a nation of readers for an amount of time.
- **Newspaper's agenda:** stories that fit the point-of-view or attitude of the publication, appealing to the emotions of its readers.

Task 1.3

Look at the headline (front page) stories of three newspapers and evaluate the news values at play. Is there more than one news value in each story? How much of an impact does the story have upon you?

Sourcing information

Broadly speaking, there are two types of source from which news stories emerge: 'on-diary' and 'off-diary' (Pape and Featherstone, 2005: 137–8). On-diary sources include those who are contacted regularly as a matter of routine, or those contacted to provide information about an event, such as the emergency services, council, courts, press conferences, reports from public bodies, schools and universities. Sometimes news stories are planned well in advance, such as up-coming events, conferences, visits, etc. Off-diary sources are those that give unexpected, unforeseen news stories, and can come from a number of places such as cuttings, experts' views, the media, the public, press releases, readers' letters, victims and witnesses. Whether planned or unplanned, it is important always to consider ways in which information can be gathered in order to 'fuel' the news story in question. Such information, from a quotation to a statistic to a witness account, can usefully illuminate the known basics and 'is what generally makes the difference between an ordinary version of the story and a good one' (Randall, 2000: 43).

Randall (ibid.) posits the following four principles about sourcing information for newspaper journalism:

- Collecting detail is crucial to good research.
- The best kind of anecdotes in news reports are often incidents or episodes summarized in one or two sentences.
- Background should be collected for any story, even the briefest ones. You should be looking for setting, context and relevant parts of the history of the subject or issue.
- Context can sometimes be the vital part of the story, putting facts of developments into a proper, even far less dramatic, perspective.

In some cases, it will be relatively easy to access the information required to write a news story. For example, the Internet and newspaper archives make it relatively simple to trace the history of a person or event currently being written about in a new context. Similarly, a local protest about council tax may be easy to research if it is known what, where and who is involved; a reporter may even be able to get to the protest within a matter of minutes. Other stories, however, will not be so simple to research, and it is here that a journalist's quick-thinking, effective planning skills come into play. Randall uses the example of a major international disaster to remind us that sourcing information may be problematic, especially for the journalist based in a different country: 'even to the authorities it is often unclear, for many hours or even days, exactly what has happened. Disasters can happen in inaccessible places, in countries where communications are poor, or where authorities are badly organised and secretive' (ibid.: 112). As such, it is down to the journalist to think quickly of a way of accessing as much information as possible to make the story work. Using the specific example of a plane crash, Randall (ibid.: 116–18) suggests the following guidelines for trying to source as much information as possible:

- Obtain a chronological narrative of what happened.
- Get eye-witness reports.
- Find out the cause.
- Check the safety record of the aircraft.
- Obtain the profile of the airline.
- Obtain the profile of the pilot.
- Get the life story of anyone prominent who was involved or died.

- Check casualties: who they are, not just statistics.
- Find out about the rescue.
- Get a chronology of recent crashes.
- Obtain a description of the scene.
- Try to get an expert's view.
- Write the anchor piece: all the best information from above, compacted into a long, comprehensive account of the crash.

Not all of these facts may be accessible, of course, but as a guide they provide a strong sense of the type of information deemed newsworthy for newspaper coverage.

Task 1.4

Write a list of the steps that might be taken to construct a news story about one of the following: an air-sea rescue; a major sports tournament win; a murder.

As well as knowing how to source information, it is worth considering how not to source information. It is vital that a journalist ensures all of his or her information is correct and fair, even to the point of verifying and then verifying again. Poor gathering of material can result in a poor, inaccurate news story, which as well as potentially misleading readers can ultimately affect the credibility of a journalist and the stability of his or her career. As such, we would like to highlight the eight common causes of error as offered by Randall (ibid.: 124–6):

- False information from sources.
- Poor note-taking.
- Failure to double check 'facts' with sources.
- Reluctance to check 'sensational' facts or developments.
- Failure to read a story once written.
- Failure to listen to your own anxieties about a story.
- Omission of facts not fitting with a preconceived (or too rapidly conceived) theory.
- Rushing into print too early.

Interviewing

Conducting an interview, whether it be the subject of a story, an eye witness to the event or someone related to the subject, can be a very useful source of information. Sometimes we think we know everything about a situation, but only when speaking to someone else do we realize that there are holes in our knowledge. As such, taking the time to interview someone who might be able to offer something interesting and useful to a story is a defining quality of a good journalist. Keeble highlights four types of interview (1994: 62–3): a *quickie* or *grabbed*, which can literally be asking something to a passer-by or grabbing a snatch as someone is eagerly trying to get away; a *vox-pop*, usually conducted as a street interview where one question is asked and members of the public give their opinion; *doorstepping* or *ambush*, usually used with celebrities, where journalists wait outside their houses or workplaces; and *telephone*, increasingly used as it is quick and cost-effective. A journalist may also undertake a longer, quality interview, where questions may have been preplanned with the intention of obtaining more of a 'narrative' rather than a 'sound bite'. This type of interview is usually preferred for a feature article, which is longer in form and discusses the topic in much more depth than a regular 'hard news' story.

Whichever form of interview is taken, it is essential that what is said by the interviewee is noted down accurately. Most newspaper journalists are trained in shorthand, which is a form of note-taking based on phonetics. Extensive training is needed in this, and the most popular models followed are Pitman's and Teeline. Increasingly, journalists will use a recording device to capture an interview. On today's market, high-quality digital Dictaphones can be purchased for less that £50, many of them with the ability to store hundreds of hours' material on them. When using such a device, however, it should not be intrusive to the flow of the interview, and the journalist should tell the interviewee that it is there. Regardless of ensuring accurate recording, however, there are many interviewees who will be unhappy about how their words have been used and divided up in a story. Although this may be a concern for interviewees, we must remember that 'the journalist's point of view is not necessarily the same as theirs'; rather, the journalist 'is assembling a mass of information of which the interviewee's comments form only a part. The journalist has other views, historical information or observations to add to the mix' (Fletcher, 2005: 165). Therefore, although problems may be encountered with interviewees' reactions, as long as the words themselves are accurate and there is proof of the conversation as quoted, the journalist is safe.

Finally, these twenty interviewing tips offered by Clayton (2000: 125–8) act as a solid starting point for any journalist considering the interview as a research tool:

1. People love to whinge, and discussing hates can be revealing.
2. Another revealing question is 'What do you see yourself doing five years from now?'
3. To keep in control, ask how much money someone got paid for a film/play/book if they won't stop talking. It's the one thing most people won't talk about.
4. If the person is not articulating well, you can always put a good quote in their mouth by prompting them with: 'would you say that ...?'
5. Avoid multiple questions; ask one at a time.
6. Take with you more questions than you need.
7. Take enough questions for more than one write-up. Work out beforehand how many separate profiles or features you can get out of one interview.
8. Unless it is specifically relevant to the piece, do not ask someone's age or weight; they are taboos and the interviewee will usually lie.
9. Don't talk too much.
10. A little knowledge is dangerous; do not pretend you know things.
11. Make absolutely certain that you understand the answers, both for accuracy and professionalism.
12. Use language your subject can understand.
13. Try not to be superior or ironic as it will probably make the interviewee hostile.
14. Use 'why' often, especially after a question answered yes or no.
15. Don't waste time asking questions that won't get you the information you need.

16. Don't bore the subject with petty questions like 'what's your favourite colour?' unless it is directly relevant to your angle.
17. Try to make the interview as casual, relaxed and close to a social conversation as possible.
18. Don't be afraid of interrupting your subject if they aren't giving you the information you want.
19. The person's speciality may not interest you but newspaper reporters can be sent to interview anyone on any subject. Force yourself to be interested in what they say.
20. Don't be shy about asking questions.

Task 1.5

Plan a list of twenty questions that you would ask each of the following: a successful sports star; the victim of a hit-and-run accident; the father of a missing child.

Finding the angle

As already discussed, news values play an important part in writing a news story. Sometimes the way that a story should be pitched is not necessarily in the obvious content, but in the angle or approach taken. If many newspapers are running the same story on the same day, then what makes a journalist's story stand out from the rest is the angle: the slant to the story that someone else has missed.

Consider the following basic premise of a news story:

A woman was abducted and held to ransom because the man she had just married used to be part of a dangerous gang. He owed them thousands of pounds.

Although this is a shocking and disturbing story, it is rather bland. In fact, it may not attract a reader's emotional appetite at all: people get abducted every day, so what is different about this woman? The fact that her husband used to be in a gang could be interesting; there may be mileage in this 'Hollywood' type of event. Again, though, it is perhaps not that interesting. Another way of looking at the story may be the fact that she had just married her husband. When did she marry him, we might ask. Consider this revised version:

> A woman was abducted and held to ransom only hours after she had married her husband. He used to be in a gang, and owed them thousands of pounds.

Straight away we can see that this is more interesting because it has more of an angle to it. Here we learn that a woman was abducted only hours after wedding; so, would she still be in her wedding dress? Would she be on an emotional all-time high? Considering the husband, why did he owe them thousands of pounds? What did he spend the money on? The wedding? These are, of course, hypothetical questions for a situation that might be nothing like this; however, the point is that finding the angle to the story, something that might be more interesting to readers and 'hook' them in, is a useful way of approaching newspaper writing.

Irony is another way of angling the news story. We all love to read about people and scenarios where something 'just cannot be': a juxtaposition of ideals and values, often humorous. Although we would warn writers against trying to find the irony in every story, we would argue that it is a highly useful tool in creating emotional engagement with readers. Consider the following examples:

- The world's fastest runner is fined for driving too slow on the motorway.
- A slimming competition winner is arrested following a brawl in a fast-food restaurant.
- A crime journalist is sentenced to prison for embezzling money from a newspaper.

Of course stories such as these lend themselves well to creative headlines and the use of puns throughout the story, especially in tabloid newspapers.

Types of news story

Having considered in-depth what lies behind the creation of news stories, let us now look specifically at constructing and writing them. First of all, we must consider the difference between the two major types of story found in a newspaper: *hard news* and *soft news*. Hard news stories 'are those that deal with topical events or issues that have an immediate or catastrophic or life-changing effect on the individuals concerned' (Pape and Featherstone, 2005: 22). Hard news is normally bad news, printed towards the front of the newspaper, and can include things like natural or man-made disasters, murder, riots, rape, child abuse, financial crises and political upheaval. Soft news, on the other hand, 'has more of a human interest focus and, although, short term at least, events may be equally immediate or important for the individuals concerned, they are rarely life-changing in quite the same way' (ibid.). Soft news tends to be less urgent than hard news, perhaps more reflective, and can include things like a victim's story some time after the accident, an anniversary of something important, the repercussions of a disaster, or a celebrity's struggle to regain his or her credibility after widespread allegations.

Soft news often appears as a *news feature*; a story that is not so vehemently sold to the reader, but rather written for a sense of interest and longer-term engagement. News features 'can breathe a little. They are longer – typically between 700 and 1000 words – with a more leisurely pace and structure that allows for more detailed analysis and assessment of people, issues or events that would be appropriate in a news story' (ibid.: 116). They can include cultural or social comment, eye-witness accounts, description and historical background, and can have an entertaining or humorous tone.

Other types of news story are identified by Keeble (1994: 95–6):

- **Timeless feature:** with no specific angle, the interest is provided by the subject or the sources.
- **Backgrounder/preview:** this focuses not so much on the news, but sets the scene for a forthcoming event.
- **Colour feature:** an article of feature length, concentrating on description, eye-witness reporting and quotations.
- **Eye-witness feature:** this is based on the reporter's observations of a news event, where 'I' is used.
- **Sketch:** opinionated, colourful, light piece, usually associated with Parliament.

- **Opinion/think piece:** this conveys the journalist's views and experiences in a controversial manner. Regular writers of these are known as columnists.
- **Diary items:** gossipy news items generally grouped together by a single byline (the name and position of the writer).
- **Profile:** a description of a person, usually based on an interview.
- **Reviews:** description or assessment of works of art, television programmes, films, books, music, etc.
- **Lifestyle features:** these include advice columns, shopping or travel features.
- **Editorials:** commentary reflecting the institutional voice of the newspaper.

As well as these main types of news story, some of which will be discussed below, there are other, smaller types of story that appear on the pages of a newspaper. McKane (2006: 148–57) summarizes these:

- **The write-off:** a self-contained story, usually eight to a hundred words, featuring on the front page and then continued in detail later on in the paper.
- **Sidebar or box:** a boxed-off piece of information or story based upon the same issue as the central story.
- **The add:** a sentence placed at the end of a story, when a smaller but related event to the main news event is mentioned.
- **The wrap:** a combination of several stories, normally from different countries or counties, compiled together for a sense of coherency.
- **The running or breaking story:** usually used to re-top a story with the latest important developments (timelines, bullet points, etc.).

Structuring the news story

Like many other forms of media writing discussed in this book, structure is everything. Although words are vitally important, with no structure to hold these words in place the news story falls to pieces. Quite literally, a reader must be guided through the process of reading about a situation, ensuring that all of the information is intelligible and 'plotted' in order to create maximum impact. From the very start, the structure of the news story must be crafted carefully in order to attract, and subsequently satisfy, the reader's curiosity about the subject, which will have often been aroused by the use of a headline. Pape and Featherstone tell us that 'a news story never starts at the chronological beginning, but, rather, with the ending to the latest, most dramatic or interesting thing to have happened' (2005: 28). Harris and Sparks tell us that an introduction ('intro') should not usually be more than twenty five words long; anything longer 'will blur the sense of drama and no larding with 'sensational', 'dramatic', 'tragedy' or other pseudo-exciting words will save it' (1997: 61). If we think of the expression 'you'll never guess what just happened', then we can glean a strong sense of what the intro of a news story must do: attract; hook; shock.

The *inverted triangle* or *pyramid* is a much-used technique for structuring a news story: it starts big and then gets narrower as it moves down. What this means for structure is that the most crucial, essential information comes first (who? what? where? when? why? how?); this is information that must be given, otherwise the story fails to make sense and misses something crucial. Eventually, as the triangle or pyramid narrows, less important information can be given that could potentially be cut by a subeditor, with no sense of the story having been lost. As McKane reminds us: 'many news stories are not read to the end. If the story has been written in the inverted pyramid style, and readers move on to something after the first few paragraphs, they have still been told the most important points' (2006: 48).

The top of the triangle or pyramid, then, should quickly and effectively tell a reader who the story is about, what the story is about, where and when it happened, why it happened, and how it happened. For example:

A 73-year-old man was rushed into hospital today after tripping over a manhole cover and falling onto a load of broken glass. Norman Brown, from Hawley, was going to collect his pension just after 9am when he stumbled on the loose cover. Council authorities refused to comment, but local residents say that an accident like this was waiting to happen.

The rest of the story develops as points are expanded upon and 'filler' information is added to embellish the story. For example, this story might go on to talk about how many complaints have been made to the council about the bad upkeep of pavements. It might provide further details of Norman's accident, and the resulting damage. It might list similar accidents that have occurred in the same vicinity. It would almost certainly provide a range of quotations about the accident, perhaps from local residents, street cleaners and even Norman himself.

Task 1.6

Take the 'abducted bride' story from above and make a list of what would be the most important parts of the story. Put them in order of importance, and begin to structure them using the inverted triangle/pyramid structure.

Newspaper language

When it comes to writing the actual words of a news story, there are certain considerations that must be made by the journalist. Unlike creative writing, where writers are usually free to express themselves in a way they deem appropriate, newspaper writing has 'rules' that need to be followed. The overall aim of a news story is to 'help the reader by relating new information to what they already know' and will thus use 'non-expert language and take the reader step by step through the information' (Harris and Sparks, 1997: 66). Logic and precision are thus at the core of newspaper journalism; there is no time for flannel, and no time for confusion: 'it takes much longer to make a piece of writing as clear and precise as possible; it is far quicker to produce something wordy and waffly. Getting a story down to very few words, yet keeping all the action, drama, colour and human interest takes a lot of practice' (McKane, 2006: 105).

'Newspaper English needs to be simple and straightforward, the sort of English a busy person would prefer' (Harris and Sparks, 1997: 77), and so even though the journalist may naturally have a creative, imaginative voice, this must be avoided in favour of concise, precise and highly targeted language that will be understood by the masses.

References to 'me' or to 'I' are usually avoided, as well as the journalist's personal opinion. The active voice ('he decided to go') is used over the passive voice ('it was decided that he should go'), and much use is made of the verb: people doing things; things happening. Long, complicated words tend to be avoided, as well as use of unfamiliar jargon. Writing should avoid assumption and speculation, and anything that could otherwise be deemed non-attributable. Slang should be avoided, unless a particular point is being made, and exclamation marks, adverbs and euphemisms should be avoided. Harris and Sparks (ibid.) list some other useful rules:

- Use specific words over general words ('red', not 'brightly coloured').
- Use concrete words over abstract words.
- Use plain words ('said' not 'commented').
- Use positive words.
- Don't use unknown quantities ('very' or 'really').
- Don't use 'should', 'might' or 'may' unless you have to.
- Don't use words thoughtlessly.
- Never qualify absolutes.
- Only use adjectives if they have something specific to say.
- Answer questions, do not create them.

Task 1.7

Read the front page story of a newspaper and consider how the rules above have been applied. Is the story still effective, even though it is written in a pared-down way? Can you think of a way to sharpen the writing even more?

Using your imagination to create hypothetical people and events, write a 250-word hard news story based upon either the 'abducted bride' story or Norman Brown's accident.

Finally, it is extremely useful to find out whether the newspaper being written for offers any *style guidelines* for journalists. Some newspapers may offer these to journalists for free, either in electronic or hard copy. A useful general style guide for UK journalists is *The Style*

Guide offered by the *Guardian* (see Web resources below), and for American journalists there is the *US News Stylebook*.

Writing the headline

We all know a good headline when we see one. Usually it will be punchy, powerful, funny, shocking or ironic, and in just a few words summarizes not only the story to be told, but the attitude or point-of-view towards it. Tabloid newspapers are often home to the best headlines, especially where there is a hint of salacious scandal, and it is not uncommon for writers to be employed mainly because of their ability to construct such good headlines. Clayton advises that headlines should attract, entice and inform, often making use of a verb to create a sense of immediate action (2000: 99). Hodgson notes that headlines should be 'refined into a simple "read-me" message' (cited in Burns, 2002: 133), to which Burns adds that they 'may also engender strong emotions in the reader such as amusement, sorrow or anger' (2002: 133). To this we would add the following techniques as useful to consider when creating headlines:

- **Alliteration:** Constable's Kinky Confessions; Footballer's Foreign Frolics.
- **Assonance:** Go Down Town, Clown; Hip, Hop ... No More Shop.
- **Puns (on single words or common expressions):** Three Men and a Cry Baby; Row, Row, Row Your ... Goat?!
- **Irony:** Mr Muscle in Drag Queen Shock; Crime Reporter Behind Bars for Stealing.
- **Single, dramatic words:** Defeat!; Gone!
- **Questions:** Is She mad?! Would You Leave Him to Die?

Task 1.8

Create at least five possible headlines for the story you have written for the task above.

Feature articles

According to Randall:

You are the reader's ears, eyes and nose. Almost every day you meet people and see things readers will never experience. If you don't tell them what these things are like, they will never know. If, for example, you are interviewing a well-known politician, readers will want to know what his or her office is like. Is it grand, or surprisingly modest? How is it decorated? Are there any interesting personal possessions about? Is the person nervous or calm? How do they appear to threaten those who work for them? You cannot rely on a photograph in the paper doing these things for you. Instead, you have to paint a word picture, however brief. And your words can convey things that pictures cannot. (2000: 182)

Feature articles, then, can be an exception to the rule in newspaper journalism. They are clearly soft news, not hard news, and will often appear either in the later pages of a newspaper or a supplement of some sort. Many readers save feature articles to read later in the day than the main news, perhaps waiting until they have more time to read them in a state of relaxation. As such, the language can be more in-depth and 'colourful', and rules about precision and concision can be loosened slightly. The use of description can bring the story of a feature alive, taking readers to where the journalist has been and evoking a strong sense of atmosphere. 'It can put flavour in the most arid and dry news story and make the difference between a report that satisfies and one that does not' (ibid.).

Some types of feature article have been discussed above, but here are some more examples, offered by Pape and Featherstone (2005: 122–9):

- **News backgrounder:** more background and detail on people or events in the news.
- **Colour piece:** behind the scenes of an event for something amusing or entertaining (such as clothes worn at an awards ceremony).
- **Leader page feature:** analyses, comments upon and delves deeper into an important news story.
- **'Watch me' feature:** reporters recounting their experiences, such as bungee jumps, rally car racing, spending the day as a personal shopper.

- **Advertorials:** in-depth discussions of a product or service; an advertisement disguised as an article.

Task 1.9

Select a story from a newspaper and think of three spin-off feature articles that could come from this. How would they relate to the main story? Would they appear in the same issue?

Reviews

Reviewing for a newspaper can be a rewarding job: not only does the journalist gain free access to films, plays, music gigs and other events, he or she can enjoy the liberty of thinking creatively and asserting his or her own opinion. Whereas news stories have to be written objectively, reviews only work properly if they are written subjectively. As Harris and Sparks note, 'reviews share the timeliness of reporting in that they are concerned with the first night of a dramatic production, musical concert or film etc.'; yet, in another respect, 'they should be approached as a feature: they can contain comment, opinion, assessment, reference to background material and an element of persuasion' (1997: 192). Many journalists have made a name for themselves by working as reviewers, their writerly voice denoting a sense of authorship and 'personality'. Examples include Charlie Brooker, Gary Bushell, Pauline Kael, Clive James, Jonathan Ross and Mark Kermode. As such, a good reviewer will make the writing entertaining and engaging as much as it is relevant to the product being reviewed. After all, if persuasion lies at the centre of a review ('go and see this'; 'do not buy this'; 'you cannot afford to miss them'), then subjective, personality-driven writing is a must.

When reviewing a product or artefact of any kind, the following should be observed:

- What were the aims of the creator(s)? Have they been achieved?
- How did you feel when you were engaged in the product?
- What was the first thing you noticed about it? What was the last thing you noticed about it?

- Which bits stood out the most, both good and bad?
- Who were the main people involved in putting the product together? What are their backgrounds?
- How did they work together? What effect did their relationship create?
- How much did this product cost? Was it worth it?
- When is this product available to the general public? How can they access it?

Background research is also useful when reviewing because it can provide a much wider context from which to draw observations. For example, if reviewing a film it would be useful to research the director (background, credits, future productions), screenwriter (background, credits, relationship to the story), principal actors (credits, typecasting, relationships) and other related aspects (setting, location of filming, costume, soundtrack, production contexts, financing).

The personal column

Occasionally, newspapers employ a writer to act as a columnist; someone with a strong authorial voice, writing regularly (usually weekly) and in the same style and format. Some columnists are famous or well-known figures, often from the world of media, and because readers become accustomed to their work, from the point of view of the newspaper this is a useful marketing tool. The personal column can thus be understood as a voice-driven sketch; a weekly or monthly 'blog' dedicated to entertaining the reader and letting them into his or her personal life for a few hundred words or so. One only has to think about the character Carrie Bradshaw in *Sex and the City* to be reminded of the effectiveness that a personal column can have. In fact, sometimes these columns are collated and published as a book, much like a collection of short stories. Keeble (1994: 216) provides us with some thoughts about the personal column, and how the writing of one can be approached:

- They 'work' when there is an original tone. This may be witty, controversial, no-nonsense, hard-hitting, eclectic, quirky, bitchy, etc.

- Their personality will always shine through.
- A kind of relationship is built with the reader.
- Their language and tone will be appropriate to the newspaper, and they make up and are influenced by the overall 'personality' of the newspaper.

Task 1.10

Imagine that you are asked to be a columnist on a local newspaper. What kind of 'voice' would you adopt? What types of things would you hope to talk about? Practise this by writing a five-hundred-word column about something that has interested you this week.

Writing for online formats

For those journalists embracing the developments that digital technology has afforded, there are some key principles related to different working practices that must be duly considered. Firstly, the delivery of news via the Internet is markedly different to that in print because there is no, or limited, restriction on space. As such, greater avenues for news presentation are available, as highlighted by Wilkinson *et al.* (2009: 145):

- **Interactive content:** where users can choose which elements of a story to see or read, and in what order to see them.
- **Hyperlinks:** allowing a user immediately to obtain more information on any component of the story.
- **True media:** combining video, audio, text, graphics, photos and other content.
- **Archives:** previously published content, including news, photos, features and editorials.

Central to any news website is its home page or welcome page. As Harrower explains: 'just as the front page is a doorway to the printed newspaper, the home page is a gateway to the online news. And because the home page links users to every related page, it must be comprehensive, yet easy to navigate: busy, yet *clean*' (2007: 155).

The home page should thus be attractive and engaging, giving a clear sense of the day's headlines as well as the other options available to the user: archives, related stories, developments of running stories, etc. The home page is usually constructed by the following elements:

- Time and date.
- Index, usually in categories such as 'UK News', 'World News', 'Finance', 'Sport', etc.
- Lead story.
- Navigation buttons, usually as hypertext, in bold or a different colour.
- Search engine.
- Links to both internal and external web pages.
- Interactive extras, such as blogs and photo albums.

Navigation is probably the most important feature of a website, one where the user is able to make his or her own pathway through the news that he or she wants to read, hear and see. Navigation thus allows stories, images and digital extras to be 'linked together as layers, with related options just a click away'; they are 'sites that let users roam at random, poking their noses into every intriguing corner, following their curiosities to customize their news' (ibid.: 154). Hypertext is the mainstay of user navigation, presenting a network of textual fragments that open up new possibilities for learning more about a story simply by 'clicking away'. Users may feel empowered by the opportunity to 'move through the text by clicking on buttons, and, since most fragments contain many buttons, readers have a choice of many different itineraries' (Ryan, 2004: 340). We have to consider, of course, that although empowerment may be felt by the user, there in fact is only a limited choice of stories to navigate to and from: those stories already decided for us by those filling the website with content.

Perhaps the biggest development of digital journalism is the idea of web stories and timeliness, often appearing only minutes after the event has happened (Harrower, 2007: 154). Unlike a newspaper, which may print a day's stories in the evening but more likely overnight, web journalism can be consistently updated, twenty-four hours a day. This means that as soon as a story breaks, coverage of it can be produced and the consumption of it begun. For example, it is common to see news websites throw a 'breaking news' story to the top of their home page, perhaps with only a paragraph or two about what the general gist of the story is. Although incomplete, this is enough to rouse a user's attention and, probably, ensure that he or she keeps checking the website for regular updates. When a full story is completed, much like that of a newspaper, it can be 'published' and updated throughout the day as and when developments occur. Sometimes the same story will be updated or tweaked as necessary; sometimes a whole new story will be written. According to Hudson and Rowlands, such web stories on the *BBC News* website are written in just four paragraphs, commonly with a maximum of two hundred and fifty words. Similarly, *Sky News Interactive* uses stories that are between eight and twelve paragraphs long (ibid.: 161).

When it comes to the writing of news stories for the web, then, the following five tips should be considered for creating user-friendly content (ibid.: 160):

1. **'Chunk' your information:** use short, bite-sized sections. Use shorter paragraphs to get most attention.
2. **Tweak your type to make it easier to scan:** think like a text designer, using bold fonts, subheadings, bullet points, etc. Lift out quotations and punctuate ideas.
3. **Rethink what a 'story' is:** not one long text story, but a web package – a way of constructing the entire story, with page links.
4. **Enhance your story with extra elements:** think about multimedia, interactivity, links, sources to download, etc.
5. **Collaborate:** use other people to help with the different elements of the package; work together to enhance the story.

Above all, the central consideration when delivering news via an online format is 'the nature of the audience, their wants as well as their demands' (Wilkinson *et al.*, 2009: 146). In other words, who is the audience and what do they want? If research finds that most users are of a young generation, for example, then the content must be suitable to what they are used to and able to handle: short paragraphs, lots of images, different colours, sound bites, downloadable material, etc. Failure to adhere to the target audience's desires and capabilities will ultimately lead to an unusable website that generates a low number of user 'hits'.

Career opportunities in print journalism: Newspapers

Many journalists begin their careers by working on a local or small-scale newspaper. Here the 'craft' of writing news stories can really be learned, and unlike with major national newspapers slight hiccups or errors in judgement are not as detrimental to a career. Working on such a newspaper can also help you to experience a wide range of duties and responsibilities, from entering the community and finding stories to interviewing local 'stars' to covering an important sports event. Whilst working on a small-scale newspaper, you may find your specialism, or your natural writing voice: crime; politics; human interest; entertainment; sport; etc.

From here, you may then want to move on to a bigger newspaper, such as a daily tabloid or broadsheet. As is also the case with local and small-scale newspapers, a job here may be in-house or freelance. In-house journalists are likely to be given a certain responsibility, such as working on the news desk or investigating crime stories. Freelance journalists face a bigger risk in finding regular work, but armed with a wealth of story ideas and a professional approach to assignments, opportunities can be very forthcoming. Working freelance also enables other work to be undertaken, such as freelance copywriting or part-time teaching.

If you are a student of journalism, then there is no better way to learn the craft of journalism than by working on a university or college publication. Most universities have their own student newspaper or magazine, and working on this whilst studying will enable you to build a really good portfolio. Work experience is also a viable option whilst studying, and many towns and cities have a variety of newspapers and similar publications that are crying out for voluntary (or even paid) work.

Further reading

Bromley, B. (1994) *Teach Yourself Journalism*, London: Hodder & Stoughton.

Burns, S.L. (2002) *Understanding Journalism*, London: Sage Publications.

Clayton, J. (2000) *Journalism for Beginners: How to Get into Print and Get Paid for It*, 2nd edn, London: Piatkus.

Fletcher, K. (2005) *The Journalist's Handbook: An Insider's Guide to Being a Great Journalist*, London: Macmillan.

Harris, G. and Sparks, D. (1997) *Practical Newspaper Writing*, 3rd edn, Oxford: Focal Press.

Keeble, R. (1994) *The Newspapers Handbook*, London: Routledge.

McKane, A. (2006) *News Writing*, London: Sage Publications.

Pape, S. and Featherstone, S. (2005) *Newspaper Journalism: A Practical Introduction*, London: Sage Publications.

Randall, D. (2000) *The Universal Journalist*, 2nd edn, London: Pluto.

Web resources

www.nctj.com
Official website of The National Council for the Training of Journalists.

www.nuj.org.uk
Official website for the National Union of Journalists.

www.pcc.org.uk
Official website for the Press Complaints Commission.

www.journalismcareers.com
Useful resource for those wishing to pursue a career in journalism.

www.guardian.co.uk/styleguide
Offers style guidelines for journalists, useful for any newspaper writing.

http://shorthand.cemp.ac.uk
Online games to improve the learning of shorthand

Print Journalism: Magazines 2

Prospects, the online careers advice website, gives a helpful explanation of what working in the magazine industry might involve, although this is just a very brief overview:

> Magazine journalists research and write news and feature articles suited to a magazine's reader profile. The readership of a magazine is often defined by a common need or interest. There are nine thousand magazine titles in the UK covering a diverse range of topics ranging from glossy magazines to trade newsletters. Most fall into four categories: business, professional, consumer and specialist consumer. The three main branches of magazine journalism are news writing, feature writing and subediting. Although generally in paper format, many magazine publishers increasingly produce material in new media (for example CD, web or audio) in addition to hard copy. The nature of a journalist's work varies considerably depending on the size of the employing organisation and the subject matter covered by the publication. It may also be affected by the medium through which the magazine is produced. Typical work activities include: researching a subject or story, talking to people, generating ideas for stories, meeting with colleagues to plan the content of the issue and the character of the publication. (www.prospects.ac.uk)

According to Davis, there is disagreement on precisely how many magazines are published in the UK because 'there is no universally accepted definition of a magazine other than it should contain articles or stories by different authors and that it should be published at regular intervals ... what most readers understand by a magazine is a publication with a colour cover and stapled or stitched pages' (1995: 3). There is a huge diversity today in the range of magazines published in the UK. We find magazines catering for every conceivable topic, from Zionism to zoology. The magazine industry is constantly evolving: new titles spring up in response to new trends; old titles get shelved or merged; and new technology makes production cheaper, resulting in an expansion of titles.

By the end of this chapter, you should be able to:

- Understand the practical and commercial considerations of writing for magazines.
- Consider where ideas for features come from.
- Recognize how to outline and structure a feature article.
- Be familiar with the different types of 'leads' and conclusions for magazine features.
- Recognize how to research and write the feature interview.
- Understand how to present and market the magazine feature article.
- Be familiar with other types of magazine writing, such as short fiction, opinion pieces, columns and reviews.
- Understand some of the legal considerations surrounding writing for magazines.

The magazine world

The first periodical to be published in England was in 1682. It was named *Weekly Memorials for the Ingenious* and consisted of eight pages of book extracts, reviews and woodcuts. Women's magazines began with a sister paper named *The Ladies' Mercury* in 1693. This was full of advice to the lovelorn on dress and marital behaviour. The eighteenth and nineteenth centuries saw a proliferation of new magazines, including many professional titles such as *The Lancet* (medical), *The Economist* (financial), *Nature* (scientific), *Law Quarterly* (legal) and *Studio* (art). In America, *Harper's Bazaar* was published in 1867, followed by *McCall's*, *Ladies' Home Journal*, *Good Housekeeping* and *Vogue*. Teenage magazines found their niche in Britain in the

1950s with titles such as *Valentine, Roxy* and *Boyfriend*, offering romantic fiction in picture-strip form. New consumerist titles were published from the late 1950s including the *Which?* series. Colour supplements distributed with the Sunday newspapers began in 1962 with *The Sunday Times Magazine.*

According to Davis (1995), the biggest category of periodicals today comprises trade, technical and professional magazines; nearly six thousand of them in Britain, with the remaining three thousand made up of consumer titles. Other groupings of magazine titles include: 'lads' mags', children's publications, journals of opinion such as the *Spectator* and *New Statesman*, alternative, underground and cult magazines such as the satirical magazine *Private Eye*, listings magazines such as *Time Out*, feminist and gay rights magazines such as *Spare Rib* and *Attitude*, and visual-oriented youth culture magazines such as *Blitz, i-D* and *The Face.*

The majority of magazines are termed 'news trade titles' and are sold by newsagents and in supermarkets. Perhaps the fastest-growing sector of publishing, however, has been the 'freebie': the give-away magazine such as those seen at airports and railway stations. Unfortunately, their over-reliance on advertising often means that they are the first to fold in any recession. The content of most magazines is divided between fiction (short stories, serials, poetry) and non-fiction, with a tendency towards the latter. Non-fiction embraces a wide range of writing, usually known simply as 'features'. The most common type of feature in all magazines is the interview feature: profiles that are based on interviews yet delve deeper into the subject matter. Other types of feature include: the 'descriptive feature', which are stories about places, animals or events; 'investigative features', which cover scandals or causes for concern; 'accounts of personal experiences', which cover everything from an explorer's latest journey to a son's personal story about caring for his elderly parents; and 'service features', which cover topics such as gardening, cookery, motoring, health and beauty, fashion, sport and medical advice. Other types of feature include gossip columns, opinion pieces, quizzes, reviews, humour, competitions, promotional offers, horoscopes, problem pages and readers' letters.

The purpose of magazine feature articles

Newspaper and magazine features are similar in structure but different in purpose and intent. Firstly, let us look at what they *do* share:

- They are both organized pieces of flowing facts and ideas.
- They are both well-researched and well-written, giving a sense of conviction.
- They both use quotations and narrative description.
- They both range in length, from a few hundred to a few thousand words.

Now let us look at how they differ:

- The main difference is the *character* of the magazine feature. While newspaper articles are newsworthy stories based upon objective facts and figures, magazine features tend to take a subjective point of view, opening up and developing factual topics.
- Whereas straight news stories are told from the third-person point of view, it is not uncommon for a magazine feature to be told in the first person. The writer will often detail his or her interactions with interview subjects, making the piece more personal.
- Feature stories are descriptive and full of detail, and generally have a strong story driving the narrative.
- Feature articles combine facts and opinion with a focus on the human interest angle of the story. While they can report news, the news content is not of primary importance.

Another major difference in magazine articles is the paragraphing and page layout. In general, magazine paragraphs are longer and more formal than those found in newspaper features, which tend to be shorter and punchier. Magazine leads are also longer than newspaper leads, taking more time to get to the crux of the story. They are meant for leisure reading, to entertain and to inform. The magazine feature still needs the necessary 'hook' to lure readers in, of course, but it has more time to 'tease' readers and has the added advantage of vivid photographs to accompany them.

Take two magazines, one trade and one consumer, and list how many different types of features (investigative, interview, descriptive, service, other) there are. Note anything unusual or innovative about them.

Feature ideas: Where do they come from?

An idea is a specific angle or approach to a subject, and garnering ideas is one of the most important jobs of the magazine features writer. Ideas should be both creative and original; no editor is interested in predictable, rehashed, stale ideas. All feature writers should carry a notebook around with them for jotting down those all-important ideas. Interestingly writers will often find that their ideas reflect their interests, which is useful for freelancers wishing to write for niche magazines. Many publications hold 'think tanks' where staff writers are encouraged to brainstorm ideas, find links and add value to stories. However, freelance writers will be dependent upon themselves for ideas.

A common dilemma for the writer may be: should I get the idea first and then find the market? Or should I find the market first and then get the idea? Whereas many new writers tend to get an idea first, more experienced ones should be able to source and research information for any publication on demand. Staff writers should source ideas from the news and features that their readers are currently interested in. No matter what the experience of the writer may be, it is always essential to keep up to date with current affairs, read the newspapers, watch television, listen to the radio, surf the Internet, note conversations, observe events, read reference books and use libraries. The world is full of ideas, and writers should keep their eyes and ears open. Dick offers the following advice for germinating ideas:

> It's just a matter of being on automatic alert: noting all that happens, thinking backwards – and forwards, seeing and hearing through new eyes and ears. What gladdens or saddens, interests or reassures, consoles or explains, intrigues or inspires? To help

germination take place ask yourself searching questions: why? who? what? where? when? and how? Twist the questions round too: why didn't? when did? what if? (1996: 16)

Topicality and timing are crucial in getting a feature article published, and so it is important to know the magazine's lead time; that is, the time it takes from inception to publication. In general, a well-established monthly magazine will have a lead time of at least six months, sometimes eight. Lead times are much shorter for weekly magazines, perhaps only one or two months. When planning ideas around anniversaries, commemorations, seasons, national events, etc., writers need to allow plenty of time between researching, pitching, writing and publication date.

Several different features can often be developed from one single idea, and so writers need to think broadly and creatively. Dick (1996: 23) offers a useful example of how this works in practice. Having visited the hairdresser one day, she mused on the amount of hair cut and thrown away. This led to a string of articles in a variety of magazines on the following themes:

- Hair care and cleanliness in the eighteenth century: a hair-raising account of women's hair fashions.
- Why men make top hairdressers for women.
- Your mirror image: what does it reveal? – facts and figures about left and right handedness.
- Hair today, gone tomorrow? What to do with hair we throw away: suggestions ranged from mixing it with tarmac for absorbing rain on roads, to composting it into a new thatching material.
- Your hair is what you eat: an article on diet for health.
- Models never complain: dressing the hair of dummies in museums, etc.

As we can see, such a simple task like having a hair cut can inspire a myriad of ideas that would appeal to a broad spectrum of magazines and their readers.

Task 2.2

Think of something you have done or seen today. With a partner, brainstorm how many potential magazine articles you can get from this single idea. Evaluate the ideas and choose which ones might be of most interest to readers.

As may have been experienced from the task above, it is important not to jump straight into writing the first ideas discovered, but to allow time for them to breathe and develop. Sometimes what may seem a brilliant idea one day may seem absolutely ridiculous the next. Hennessy (2006: 57) provides a list of useful considerations which can be used to test the viability of a magazine feature idea. These include:

- The scope of the idea: its broadness or narrowness.
- The freshness of the idea, or an ability to update an existing idea.
- The appeal of the idea to the target readers.
- The clarity of the theme/angle/point of view.
- The significance, importance, relevance and timeliness of the idea.
- Potential libel, legal or ethical considerations.
- How much the feature will cost the writer in money and time.

Many magazine writers are inspired by other articles they have read in magazines and rewrite the feature, giving it a different spin, outlook or argument. There is no copyright on ideas, but in no circumstances should writers steal the words of another writer and attempt to pass them off as their own. If they do, they will soon find themselves (and the publication they are writing for) in deep trouble, with their wonderful careers as magazine writers over.

The writing process

The priority for magazine writers must be immediate communication. Writing should be simple, direct and vivid. The writer must have a solid grasp of his or her intended message and the purpose behind that message. Is it to entertain, to persuade, to argue, to inform, to shock or to provoke? The essentials of good magazine writing are to:

- Begin with a lead that hooks the reader in, and keeps them.
- Choose the right word, but remember that precision takes time and effort.
- Be simple and concise; simplicity is the key to all effective messages.
- Use the familiar word rather than the unfamiliar, and avoid jargon unless absolutely necessary.
- Use the concrete rather than the abstract, and create involvement rather than theorizing. Be specific as well as general; give facts as well as figures.
- Avoid using clichés. They are lazy journalism, and usually consist of overworked metaphors.
- Be honest and positive but beware of giving a story more attention than it deserves by exaggerating events. Equally, avoid getting bogged down in euphemisms and political correctness.
- Write as you speak. Avoid pomposity, preachiness and ostentation.
- Vary the pace and rhythm by writing sentences of varying lengths. This prevents monotony and reader boredom.
- Avoid unnecessary adjectives and adverbs; they are often the first to be blue pencilled out by editors, and are the mark of an amateur writer.

Hennessy claims that 'simplicity, directness and the resulting clarity (of communication) will result from keeping to the same subject as far as possible. (Don't change the subject too often.) ... Putting the meaning where possible into active verbs rather than in passive ones or in abstract nouns ... and keeping subject and verb near each other' (2006: 201). He also suggests that during the editing process, writers should look for irrelevancy, digressions, self-indulgent writing, superfluous modifiers, circumlocutions and tautologies.

Structuring the magazine feature article

By the time all the necessary background research for a feature article has been completed, there will be an overwhelming amount of information to work with. The next task is to then use this material to plan the structure of the article. Structure is a 'blueprint' or a map that gives both writer and reader a direction to follow. In general a writer will need to develop between two and four main points or threads, depending on the length of the article. In turn these points will need to be supported by quotations, facts and figures, anecdotes, case histories and other material. Some writers argue that overplanning makes for a dull story and destroys creative inspiration. However, if a writer does not know what his or her main points are, then neither will any potential editor. Some articles need little outlining, such as a how-to story; others, such as in-depth informative pieces, require serious thought and planning.

The writer should begin the plan or outline of his or her feature with the working title. This should be followed by the storyline (theme/idea) and lead (hook). From here, the writer will launch into his or her main points, supported by any back-up material. Finally, the outline should be finished with the story's ending. The article itself should begin with the most important point, and work downwards in logical relevant importance, with each point flowing naturally into the next.

Longer features require more complicated outlines. These should include at least three main points, each followed by at least one subpoint which is substantiated by facts, figures, quotations, background information, interviews, etc. If the outline appears top heavy with main points or bottom heavy with too many supporting points, then the outline should be rethought.

A typical outline for a magazine feature, then, may look something like this:

Storyline (theme)

This is the 'big idea', the driving force of the article. It should allude to what the writer wants to say.

Lead

This is the opening paragraph, and should include the 'hook' to draw the reader in effectively.

Main point 1

This is the most important subject of this article. It should explore what is involved, by whom, where and when, along with questions of how and why.

Subpoint(s)
Facts, figures, quotations, interviews, anecdotes and any other support-ing evidence to back up the main point.

Main point 2
This evolves from main point 1. It is of secondary importance, yet crucially develops the article's narrative. It may bring into question an ancillary topic or subject (person).

Subpoint(s)
Facts, figures, quotations, interviews, anecdotes and any other support-ing evidence to back up the main point.

Main point 3
This evolves from main point 2. It is of even less importance, yet devel-ops the article's narrative in a further direction. It may bring into ques-tion yet another ancillary topic or subject (person).

Subpoint(s)
Facts, figures, quotations, interviews, anecdotes and any other support-ing evidence to back up the main point.

The rules for the outline are not set in stone; they can be varied to avoid conformity and add vigour, but any deviation must still lead to an organized and flowing narrative. The article must sound as if it grew organically, not a cobbled together set of points, views or instructions. Hamilton suggests that 'growth occurs naturally, with-out interruption: each element stems from the element preceding' (2005: 109). Writers can achieve this by linking paragraphs with tran-sitions, those words and phrases that alert the reader to a linkage. Examples include 'meanwhile', 'at the same time', 'in addition', 'also', 'but', 'firstly', 'secondly', 'finally', 'however', 'consequently' and 'subsequently'. These transitory words allow the article to read as a succession of related thoughts packaged into paragraphs, each paragraph expressing and expanding on a single thought: 'the tran-sitions from one thought to another, one graf [paragraph] to another, signal shifts in time, space, place, speakers and action, making the story understandable because the connections among the grafs are clear' (ibid.: 111).

Select a magazine feature article and plot the outline on a piece of paper. Note how the article (a) conforms to the standard outline or (b) deviates from the standard outline. How does this affect your feeling towards the topic discussed?

Using the same article, highlight all the transitional words and phrases linking points and paragraphs. How successful do you think these transitions are?

Writing the lead

The lead is designed to hook the reader in: to attract and to hold. The opening lines are the most important, a deciding factor as to whether the reader carries on reading or discards the article and moves onto something more interesting. The lead is a promise of what is to come, and you must not let the readers down by breaking that promise. Hamilton offers us a pertinent metaphor to describe the lead of a feature article describing it as like the 'trunk of a tree, [growing] out of the material and the storyline that root it. The rest of the story – branches, buds, leaves, fruit or flowers – flows from the lead' (ibid.: 114). Likewise, Ruberg suggests that:

> the lead is like an audition. An aspiring Broadway actress sings her best ten bars on stage, hoping she'll be asked back for a second round. It's only ten bars, but they're the first and only notes the director will hear if she doesn't knock his socks off. Similarly, writers need to present their very best information in those opening ten words to get 'called back' by their readers *before* they can get to the research and the details. (2005: 131)

There are many different types of leads to choose from, but writers must select the one most appropriate to their story and its purpose. They should put themselves in their readers' shoes and consider which type of lead they will most appreciate, and which type of lead is most appropriate for the story's theme and tone. Common types of lead include:

- **Question and answer.** This begins the article with a question, but must answer it either immediately afterwards or at some time in the body of the article. Question and answer leads should be short, snappy and strike at the heart of the reader's interest.
- **Case histories.** These are specific stories that will add the human touch to the article and help to illustrate the main points. Any case histories chosen must be relevant to the main message of the article.
- **Narrative description.** This lead presents itself as a narrative or story, usually told in the third person.
- **Narrative description in the first person.** This is used for immediacy and draws the reader into the article.
- **Comparison and contrast.** This type of lead is effective at hooking the reader. It can compare the way things used to be with the way things are now or the way we used to think with the way we think now. It can rely on binary oppositions, for example, good versus bad, beauty versus ugliness, health versus illness.
- **Historical comparison and contrast.** This takes a notable moment, event or person from history and then contrasts it with the way things are now.
- **Literary reference.** This begins with a literary quotation, idea, reference or fact to highlight the message of the feature article.
- **Figure of speech or play-on-words.** This begins with a pun or verbal 'joke'.
- **Prose poetry.** This waxes purple in its allusion to something dear to the reader's heart. Borrowed from the novelist's craft, the prose-poetry lead is used to set the tone or mood of the article.
- **Dialogue.** This creates a situation or establishes character.
- **Teaser.** This is provocative and exciting. It engages the reader with tight wording and graphic images.
- **Delayed.** This withholds identification of the person, group, place or event that is central to the story. Identification is usually delayed for only a few paragraphs, but sometimes can be suspended until the end of the article.
- **Descriptive.** This is similar to the narrative lead in that it simply paints a picture of a person, place or event. The descriptive lead is sometimes called a **situation lead** if a scene is set or a particular atmosphere is created.

- **Direct address.** This talks to the reader by addressing them as 'you', designed to involve the reader in the story without actually introducing the writer.
- **Expression.** This uses aphorisms, proverbs, mottoes or other traditionally well-known illustrations of basic truths to introduce the article.
- **Prediction.** This predicts a situation or issue soon to arise based on forecasts from reputable sources.
- **Relationship.** This describes cause and effect and how one event triggers another.
- **Surprise.** This is also known as the **punch lead** and is intended to shock the reader. It should be used to lead the reader astray initially, but like any good lead, should tease, promise and deliver.
- **Summary.** This sums up in a few sentences or a couple of paragraphs the essence of the feature article.

Task 2.4

Select a number of magazine feature articles from different types of magazine. Identify the various leads used. Rewrite the leads using a different lead type and evaluate their effectiveness.

Writing the ending

Unlike news stories which can just stop, feature articles usually have a definite ending. It is useful to consider the idea of a circular narrative, where the article can begin and end with the same idea or indeed the same question; what has moved on is the reader's understanding of the subject. As such, the ending can be just as important as the lead. As Hamilton tells us, 'the ending serves a definite purpose. It closes the story loop, tying up all the loose ends and leaving the reader emotionally satisfied' (2005: 124).

When considering the practicalities of writing the ending, Bugeja (1998: 149) suggests a consideration of the following basic requirements:

- It echoes or answers the introduction, fulfilling the contract promised in the title of the work.

- It has been prepared for, or foreshadowed, via preceding thematic statements.
- It contains a final epiphany or peak experience for take-away value.
- The epiphany is expressed in an open or a closed manner, depending on the piece.

The decision to use either an open or a closed ending is important as it will affect the overall feel of the article. Writers should consider an open ending if they want to leave their readers guessing or pondering on their truths; a closed ending, rather, resolves the topic or theme of the article. Writers should consider a closed ending if their aim is to satisfy their readers or entice them to think or act in a certain way.

Endings should be carefully crafted and not just tacked on as a swift conclusion. They should be relatively short, with one or two paragraphs, and tightly written. As with leads, there are a number of endings to choose from, ranging from a single word to something more descriptive and evocative. Other endings include the straight question, the rhetorical question, the onomatopoeic ending, the play-on-words, a summary quotation, the echo conclusion (echoing something written in the lead or body), the twist, the stand-alone quotation and the statement ending (the writer's final perspective on the situation).

Task 2.5

For the articles previously selected, identify the types of ending used. Rewrite these endings using a different type and evaluate their effectiveness.

Choose a topic that interests you and write a feature article of one thousand words. Craft a suitable lead, body and ending.

Researching and writing the feature interview

The magazine feature interview is often more thorough than the newspaper interview because the writer is not subjected to harsh deadlines and has more time to research and organize the interview. Interviews can be conducted personally, by e-mail, by letter or by telephone. Personal interviews should yield good quotations, accurate descriptions and insight into the person being interviewed or the issues being addressed. The main disadvantage of the personal interview is that it takes time to arrange and often time to gain the interviewee's confidence. The telephone interview is usually used for re-interviewing primary subjects or for garnering extra information. The main disadvantage of telephone interviews is that the writer cannot see the subject and therefore is unable to comment on body language, setting or environment. It is also difficult to establish rapport.

Once it has been decided whom to interview, the next step is to ask for the interview. One should explain quickly and simply who one is, why one wants to interview the person, which publication one is writing for, the idea behind the interview, and how much time will be needed. It is absolutely crucial to be honest about the intention of the interview; never mask the true agenda behind it, otherwise trust will be lost and the writer's reputation may be damaged. Once the interview has been granted, the writer will need to research both the interviewee and the type of interview he or she aims to conduct. The research process may include trawling through newspaper archives, websites, city or academic libraries, electronic databases or film archives. The writer will need to begin the planning of the interview armed with detailed information about the interviewee. In this way, time can be better spent asking the interviewee more interesting questions, who in turn will be impressed by the writer's knowledge.

Asking questions

Most writers, new as well as long standing, write down the questions they want to ask the interviewee beforehand. That said, the writer should be prepared to deviate from the planned questions if and when the need arises; flexibility can lead the writer to some exciting places. Following the interviewee's lead can enable spontaneity and the opening up of a new, perhaps better, angle to pursue; interviewers must be able to think on their feet.

Questions come in a variety of styles, each with their own purpose and effect. Below are some of the most common and useful types:

- **The open question** allows the respondent to answer in a variety of ways. It allows the subject to open up and expand on an idea or issue. For example:
  What's your opinion of the current economic climate in Higher Education?

- **The closed question** requires a more narrow and focussed reply. For example:
  Where do you spend most of your working day?

- **The probe question** asks for clarification or amplification of an incomplete answer. For example:
  What is it about your work that you particularly enjoy?

- **The mirror question** repeats part of the interviewee's answer. Consequently the interviewee is forced to amplify and expand on his or her answer, which often elicits more interesting information. For example:

  Writer:
  Why do you recommend books by Sandra Cain and Craig Batty?
  Interviewee:
  Because they are interesting and well written.
  Writer:
  You say they are interesting and well written ... in what way do you think this will be helpful to students wishing to study media writing?

  Use mirror questions sparingly. Their purpose is to slow down the pace of the interview and to clarify quotations.

- **Hypothetical questions** should also be used sparingly. Their purpose is to allow the respondent to think about or comment on particular developments or issues. For example:
  It's been suggested that electronic books will do away with the need for traditional publishing altogether. What's your view on this?

There are three types of questions that the writer of feature interviews should avoid. These are:

- **The yes and no question.** This allows the respondent to answer either 'yes' or 'no'. As they fail to yield a detailed answer, they are useless for magazine interviews.
- **The leading question.** This can be unethical because it suggests a *right* answer. For example:
  Everybody in this town that I've spoken to suggests that the proposed new library is an excellent venture. What's your opinion?
- **The loaded question.** This is designed to provoke a respondent. Loaded questions can be divisive and manipulative. For example:
  You are a successful writer, but most people are not interested in white, middle-aged writers anymore and suggest that the field should be left open for younger, more energetic writers. What's your opinion on this?

When interviewing, the writer should be sure to ask interesting questions which add value. No reader wants to read the same old churned out information. The writer will need to ask difficult questions at times, but should avoid being offensive. The most difficult interviewees are those that do not have a great deal to say; they can be hard work. Their anxiety can often get in the way of their ability to say what they want to say, and the result is that they fail to do themselves justice and the writer is then left with little to work with. One solution is to try and establish a rapport before the interview begins, perhaps by talking about everyday matters in order to gain the respondent's confidence.

Robertson (cited in ibid.: 154) offers five interviewing tips that most writers should follow. These include the fact that writers should be prepared to change their minds about the interviewee and assume nothing. They should also keep their egos out of the interview and recognize that they are not the subject. They should actively listen and never be ashamed of saying 'I don't understand' or 'what does that mean?'. It is also important to remember that nothing is ever really 'off-the-record': everything is grist to the mill as far as the magazine interview is concerned. However, there is one exception: when the writer promises *before the interview* that something will be off-the-record and excluded from the written interview.

Task 2.6

Select a number of magazine feature interviews from the Sunday supplements. Identify the types of questions asked from the preceding list and evaluate their effectiveness.

Formats for feature interviews

Once an interview has been researched and conducted, it can be written up. Begin by ordering the material of the interview so that it achieves clarity and maximum impact. This means that the logical order of the questions asked may not be followed, but the writer should still aim for a narrative that appears conversational, not fragmented. One quick look through a selection of magazines will show that there are two main formats for writing-up the feature interview: the 'Q & A' and the narrative. According to Hennessy, the Q & A:

> is used for a serious debate leaving out personalities, but is also used as a way of ensuring that the interviewee is centre stage ... Popular magazines use the Q and A format for fast-moving, concise accounts of a person's views, a standfirst or a brief paragraph serving for the introduction ... Some interviewers use the Q and A format to get closer to the interviewee. The descriptive material can make an informative introduction. The feature then becomes more like a dialogue in a play, with feelings exposed. (2006: 279)

Conversely the narrative interview reads far more like a story and uses some of the techniques of traditional storytelling. No words should be wasted and each word used should move the story along, interspersed with quotations and interesting insights on the subject. These insights may be the result of the environment, the subjects themselves, their body language, dress or behaviour. When writing-up the narrative interview, the writer does not need to tag every question with 'I asked' or ' he said', or even place his or her own questions in speech marks (see the interview entitled *Inside Out* in the following task).

Task 2.7

Consider the article below written for *You*, the magazine supplement for the *Mail On Sunday*. What is the impact of this compared to a Q & A type of interview? Which type of interview do you prefer to read, and why? Which type of interview would you prefer to write, and why?

Inside Out

I'm waiting in a subterranean office within the dark shadow of the overpowering Channel Four building in Medway Street, south west London. I've come here to interview Paul Lewis, editor of the national newspaper for prisoners – *Inside Time*.

Paul bowls into the office apologising for being a mere two minutes late. He's a remarkably handsome man, possessing a sharp intelligence you could cut yourself on. His sixteen years spent in a prison cell do not appear to have dulled him one bit.

I ask him to tell me how the paper was started. 'Well,' he says, eyes glinting, 'the paper was started four years ago by a national charity called The New Bridge as a voice for Britain's population of prisoners. The New Bridge aims to create links between the offender and the community and they run all sorts of projects which enable them to work towards the rehabilitation and re-socialisation of offenders. The newspaper's one of these projects and was the direct result of a survey carried out in all one hundred and thirty six of Britain's jails. The paper's distributed free of charge to fifty four thousand serving prisoners.'

There were rumours that the newspaper had not been well received at first by the prison authorities. 'A lot of prison governors binned it,' says Paul. 'They were suspicious of anything new and weren't sufficiently foresighted to see the potential benefits to both staff and inmates. The paper isn't a forum for bashing the system, it's there for the prisoners – to inform and educate. Anyone has a right to comment on any subject in the paper and that goes for prison governors, officers, probation staff, grey suits from HQ and prisoners themselves. In fact prison headquarters in Cleland Street were so impressed with *Inside Time* they issued a directive to all governors to make it freely available to all prisoners in their respective prisons.'

I remark on the fact that Lady Billington and her brother-in-law, the playwright Harold Pinter are both consultants for the paper. 'Yes, that helps of course. Rachel is one of Lord Longford's daughters. Frank Longford was a founder member of The New Bridge back in the 60s. Rachel's very conscious of prisoners' rights and active in prison reform. Her whole family are ...'

I mention that Lord Longford has an unfortunate reputation as the 'potty peer'. 'Yup,' scowls Paul, 'that really gets up my nose. O.K., so he's upset a lot of people with his crusade for Myra Hindley. I don't blame people getting narked over that, but nobody bothers to comment on the years of unfailing kindness he's shown others, many of whom should never have been in prison in the first place. He and his family have been very kind to me and welcomed me with open arms. I'm hoping some of their compassion – not to mention some of their literary genius will rub off on me,' he laughs.

So, how did Paul Lewis get himself involved with *Inside Time*? 'Through the back door and by a stroke of luck really. The whole episode has saved me from further offending. I've served five separate prison sentences totalling sixteen years. All my crimes were burglary. I did big houses in the Southampton area and was known by the local cops as 'the gentleman burglar. Knew my stuff you see ... and never left a mess. But God, did I waste my life. I've also been a good communicator and I wrote a lot in prison. Men discover long buried or unknown talents when they're locked away. Soon after I was released I was asked to go on the 'Kilroy' programme on T.V. They were doing some show on the criminal justice system. It was there I met some people from The New Bridge and with their help I was encouraged to start lecturing in schools and colleges on the futility of crime and the utter waste of life it results in. I was fourteen years old when I started offending and if someone had been there to tell me the stark and brutal realities of prison life I like to think I would have stopped there and then. I began life as a nice middle-class kid you know – I was never disadvantaged. I disadvantaged myself as I grew into a life of crime. Anyway, the lecturing was successful and I was soon invited to talk to the students at all the public schools – Harrow, Marlborough College, Westminster, Cheltenham Ladies' College. The editor of *Inside Time* was then a young woman called Anna Sway who'd been given a life sentence at the age of eighteen for killing her mother. She served two years on appeal, worked on the paper, went on to write a novel and a couple of successful plays. She got too busy to carry on with the paper so The New Bridge offered me the chance of editing. They needed an ex-offender in the role of editor; it looks more convincing and less patronising to the average con who's going to read it.'

I remark that there had been talk of the paper folding due to lack of funding. 'Yes, well it is a free paper after all,' says Paul. 'We were lucky, the Paul Getty Foundation and the Tudor Trust came up trumps, so we have enough money to see us through the next couple of years now. All the printing is done at cost at Kingston prison in Portsmouth; they have their own print works. We did think of taking advertising in order to secure revenue, but the only people willing to purchase space in a newspaper for prisoners were solicitors.'

And what of Paul's future plans? 'Well, I hope to carry on lecturing for a while yet, though of course I do realise I have a sell-by date and can't keep trading on the fact I was once a crook, albeit a reformed one,' he grins. 'People would soon accuse me of playing the system. Some people already say things like, "crime certainly pays then, Paul", especially when they find out I make a comfortable living from lecturing. But I think that's unfair. I really am trying to prevent young people from becoming just another sad statistic, wasting their lives and costing the taxpayer a further £400 a week to keep them locked away.'

'My future?' Well, I worked with Lynda La Plante on her novel, *The Governor*, about a woman governor in a men's jail. I'd like very much to write a novel of my own one day. I've appeared on TV countless times, always on programmes and documentaries discussing issues and topics on law and order. I'd like to break free eventually from crime related work, it's rather limiting after all. I've been out of prison for almost five years now. A lot's changed in the prison system since then. We have a very right wing and punitive Home Secretary in power at the moment. You never know, I might have to go back inside for a refresher course.' Paul gives a rueful smile, '... hopefully as a writer-in-residence, not as an inmate.'

Task 2.8

Ask a friend or colleague to read you a published magazine feature interview of between one and three thousand words. Test your note-taking skills by making notes of the content. Note the main points such as facts, names and figures. Rewrite the interview using only your notes. How much does your rewritten example differ from the original? How effective are your note-taking skills?

Interview a friend or colleague about an important event in their life. Write up the results in an eight-hundred-word narrative form of interview. Read it back and ask whether he or she thinks it is a fair representation.

Marketing the magazine feature

A writer should always sell the idea first rather than the actual article itself. This is because magazine editors may not be looking for that particular topic at that particular moment, or have already covered it in a recent edition. Feature editors buy ideas, rather than finished articles. Writers are advised to pitch several ideas to the features editor rather than just one, and preferably by e-mail. It is important to state the ideas simply, the reasons for writing the proposed articles at this time, and an indication why you are the best person to write the article; perhaps you have experience of the issue, or are an expert on the topic. Once the commission is received, the word count and deadline should be established. Deadlines are extremely important: failing to deliver on time may mean that future commissions may not be offered. A decision about the sourcing of the photographs that will accompany the article must also be made, as these are the writer's responsibility. The basic rules for manuscript presentation are that they should be typed, double spaced, presented with large margins on either side (3–4 cm), on white A4 paper, in Times New Roman, Ariel or Courier, and be at least 12 pt. Before sending out the manuscript, we advise that the following simple questions are considered:

- Will the readers of the publication actually find this article interesting?

- Has anyone read the article critically and suggested improvements?
- Has the article been proofread carefully?
- Have the basic rules of presentation been followed?
- Does the manuscript contain a name, address and e-mail?
- Does the manuscript state the word count?
- Are the enclosures, such as photos with captions, complete?
- Is the postage sufficient, or is the editor's e-mail address correct?
- Is there an opportunity to suggest further article ideas?

The following quotations from magazine editors, collected by the authors of this book, usefully highlight common 'hates' about freelance writers. In order to impress any commissioning editor, read, digest and avoid.

- Ignoring the brief and not bothering to read the magazine.
- Sending articles without bothering to check if we have already published a similar article on the same subject in recent issues.
- Poor writing technique.
- Long CVs included with their work and lengthy, involved letters.
- Freelances who promise features and then sell them to competing titles.
- Freelances who lecture me about how I should do my job. Freelancers who acquire my home phone number and call me in the middle of the night 'for a chat'.
- Not knowing who they are writing for.
- Failure to deliver or not delivering to the agreed brief.
- Missing deadlines and exceeding word count limits.

When the same editors were asked what they thought made a good freelance feature writer, their common responses were:

- Ideas.
- Well-researched articles.
- The ability to write well and deliver on time.

Other types of magazine writing

Magazine writers wishing to branch out from feature articles and interviews should consider writing columns, opinion editorials ('op-eds'), reviews or short stories. Reviews and short stories provide a market for the freelance writer, but most columns and op-eds are written by magazine staff, including celebrities, opinion leaders and experts. An editorial represents the views of the magazine and is usually written by the editor of the magazine or one of the staff writers on their behalf. Editorial columns also feature other people's opinions on the same or similar subjects. These are known simply as 'columns'. Editorial pieces have an introduction, which should state the problem to be addressed; a body, which should express an opinion; a solution – to the problem; and a conclusion, which should emphasize the main issues addressed. As well as having a timely news angle, they must also offer an objective explanation of an issue, especially if that issue is complex. Editorials can also include opinions from the opposing viewpoint that directly refute the same issues that the writer is addressing. Good editorials engage issues, not personalities, and refrain from name calling or other tactics of petty persuasion. Anyone can gripe about a problem, but a good editorial should take a proactive approach to making the situation better by using constructive criticism and offering alternative solutions. Finally, an effective editorial should end with a concise conclusion that powerfully summarizes the writer's opinion: 'punch'. Editorials fall into four types:

- **Editorials of argument and persuasion:** take a firm stand on a problem or condition. These tend to attempt to persuade the reader to think the same way as the writer. This type of editorial often proposes a solution or advises taking some definite action.
- **Editorials of information and interpretation:** attempt to explain the meaning or significance of a situation or event. There is a wide variety of editorials in this category, ranging from those which provide background information to those which identify issues.
- **Editorials of tribute, appreciation or commendation:** aim to praise a person or activity.
- **Editorials of entertainment:** can be a short, humorous treatment of a light topic, or a slightly satirical treatment of a serious subject.

Task 2.9

Select a magazine which includes an editorial piece at the beginning. Analyse and place it in one of the above categories.

Writing a column

The regular column is always popular with magazine editors: they provide security, depth and perspective to the consideration of issues or events. They aim to provoke, amuse, entertain, annoy or inspire readers. Columns can range from lifestyle pieces to the deadly serious, and Hennessy (2006: 292) suggests that they can fall into four main types: the world at large; lifestyle; argument and provocation; humour, parody and fantasy.

Columns may fall under different categories, but, as outlined in the previous chapter, they have one thing in common: they are alive to the writer's voice, and are often instantly recognizable to the reader. Celebrities or well-known figures can be synonymous with column writing, highlighting the desire for editors to have a 'brand image' attached to their publication. It is therefore highly unlikely that a well-established magazine will commission a regular column from a new writer, but publications such as local, county and student magazines may. Maintaining a column over several months, or maybe years, is hard work. The writer must have a wealth of ideas and know the publication they write for, or intend to write for, inside out.

Task 2.10

Select an inside-page home-news story from a national newspaper, and write a one thousand word argument around it for a general interest magazine.

Writing reviews

The main problems with reviews, be they for plays, music, books, film, television or exhibitions, is that there are production schedules, particularly on monthly magazines. By the time the magazine gets published the creative output to be reviewed is past its sell-by date. Books present the least problem as copies or proofs are sent well in advance for review before their own publication. Television programmes are particularly difficult because there may be only one opportunity for viewers to see a programme. Consequently programmes are usually previewed rather than reviewed in magazines. However, there is ample opportunity for new writers to review local theatre, films, art, events, books, etc. for local magazines. The pay is measly, consisting usually of a free ticket to the event or a free book, but the writing is fun – and free tickets to anything is always a bonus!

Reporting is the basis of reviewing in the sense that 'facts' are being given to an audience, and as such Hennessy (2006: 310) offers the following preliminary guidelines for magazine reviewers to consider:

- What is it (the artefact) called?
- What is the genre? (Literary novel or thriller, tragedy or comedy, art-house or blockbuster?)
- What is it about? What does it mean? What does it represent?
- What is it like?
- Who created it?
- Who produced/directed it?
- Where is it showing? Where can you buy it?
- When and where does the action take place?
- Why was it written/painted/composed?
- How much is it?

The most interesting part of a review, of course, comes from the reviewer's actual engagement with the artefact being reviewed. Readers enjoy being given not only factual information, but personal reactions that may inspire them to also participate in the artefact. In order to achieve this, a magazine reviewer offers evidence to substantiate his or her thoughts and feelings. Hennessy (2006: 311) gives further guidance on this:

- What are the work's merits/defects?
- Is it worth your time and money?

- Did you like it?
- Will you like it?
- What sort of people will like it?
- Is it informative/inspiring/interesting/entertaining?
- What are the significant elements and how do they compare generally with other works in the genre (plot or characters, well-made play or postmodern experiment, message or slice of life, melody or in the raw)?
- How does it compare with other works by this creator/producer/director? What about with contemporaries' work? What about work of a similar kind in the past?
- How far does the creator succeed in achieving what he or she set out to do?
- How well has the work been served by the interpreters involved: actors, directors, set designers, musicians, etc?
- If known – how did the audience react to the work?

Task 2.11

Analyse a number of book, art and music reviews in a consumer magazine. How many of the above questions do you think the reviewer has considered? Have a go at writing your own review for a local event or a book that you have recently read.

Writing the short story

There is still a strong market for short stories in women's weekly consumer magazines, although this is a very competitive area of writing. Although such magazines vary in style, tone and readership, the prevailing style of short story is light-weight and formulaic: romantic, aspirational, domestic, etc. A short story is not a smaller version of a novel; there are set guidelines for structure, and sometimes even the topic. If interested in writing short stories for magazines, it is important to check the magazine's on-line guidelines for writing and submission first. The short story is an illustration of one aspect of human nature or the human condition. The story does not have to explain the meaning of life, but it should show how a character alters in some way or undergoes a change in attitude to life or a problem. The short story shows the development of the character in some way towards, or away from, a pre-established goal. The framework of the short magazine story relies on limited exposition, limited scenes, a short time span and few characters. However, like the novel, the short story must still contain an element of conflict: something or someone must interrupt the protagonist from reaching his or her goal, which the protagonist usually overcomes in the story's resolution.

Conflict can come in several forms. The most common is between two characters or 'man versus man', as in boy meets girl, boy loses girl, boy gets girl back. Short stories do not have to rely on romantic conflict, though: the conflict can be between neighbours, siblings, colleagues or even big business verses the little man – the David and Goliath form of conflict. Conflict with circumstance is where life is going wrong for the protagonist; it may or may not be his or her fault. Inner conflict is where the character is fighting with himself, perhaps trying to overcome a flaw in his character or battle with his own conscience. Conflict with the elements usually includes a strong character who is battling with the environment in some way. Perhaps he or she is struggling to sail across the Atlantic in a storm, or is in danger of being eaten by lions. Some stories contain a mixture of these types of conflict; they are not exclusive. Short stories for magazines should contain a plot, believable characters, some dialogue and a satisfying ending. To summarize, a short story illustrates one facet of human nature, illustrates a moment of change, has a type of conflict at its core, and makes direct links between the conflict and the moment of change.

Task 2.12

Read a number of short stories in a selection of women's weekly magazines. Analyse the type of conflict they present. Have a go at writing your own short story (800 words) aimed at a female audience.

Career opportunities in writing for magazines

The world of magazine writing is very competitive, and editors are seeking the best writers that they can get their hands on, hence the proliferation of new degrees in British universities offering courses such as 'Magazine Journalism', 'Media Writing' and 'Creative and Professional Writing'. There are two ways into magazine writing: you either freelance and pitch to any magazine you think you have something to offer; or you become employed as a staff writer by a particular magazine. Should you choose to follow the freelance route be mindful that there are plenty of other writers out there seeking to do the same. However, talent will out, and good writers with excellent ideas will always find work. A good source for markets for freelance magazine writers is *Writers' News*, a subscription based writing magazine which publishes several writing opportunities each month.

If you want to start in-house, the best route is to begin as an editorial assistant for a magazine publishing house. This will allow you to develop your skills and make contacts in the industry which is important as many journalism vacancies are not advertised. Some larger publishing houses often have structured on-the-job training schemes, but demand for acceptance on these is huge. You should consider completing a pre-entry journalism or degree course before looking for work. Qualifications recognized by the industry are accredited by the Periodical Training Council, the training section of the Periodical Publishing Association (PPA) and the National Council for the Training of Journalists (NCTJ). The NCTJ also runs distance learning courses including *Writing for the Periodical Press*, which gives a basic understanding of the magazine industry.

Whatever your entry route to magazine journalism, be proactive and persistent. Consider unpaid work internships, as the key to a staff post is practical experience. Other ways to gain experience and build up a portfolio of published work include contacting editors directly with ideas for relevant articles, writing reviews for film, plays, books and products, working as a correspondent on a local paper, writing for a student magazine or newspaper, or volunteering to work on the newsletter of a not-for-profit organization.

Visit the PPA website for advice on finding work experience and applying for jobs. As a member of the PPA, you can take the PPA Professional Certificate in Journalism, which covers both print and on-line publications.

Further reading

Baker, D. (1995) *How to Write Stories for Magazines: A Practical Guide*, 3rd edn, London: Alison & Busby.

Bugeja, M. (1998) *Guide to Writing Magazine Non-fiction*, Boston, MA: Allyn & Bacon.

Crone, T. (2002) *Law and the Media*, Oxford: Focal Press.

Hall, C. (1999) *Writing Features and Interviews*, 2nd edn, Oxford: How To Books.

Hennessy, B. (2006) *Writing Feature Articles*, 4th edn, Oxford: Focal Press.

McKay, J. (2006) *The Magazines Handbook*, 2nd edn, London: Routledge.

McLoughlin, L. (2000) *The Language of Magazines*, London: Routledge.

Pape, S. and Featherstone, S. (2006) *Feature Writing: A Practical Introduction*, London: Sage Publications.

Ramet, A. (2007) *Writing for Magazines: How to Get Your Work Published in Local Newspapers and Magazines*, Oxford: How To Books.

Ruberg, M. (2005) *Writer's Digest Handbook of Magazine Article Writing*, 2nd edn, London: Writer's Digest Books.

Strunk, W. and White, E.B. (1999) *The Elements of Style*, 4th edn, Harlow: Longman.

Welsh, T., Greenwood, W. and Banks, D. (2005) *McNae's Essential Law for Journalists*, Oxford: Oxford University Press.

Web resources

www.ppa.co.uk
Magazine-specific resource for journalists.

www.nctj.com
Official website for the National Council for the Training of Journalists.

www.nujtraining.org.uk
Official website for the National Union of Journalists (Training).

www.nuj.org.uk
Official website for the National Union of Journalists.

www.writersnews.co.uk
Writers' News and Writing Magazine, filled with services for established and aspiring writers.

Broadcast Journalism 3

Unlike print journalism, broadcast journalism is written to be heard and, in the case of television, seen. Broadcast journalism acts as the eyes and ears of the audience, taking in the knowledge of local and world events and processing them to create meaning. As such, broadcast journalists must have a passion for storytelling and a passion for touching the emotions of their audiences. They must be quick and effective in meeting tight deadlines, and have the flexibility to multitask. They must recognize that broadcast journalism employs a particular structure and uses specific language, and that this will vary between story types, from an international 'hard news' event to a regional 'soft news' tale of human interest. Therefore this chapter will build upon the ideas already presented in the first two chapters of the book and examine the precise nature of writing news stories for the broadcast medium.

By the end of this chapter, you should be able to:

- Understand the qualities required of a broadcast journalist.
- Recognize the ethical considerations underpinning broadcast journalism and begin to apply them to hypothetical news stories.
- Evaluate the importance that news values play in constructing a news story.
- Recognize the uses and limitations of the different ways that broadcast news stories are sourced.
- Understand how broadcast news stories are structured and apply to them the specific principles of broadcast news language.
- Demonstrate a familiarity with specific types of broadcast writing, such as hard news, soft news, sports broadcasting and radio broadcasting.

The principles of broadcast journalism

We could ask, why do we need to see and hear news when we can read it? A simple answer is this: 'broadcast journalism, through the power of dramatic video and engaging audio, offers emotional appeal, realism and immediacy that printed stories can't match' (Harrower, 2007: 164). Seeing live images and hearing live sounds makes broadcast journalism akin to screenwriting, where the action takes place before us and we are pulled into the world of the story. Although print journalism does its best to create emotional engagement between the text and its reader, broadcast journalism has an easier job. Simply, its visual and aural form promotes an inherently visceral appeal. For Wilkinson *et al.*: 'television is a dramatic, emotional medium that best covers accidents, emergencies, rescues, and events unfolding before the viewer. Television also works best when the viewer can see other people moving or being active on the screen' (2009: 115). Thus, broadcast journalism allows events and people's reactions to events to be captured in a moment and presented to an audience as if they were there; a shared experience.

Like print journalism, broadcast journalism is collaborative in nature and utilizes a range of roles to create the finished 'package'. From news editor to reporter, cameraman to sound technician, the idea that 'many hands make tight work' (Bell, 1991: 34) holds strong in a medium that is increasingly driven by ratings. However, unlike print journalism, there are three principles (Wilkinson *et al.*, 2009: 111) that specifically define broadcast journalism as its own entity, and are crucial to remember for anyone wishing to work as a broadcast journalist:

1. **Stress the visual:** pictures dominate the screen and 'tell' the story. Sight and sound should be woven into a unified whole.
2. **Stress the moment:** it 'just happened'. Going 'live' to a reporter within a news segment also offers excitement and immediacy.
3. **Stress the simple:** offer linearity in speech. Viewers cannot go back and read the script, so broadcast news must be presented simply and coherently.

Qualities of a broadcast journalist

The traditional skills of print journalism are still very relevant for broadcast journalism. According to Hudson and Rowlands, 'uncovering information, interpreting it, and presenting what is truthful and relevant to as many people as possible' (2007: 4) is the mainstay of the broadcast journalist's role. Quite simply, 'a good journalist "gets good stories" or "knows a good story"' and, further along the career path, 'a critical news editor asks: "Is this really a story? Where's the story in this?"' (Bell, 1991: 147). When brought into the visual and aural medium of broadcasting, these qualities are somewhat expanded upon. For Hudson and Rowlands, audiences 'want journalists to interpret the world around them and tell them what's going on, because they don't have the time in their busy lives to work it out for themselves' (2007: 4). Although this statement may not hold true for everyone, the fact does remain that in a world where people lead busy work, domestic and social lives time is at a premium; as such, the broadcast journalist plays a key role in creating a summary of the world's news and affairs. The danger, of course, is that the 'truth' purveyed, however skewed, is likely to be taken as writ; people do not have time to 'work it out for themselves', so they simply accept the facts given to them.

With this 'burden of duty', then, the broadcast journalist must possess a whole host of skills and qualities needed to succeed in such a competitive industry. Boyd *et al.* (2008: 4) believe that a broadcast journalist should have a passionate interest in current affairs, be a team player, be comfortable working in a fast-moving, pressured environment, possess flexibility and adaptability, and have an understanding of audience needs. More specifically, Helen Boaden, Director of BBC News, tells us what employers look for:

> You want curiosity. You want the capacity to challenge, to see stories laterally, to ask difficult questions of everybody. You want people who are interested in people they're likely to be interviewing but also the issues of the wider world. (Cited in Hudson and Rowlands, 2007: 10)

Task 3.1

Write down any examples where you can demonstrate the skills and qualities outlined above. How would you talk about these in a potential interview setting? Do you think you would make a good broadcast journalist?

Types of news

Although many broadcast journalists develop a specialist field through their career, such as ITN Royal Correspondent or BBC Political Editor, it is likely that they will have worked in a number of fields with a wide range of related stories before achieving this. The wide-ranging types of story that broadcast news covers makes it an exciting industry to work in. As well as news programmes obviously having to cater for their wide-ranging demographic, the variety of news types offered means that broadcast journalists are able to further their experiences of the world and so remain interested in their jobs. The main types of news are categorized by Boyd *et al.* (2008: 20–5) as:

- Emergencies.
- Crime.
- Government.
- Planning and developments.
- Conflict and controversy.
- Pressure and lobby groups.
- Industry and business.
- Health and medicine.
- Human interest.
- Sport.
- Seasonal news.
- Special local interest.
- Weather.
- Traffic.
- Animals.

As we can see, these news types are a mixture of 'hard news' and 'soft news'; that is, dramatic stories and entertaining stories. As will be discussed below, a range of news story types is essential to creating a well-balanced, textured and audience-friendly news programme.

Task 3.2

Watch several news programmes or bulletins throughout one evening and categorize each of their stories according to the list above. Is there a bias towards several of the categories? Is there a common order of news according to the categories?

When it comes to the delivery of news stories there is also variation, mainly in their style and length. Wilkinson *et al.* (2009: 119–20) list three types of common news delivery, which we have expanded upon:

- **Reader:** this is a presenter-only style of delivery, where the presenter simply reads a story to the audience. The camera remains on him or her throughout. Usually 'reader' stories run for a maximum of twenty seconds.
- **Voiceover/presenter:** this is similar to a 'reader' but contains a sound bite from someone involved in the story. The presenter will read the story to the audience and an accompanying sound bite will support what he or she is saying. Usually 'voiceover/presenter' stories run for a maximum of one minute, but can be as little as twenty-five seconds.
- **Package:** used mainly for big news stories, a 'package' contains a whole host of visual and aural elements. It will usually start with an introduction from the presenter, followed by footage, sound bites, graphs, charts and statistics as part of the (outside) reporter's own recorded story. A package will usually last for more than a minute, sometimes running to three.

The news mix

Broadcast news is just that: news that is cast to a broad range of people, who ultimately have a broad range of tastes. As such, it is important that producers of news programmes cater for diverse audiences and adopt the idea of the *news mix*: a range of news stories that differ in content, style and tone. Broadly split between hard news stories and soft news stories, the news mix gives the news programme a textured and friendly feel; it is not heavily reliant upon just one type of news story, but instead embraces a range of stories that encourage a range of feelings and emotions.

'Hard stories are those with importance, significance and relevance to the audience' (Hudson and Rowlands, 2007: 42), such as major international or national events, disasters, politics and current affairs. Hard stories are usually 'breaking' stories, with a sense of immediacy and urgency about them. Examples might include:

- The assassination of a political figure.
- An inner-city teenage stabbing.
- A hurricane.
- The meltdown of the stock exchange.

Soft stories, on the other hand, 'do not usually have a direct impact on people's day-to-day lives' (ibid.: 44), such as emotionally light, sometimes quirky, human interest stories involving celebrities, royals, children or animals. Examples might include:

- The marriage of a pop star.
- The divorce of a film star.
- A member of royalty turning twenty-one.
- The birth of a five-legged dog.

Often the news programme will begin with a raft of hard news stories used to hook the audience into the programme and to keep them on the edge of their seats. This is usually followed by lighter, soft stories used to allow the audience to 'wind down' and see that the world is not all doom and gloom. The quirkiest story may be saved until the very end of the programme, such as the 'and finally' feature made famous by ITV's *News at Ten*. The structure of the news mix can be seen as an attempt to structure the emotion of the audience: suspense, anticipation, horror and relief; or, in Aristotelian terms, pity, fear and catharsis. The news programme can thus be likened to a film or television drama, where the audience is taken on a 'ride' of emotions.

The differentiation between hard news and soft news, however, is not always consistent between news programmes. As Boyd *et al.* tell us:

> Where news ends and entertainment begins is more than a matter of house style ... Where that line is drawn will depend on the target audience for a programme and the priority that is placed on high ratings. The surest way to boost those ratings is to increase the amount of entertainment that goes into the mix. (2008: 18)

This tells us that because of the competitive nature of broadcast news, especially that on the various commercial channels, entertainment stories may be 'dressed up' as hard news stories purely to increase ratings. Conversely, hard news stories may be 'dressed down' as entertainment by including references to celebrities or products of popular culture (film, television, music, computer games). Although many may view this as a negative quality of broadcast journalism, it does for the journalist mean something else: an ability to find the popular in the niche. As such, another quality of a good journalist that we could add to the list above is the ability to find the appropriate angle of a news story to suit a particular audience demographic.

Task 3.3

Using the news programmes viewed for the task above, can you identify clear divisions between hard news and soft news? Are there any cross-overs? Have any hard news stories been angled differently to appeal to a more popular market?

As well as events of the world dictating the content and order of a news programme, a news editor's preference for types of story is likely to have an influence. Not only this, a channel's ownership, where and when the bulletin is broadcast, and the type of bulletin broadcast (rolling news, lunchtime news, main evening news, etc.) can play a crucial part in how news is packaged together (Morgan, 2008: 84). For example, ITN (commercial) news editors may have specific views about what content their bulletins should have if they consider that ratings are a high priority. This may differ from the BBC news editor, who values the quality of a story over its commercial appeal. Similarly, news producers working in specific areas 'have to consider how their programmes reflect the region they serve' (Hudson and Rowlands, 2007: 42). Both ITV and BBC have news centres in some of the country's major cities (London, Manchester, Birmingham, Leeds, Glasgow), each anchored to a particular region that will serve one or a few counties. Although the main news stories of the day may appeal to a national audience, this is not always the case in the regions, where an audience may prefer to hear about something more local. Here there are two options: either the stories presented are totally different from the national ones, reflecting a more local appeal, or some of the stories are the same, but angled with a more local appeal (a local person involved, how the incident affects the region).

Task 3.4

Watch a news programme from your local region. Identify which stories are purely local and which ones are of national importance but angled for a local audience. How effective are the latter stories?

News values

As already discussed in the previous two chapters, news values are integral to a discussion of journalism. Not only can we use them to 'judge' a piece of journalism in a critical way, we can use them to inform news practice and, specifically, news writing. In rather crude terms, a short way of understanding the news value of broadcast journalism is this: 'Does the story excite you? Do you want to know more? Will your friends and family want to hear it?' (ibid.: 20). These three questions may sound more like the selling point of a news story than its news 'value', but in fact they tell us a lot about how the broadcast journalist industry works. For example, Deborah Turness, Editor of ITN, states: 'every single news item that we do should perform some kind of emotional function ... it reassures; it explains; perhaps it shocks; perhaps it inspires fear; or perhaps makes you laugh' (cited in ibid.). This clearly tells us that the core function of a news story is to affect its audience; the list of verbs she gives frames every news story with a sense of duty. Thus the production of broadcast journalism must constantly consider the question of newsworthiness: who will care about this?

Boyd *et al.* tell us that although the premise of a story may be information that is new, true and interesting 'for it to be newsworthy, it would have to be relevant to you, the audience' (2008: 19). In other words, the story should get its audience talking; it should perform a 'have you heard?' duty. As such, some stories outweigh others in terms of news values, resulting in a hierarchy of information that news editors will want to be presented in their news programmes: 'gun sieges, violent crimes, car chases, precarious rescues – the greater the drama, the greater its prominence in conversation' (ibid.: 17). News values may also change over time according to transforming cultural knowledge and shifting audience desires. Harrower believes that 'smart' journalists 'adjust to the tastes, reading habits and news appetites of their readers [and viewers]' and, because of the competitive nature of 'selling' news, 'it's essential to monitor how effectively you're delivering your message and satisfying your audience' (2007: 18). To this end, news values and newsworthiness are in a constant flux: what might be ground-breaking and eagerly anticipated today may be banal and boring tomorrow.

Task 3.5

Can you think of any news stories that were ground-breaking at the time of first broadcast but are now common and 'everyday'? Evaluate the effect that such stories might have had upon a news editor's view of news values.

The Public Service Broadcasting (PSB) commitment of many television and radio channels is another form of news value. Here news programmes from the likes of the BBC, ITV, Channel 4 and Channel 5 are designed 'for the public benefit rather than commercial gain ... [and] include a commitment to covering a diversity of interests and tastes, including minority interests' (Hudson and Rowlands, 2007: 22). The overarching idea with PSB is that news should be of the public interest, and not necessarily of interest to the public. Objectivity plays a key part in this, where the journalist is encouraged to see a story from the point-of-view of a third party, and not from his or her own point-of-view. However, these ideals are not without their criticism. For example: 'complete impartiality is like perfection; an ideal for which many will strive but none will wholly attain. Even the most respected journalist can only be the sum of his or her own beliefs, experience and attributes, the product of society, culture and upbringing' (Boyd *et al.*, 2008: 33).

Franklin notes broadcast news journalism's tendency 'to retreat from investigative journalism and the reporting of hard news to the preferred territory of "softer" or "lighter" stories' (1997: 4). As such, 'entertainment has superseded the provision of information; human interest has supplanted the public interest; measured judgement has succumbed to sensationalism; the trivial has triumphed over the weighty' (ibid.). This may not come as a surprise if we consider Langer's belief that television news 'is primarily a commodity enterprise run by market-oriented managers who place outflanking the "competition" above journalistic responsibility', resulting in programmes that are 'in the business of entertainment, like any other television product, attempting to pull audiences for commercial not journalistic reasons' (1998: 1). We can thus understand this as *tabloid journalism*, visually and aurally presented, but driven by the same news values as red-top newspapers. An example of this can be seen in ITN's coverage of murdered toddler James Bulger's funeral, 'with its insensitive conjoining of the sentimental and the sensational, the prurient and the populist' (Franklin, 1997: 3). Here the processes of broadcast journalism are alluded to but the presentation of visual and spoken material is packaged together to generate a particular effect on the viewing audience. This is understood as 'newszak', Franklin's terminology to describe the dire state that he sees broadcast journalism currently in:

> Newszak understands news as a product designed and 'processed' for a particular market and delivered in increasingly homogenous 'snippets' which make only modest demands on an audience. Newszak is news converted into entertainment ... The task of journalism has become merely to deliver and serve up whatever the customer wants; rather like a deep-pan pizza. (ibid.: 4–5)

With this in mind, then, we must consider how exactly broadcast journalists 'process' their information in relation to news values, wanting to deliver a story that is both newsworthy and that pertains to public trust and the interest of the public. As part of this process, 'journalists constantly apply what's called *news judgement*: the ability to determine which stories are most interesting and most important to readers' (Harrower, 2007: 16). In a broadcast environment, news is quicker than in a print environment. As such, some news values are more specific to the visual and aural medium; a medium which also appears more frequently than the usual daily newspaper. Listed here, then, are some news values of a newsroom, as given by Hudson and Rowlands (2007: 26–37):

- **Relevance:** literally, how big is the story? What does it mean to and for the public? If it is a 'small story', how can it be made relevant and appear 'bigger'? Why does the story matter? For example: *Sliding share prices leaving millions of people short of pension funds; a local 'green' campaigner having the potential to challenge a national law.*

- **Interest:** the story needs to interest the audience as well as the journalist. News judgement is crucial here. Making a story entertaining can be a way to combat potential 'disinterest'. For example: *How might the changing of dog food supplier to the Queen be made interesting to the general public? How can humour make a story about a talking parrot interesting?*

- **Shock value:** this is all about surprise. What did someone expect, or not expect, to happen? For example: *The death of Princess Diana; Jade Goody's diagnosis of cancer.*

- **Drama:** some stories have plot twists akin to novels and films. This may relate to the unearthing of secrets in people's lives. For example: *The mystery surrounding a missing girl, with new evidence every day; more and more shocking revelations about MPs' expenses.*

- **Pictures:** which pictures are or might be available to complement the words? They can usefully capture tragedy, revulsion, emotion, etc. For example:

A picture of a crashed aeroplane; someone wearing something they should not be wearing.

- **Immediacy:** it may seem obvious, but news has to be news: it has to be *new*. Finding a new angle to make a story more immediate is a useful technique, especially with twenty-four-hour rolling news programmes. For example:
  Developments throughout the day from a big court case; identities released of the victims of a bus crash.

- **Controversy:** generated by journalists, controversy invites comment from others on an event or issue, and can sometimes initiate change. For example:
  What happens when someone in the public's trust is caught out for mass fraud? How do people react when a priest is arrested for child abuse?

- **Proximity:** this means the story's 'closeness to home'. In other words, how does it relate to us as human beings, with our own families? For example:
  Viewers/listeners are reminded about life and death when talking about war; the safety of home and family is thought about when hearing of a terrible train crash.

Task 3.6

Interview a friend to find out as much as you can about him or her. Imagine that you have been commissioned to write a news story about your friend: use the news values above to make a list of ten potential stories. Do not worry about the timing of events in your friend's life (many of them will be in the past); rather, use the ideas and give him or her newsworthiness by applying news values.

As Morgan reminds us, we must remember that editorial and operational procedures, too, dictate the viability of covering a news story. Although a journalist may think a story extremely newsworthy, there are elements that are just out of his or her control. For example:

editorial decisions (running order and importance of stories); time constraints (what can be achieved in time?); financial and budgetary constraints (what can be afforded?); geographical constraints (what can be supplied in time, via satellite, etc.?); access (to people, locations, etc.); other sources (news agency pictures or independents, etc.). (2008: 86).

As well as this, lawful regulations dictate what can and cannot be said. In the UK, Ofcom is the governing body that regulates broadcast news. As with most regulations, it asks 'to ensure decency, fairness and impartiality and to support the basic democratic concept of freedom of expression. Contrary to what some people think (or would like) you cannot say or do anything you want in broadcasting' (Boyd et al., 2008: 29). Laws prevent defamation of character through slander (spoken) or libel (published), and because television and radio news is formally presented to the public and recordable, it is classified as published, therefore libellous. The definition of 'libel' is to 'expose a person to hatred, ridicule or contempt, cause him to be shunned and avoided, lower him in the estimation of right thinking members of society generally, or disparage him in his office, profession or trade' (ibid.: 30); therefore, anything in a news broadcast that can be classified as this is within contempt of the law.

Finding a story

For all newsrooms, a 'controlled' way of sourcing stories is through forward planning. As with print journalism, this involves keeping a news diary of some sort so that specific events known to be coming-up can be covered accordingly. Planning thus lies at the centre of this type of story sourcing, where those involved must be aware of all potential outlets for coverage:

> They plan the movements of the Olympic Games, for example, for general elections, for EU summits and world conferences ... They also track the movements of foreign correspondents round the world and help ensure that as events unfold they can provide coverage for news. (Morgan, 2008: 85)

Similarly, broadcast 'district' or 'field' journalists are employed to go out into the community and find out what is happening. This type of story sourcing is more original than relying purely on press releases (Boyd *et al.*, 2008: 40), creating the potential for more 'exclusive' or original stories. Such journalists are likely to build up a bank of contacts that they can call upon at any given time, 'from politicians and captains of industry to market traders, pub landlords, policemen and members of voluntary organisations' (Hudson and Rowlands, 2007: 50). This can be a rewarding type of role because it gives the journalist a sense of community spirit and, potentially, a feeling of doing a worthy duty to the people.

Most stories, however, do not come from forward planning: they occur from events that happen spontaneously, all over the world. Such events provide stories that are classified as *breaking news*, and as soon as they happen the journalist must quickly establish the core story elements: who, what, where, when, why and how. From these initial basic elements, a story can be built-up and eventually broadcast to the audience. In some cases, such as a major international disaster or the discovery of a history of misdemeanours, 'the breaking news story may become a *running story* – one that has repercussions over the following days, weeks, months and years. It is important for journalists in a newsroom to stay abreast of running stories' (ibid.: 40). In such a case, it is the fresh, new angle, or *top line*, that becomes important to the audience: what is new about this story today, and why should anyone be interested again? Hudson and Rowlands (ibid.: 33) offer some useful considerations that ask journalists how they will approach their running stories this time, and provide them with updating techniques. Such considerations may include:

- Is the story being told for the first time, or is it already in the public domain?
- Is new information being made public? How important is this?
- Has the story changed in any way (worse, better, more at stake, etc.)?
- Are key people linked to the story talking for the first time?
- Are there any new sound clips or moving pictures of interest?

'Recognising the different angles available not only helps focus on the best way to tell the story, it offers the option of featuring different approaches in later bulletins, updating and refreshing the coverage without necessarily relying on new information' (ibid.: 39). As such, an audience should never feel that they are being presented with the exact same information, but rather a developmental journey through the story which both answers old questions and asks new ones at the same time.

Below we expand upon Hudson and Rowlands's list (2007: 52–8) that outlines where most broadcast journalists find their 'breaking' stories:

- **Press offices send press releases** in the hope that they will be turned into stories. However, it is important to remember they contain 'spin' to 'sell' effectively the press office's ideas. Thus press releases are 'copytasted' by journalists themselves to try and find an angle they wish to use.
- **Routine calls to emergency services and voice banks** are used to find out information about local accidents or incidents. Most of the recordings will be of minor incidents, but some may escalate into potentially bigger stories.
- **Freelance reporters** cover all types of story in all types of location, and thus a wide range of stories may come in to the newsroom.
- **News agency wire services** provide newsrooms, for a fee, with all the available news stories, including sports results and other facts and figures (share prices, etc.). In the UK, the Press Association and Reuters are used. However, it is always essential to double-check the information given.
- **News conferences**, such as those held by the police, can offer vital information for ongoing news stories (crimes, missing people, etc.).
- **Protests and demonstrations** are also useful sources of information because, as well as the action being seen first-hand, interviews can be grabbed and photographs taken.

In today's world of digital, participatory media, there are even more sources for obtaining the components of a news story. As Hudson and Rowlands highlight, 'the constant flow of information into newsrooms from viewers and listeners via text messages and e-mail, and journalists' access to blogs and podcasts mean there has never been so much research material available to reporters' (ibid.: 75). Whether prompted or not, everyday people try to make a stake in the newsmaking process by providing information they deem useful. This 'citizen journalism' works to empower the non-journalist, breaking down barriers between producer and consumer, them and us. However, it is important to remember that 'little of [the information] can be treated as instantly authoritative. Everyone and anyone has access to the Web and mobile phones. Few websites can be treated as reliable sources of information; text messages even less so' (ibid.). As such, any information provided via these means should be checked and then checked again for accuracy.

Task 3.7

Using the sources listed above, write both advantages and disadvantages of each way of obtaining a story. Decide upon an order of the usefulness of the sources, starting with the most useful first.

For the broadcast journalist, particularly the videojournalist sent into the field to cover a story, hard work will inevitably be undertaken in order to fit the story into the bulletin. Some will be lucky in that a segment can be recorded during the day and then edited into the main news programme; for others, however, staying out to cover the story may be the only option. Morgan writes that as well as going out to cover the story in the first instance, such a journalist may have to record and deliver the story from his or her location (via the Internet, a webcam linked via satellite, a satellite telephone or normal telephone), update it if it is an important, breaking one, and be available for 'lives' from the location to the newsroom (2008: 87). This means that for some broadcast journalism is anything but a cosy nine-to-five job.

During a routine day in the newsroom, stories will be dropped and new ones covered. This is because although a story may seem newsworthy at the time, something 'bigger and better' may come up that requires more energy and attention being paid to it. Although journalists may at first feel that their efforts have been wasted on a story that is dropped, they should not take it personally. Rather, such a

'demand for sharp reflexes, total flexibility and all-stops-out perform-
ance puts the buzz into news reporting' (Boyd *et al.*, 2008: 61).

Interviewing

> All interviews are social encounters ... During the course of an
> interview questions are posed by the interviewer to the intervie-
> wee in order to obtain information. The nature of the information
> exhibited can be verbal or nonverbal. The information can be
> factual or attitudinal. (Cohen, 1987: 13)

Interviewing for broadcast journalism has two forms: for background
research, where the interviewee may or may not be referred to, and
for primary evidence, where the interviewee will appear as part of the
report. This poses an interesting initial question: whom do we interview? Cohen notes the potential interviewee's role in society as a
major factor for deciding who to interview for broadcast news. It may
be, for example, a public official (civil servant, judge), professional or
expert (doctor, scientist), or someone elected to their position
(mayor, prime minister) (ibid.: 40). The role of this person in society
not only helps to determine their rank and thus their relevance to
the story, but in fact how the audience is supposed to feel about the
story in question. For example, experts are chosen on the basis of
their superior knowledge of a subject; therefore, if a journalist wishes
to purvey a particular angle of the story, the choice of expert made
may crucially help (or hinder) this.

When it comes to the actual interview, as with all interviewing, it
is important to ask open questions where the interviewee can
respond in a way he or she wishes. For example, asking 'Do you think
these financial irregularities are wrong?' can only elicit one of two
answers: yes or no. However, asking 'What do you make of these
financial irregularities?' opens up the question to any number of
responses, where the interviewee can tell us what he or she really
thinks and feels about the situation. This way of questioning thus
allows a narrative to form from the responses given; the story almost
tells itself, based upon various avenues that the interviewee journeys
down when speaking. Not all of the interview material will be

chosen, of course, but as a general rule the more material, the greater the choice available when it comes to editing the package together. In fact, a snippet of only eight or ten seconds may be taken from an hour's interview for final broadcast, but such a small segment from such a large interview should mean that the words used are of a high quality and relevant to the essence of the story.

An interesting dimension of the interview, perhaps more obvious with broadcast over print journalism, is the fact of obtaining an interview in the first place. Like the newspaper's 'scoop', the broadcast interview can be seen as a goal in itself, not just a goal in what it achieves. For Cohen: 'it is not uncommon for a journalist to be credited, mainly by colleagues and sometimes even by the public, simply for having obtained the interview without much consideration of what was said in it and its possible implications' (ibid.: 15). An example of this would be Martin Bashir's interview with the late Princess Diana in 1995, which although was acclaimed because of the way in which she discussed her personal life, was acclaimed just as much for having been an actual interview with Princess Diana. Interviews such as this are somewhat of a phenomenon in broadcast journalism and, for the journalist lucky enough to be given such an interview, time and care should be taken in planning both the questions and the general approach so that maximum impact can be achieved.

Writing broadcast news

According to Bell, authoring a news story is a complex business: it is formed from others' accounts of events and can include existing 'texts' such as interviews, public addresses, press conferences, press releases, prior stories on the topic, news agency copy or research papers (1991: 57). The journalist can thus be seen more as an editor, compiling all the necessary and available information to form a coherent structure, and then finding a story spine through it. It may be tempting for journalists to write what they think or feel about a situation, but because a news story is not an opinion piece, and because they have an ethical duty to their audience, they must construct the story based upon facts. There can be an angle to the story, of course, and this may be determined by their attitudes and points-of-view, but it is important that all statements are substantiated with evidence. Accuracy is thus extremely important in news writing; not only can silly mistakes flaw the journalist's career, they can sometimes be legally detrimental. As already highlighted, the newsroom is a busy, highly charged environment with tight deadlines, and it is under such pressured deadlines that mistakes can occur. Mistakes can also occur when journalists are writing about something unfamiliar to them, and they do not make the time to check facts. For example, Hudson and Rowlands cite a BBC Radio Four news broadcast which stated that HMS *Victory* is 'anchored' in Portsmouth Harbour: this is not strictly true, because Portsmouth Harbour is a dry dock (2007: 135). Therefore, journalists must always ensure that they make the time to check and double check facts, especially when writing about a subject that is unfamiliar to them.

Unlike newspaper writing, broadcast journalism requires that journalists 'write words that have to be spoken and sound natural. Their words must not sound as if they are being read out loud. In that sense broadcasters have more in common with the dramatist than with newspaper reporters' (ibid.: 128). Broadcast news stories only get one chance of being heard; unlike a newspaper, they cannot be read again if something is not understood. Therefore, a story must be clear, unambiguous, simple and clean. It must speak to a broad audience in an uncomplicated way, avoiding both difficult language and difficult expression. It should be written in an active voice, and broken up into bite-sized units (sentences). According to Harrower, broadcast journalists generally read between 150 and 180 words per minute: 'at that rate, it would take 28 hours to read a typical edition of *The Washington Post*. Most half-hour newscasts contain fewer words than one typical newspaper page' (2007: 165).

Task 3.8

Read the following broadcast news story, and evaluate what is wrong with it.

Michael Jones, a forty year old man, was arrested today because he committed an armed robbery last week. He did it in Leeds, at a jewellers', just as they were closing. The man stole jewellery worth over fifty thousand pounds, and as soon as he had it in his possession, he went on the run for a week. He was caught today after a tip-off to the police from someone who is rumoured to be in his family. When he committed the armed robbery, a female worker was hurt because Jones hit her in the face with a gun when she refused to open the jewellery cabinet. She has been off work since with shock. It has been said, by the police, that there is no way this man will be granted bail. It has also been said that they are opening old cases of armed robbery to see if there are links to him.

Like newspapers, many broadcasters offer style guidelines for journalists, providing a sense of the manner in which they speak to their particular audience. 'The difference between networks is one of tone, not the way stories are told' (Hudson and Rowlands, 2007: 134), and so it is always useful to investigate the different ways in which broadcasters achieve this. As an example, BBC News style guidelines can be downloaded (free of charge) from www.bbctraining.com/styleguide.asp. This is an excellent guide providing a wealth of useful information for the broadcast journalist.

In more general terms, here are some key points of advice for writing effective broadcast news, as offered by Hudson and Rowlands (ibid.: 129–33):

- **Use good conversational English:** interesting, understandable, entertaining and familiar expressions should be used. News presenters need to sound like they know what they are talking about, and so natural, attractive conversation is essential.
- **Tell it to your friends:** how would you tell a story to your friends? Of course, a broadcast story will not be exactly like this, but thinking in this way will give a good sense of pace, tone and structure. If viewers or listeners are doing other things at the same time, then you have to compete for their attention.
- **Be concise:** do not use padding or superfluous wording. Be straight to the point, stripping the story down to its essentials. Do not compress lots of facts into one sentence; rather, use a range of short sentences, where one idea per sentence is considered. Avoid subclauses, and read the story aloud to test it.

- **Keep it simple:** do not use jargon. It is difficult to listen to and hear complicated sentences, so consider the structure and vocabulary. Use active, not passive, sentences. Be direct and aim for a strong delivery.

Task 3.9

Rewrite the 'armed robbery' news story in Task 3.8 into a more effective piece of broadcast journalism, considering the advice given above.

Finally, we must remember when writing television news that we are writing for a visual as well as an aural medium, where the picture can speak volumes above the actual words. For Hudson and Rowlands, 'sometimes "writing" for television means not writing at all. Pictures with natural sound – the sound recorded at the scene – may be more effective in helping tell a story than the same pictures with a voice-over' (ibid.: 157). Television news has the added quality that an audience can feel like they are there, drawn into the action and thus part of the story. In such cases, excessive voiceover from the news presenter or reporter may in fact detract from the experience of watching the story rather than augment it.

Language

When it comes to the specific words used in a broadcast news story, there are even more principles to consider. In short, unlike a newspaper story, 'writing for broadcast can mean throwing away literary conventions, including the rules of grammar, so the words make sense to the ear, rather than the eye' (Boyd *et al.*, 2008: 69). Everything in broadcasting is written to be spoken, so news copy must sound 'natural to the ear and [be] easy to read out loud, without causing the reader to stumble over words and gasp for breath' (ibid.: 70). Hence contractions are always encouraged ('can't', 'won't', 'shouldn't') unless the specific point is to emphasize a word ('he could *not* have done it', etc.). Short words should always be used over long words, and short phrases over long phrases. For example, 'during' should be used over 'in the course of' and 'because' over 'owing to the fact that' (Hudson and Rowlands, 2007: 138).

Overall, the language of broadcast journalism is concerned with making a story understood the first time it is heard: 'cut the clutter and iron out convoluted writing. Sentences should be clear and straightforward, without clauses and sub-clauses' (Boyd *et al.*, 2008: 71). The audience should be able to understand the story they are told straight away, without having to spend time back-tracking sentences in their minds in order to make full sense of it. Quite simply: 'plain English does away with woolliness, wordiness, officialese and circumlocution and replaces it with words and descriptions that are concrete and direct. Plain English is about rat-catchers and road sweepers, never "rodent operators" or "highway sanitation operatives"' (ibid.: 74).

Task 3.10

Rewrite the following sentences into more effective broadcast news phrases:

- She said that she could not believe what had happened to her.
- Although lawyers cannot prosecute at this stage, they have said that they will not give up the fight to attain a sense of justice.
- Medical officials praised the actions of the aircraft's in-flight service operatives.
- The football club cannot believe the decision made by the Football Association, and are adamant that they will lodge an appeal with the relevant director of operations.

Structure

Much of the structural architecture involved in constructing a broadcast news story is shared with that of a newspaper story. For example, the 'key ingredients' of a story are: Who is involved? What happened? Where did it happen? When did it happen? Why did it happen? (Hudson and Rowlands, 2007: 147). These questions satisfy the audience's appetite for knowing the basic elements of a story first and foremost, which can then be developed and expanded as appropriate. Boyd *et al.* concur with this, arguing that in hard news stories, predominantly, the story 'begins with the most important facts, then backs them up with detail, background and interpretation, constructed to get the story across in a logical way that is clear and commands attention' (2008: 83–5). In other words, the key ingredients come first and are then further extrapolated to substantiate them. Although this may sound like the inverted triangle or pyramid technique of structuring discussed with regards to newspapers, it might be more useful here to think of a circular narrative, where rather than information 'fizzling out' so that it can be cut by the subeditor if needed, it develops strongly and finds a clear resolution at the end. In this case, Hudson and Rowlands argue for a Christmas tree model of structuring: the package starts with an intro (the tip of the tree), key information is given (the top of the tree), and then the story develops and fills out (the branches) until it fully blossoms and then comes to a resolution (the base) (2007: 153). Unlike the inverted triangle or pyramid, the Christmas tree does not necessarily denigrate information that comes later on in the story; rather, it uses such information to explore the story more fully, before pulling it all together again to produce a solid and substantial resolution.

In a similar way to this, Boyd *et al.* (2008: 87) propose a simple 'WHAT model'* for structuring the broadcast news story:

- What happened? The introduction tells the story in brief.
- How did it happen? Explain the immediate background or context.
- Amplify the introduction. Flesh out the main points in order of importance.
- Tie up loose ends. Give additional background material.

> ### Task 3.11
>
> Watch a range of broadcast news stories and make notes about the structure they employ. Is the Christmas tree or WHAT model in obvious use? How effective is it in telling the story?

---

* This model was published in Boyd *et al.*, *Broadcast Journalism: Techniques of Radio and Television News*, p. 87, copyright © Elsevier (2008).

Writing headlines

'They're the first thing the audience hears, but often the last thing to be written. The headline has to capture the attention, sum up the key points of the story, and tell people why they should want to stick with the bulletin' (Hudson and Rowlands, 2007: 148). They should be brief and punchy (perhaps only a dozen or so words), written in the present tense and with a sense of urgency. Usually a news programme will begin with a sequence of headlines, known as the 'menu' (ibid.: 149), which whets the appetite of the audience as to what is about to come. Increasingly, the menu is presented before the credits roll, which, as well as creating dramatic effect, is an attempt to grab the audience before they switch to another channel.

As discussed with regards to writing for newspapers, the headline does not only give a sense of the story's content, but can indicate the attitude or point-of-view angled towards the story. In this way, the headline works as a 'sales pitch' to the audience, inviting them to hear *their* news and not someone else's because what they are about to say is better. As such, the words of a broadcast headline should be appealing and somewhat 'exciting'. Examples might include:

- Ten dead and more injured as a school bus crashes into a river.
- Businessman jailed for stealing money and then killing his family.
- 'I do it for love.' The man accused of stalking celebrities speaks out.
- 'Game, set and match.' Britain brings home its first tennis gold medal in over a century.

What we can also see from these headlines is that they purvey a sense of the *latest* developments in a story. The headline does not introduce the story in the sense of setting the background scene, but introduces it in the sense of telling an audience where the story 'is at'. For example, the school bus crash headline tells of the 'result' of the crash: ten dead and more injured. The businessman story tells us the 'result' of the inquiry: he has been sentenced to jail. Even in the other two headlines, which use quotations relating to the story, the idea is that something has happened in the past, and now we are about to hear the latest development in the saga.

Task 3.12

Find five stories from a newspaper and write a broadcast headline for each. Experiment with alternatives to each headline, and evaluate how they offer a different point-of-view towards the story.

Writing the intro

In the UK, broadcast news introductions (intros) are also known as 'links'; in America, they are called 'leads'. As touched upon above, an intro will give the audience the 'key ingredients' of the story, such as who, what, where, when and why, and may present a clear angle from which the story will be told. Bell sees the intro as a 'micro-story' which 'compresses the values and expertise of journalism into one sentence' (1991: 176). As Boyd *et al.* advise: 'to make it easier to select the main point, it can help to choose a key word or short phrase which sums up whatever is most important about the story' (2008: 84). This will then allow the journalist to write his or her intro from the point-of-view of what is interesting about this story, such as, why now? Or, put another way, the point-of-view written into the intro 'intensifies the lens through which the story will be told' (Bell, 1991: 183).

As a general rule, an intro should not usually exceed thirty or so words. It may present all the facts at once, such as:

> Barry Price, the former Chief Executive of Shires Bank who stole three million pounds of customers' money and then bludgeoned his family to death, has today been sentenced to life imprisonment.

Alternatively it may be written in the manner of an exciting or dramatic sentence, perhaps employing a quotation from someone in the story or approaching the story from an oblique angle. For example:

> The rain may have poured and the spectators may have got drenched, but the sun was certainly shining down on Caroline Ball today as she brought home the first gold medal won by a British female tennis player in over a century.

Task 3.13

Using the five stories from the exercise above, write a broadcast news intro for each. Read them aloud to test their effectiveness.

Writing the outro

The 'outro' of a news story has to pay off; the final words used will give the audience a lasting impression about what has been presented. In short, the outro should tie up the story's loose ends, summarize it and project towards the future (Hudson and Rowlands, 2007: 152). This is important not only to portray a solid sense of the story that has been reported, but to keep the audience's ongoing attention from story to story: 'for broadcasters, it is as important to end well as it is to begin well, because you need to hold the audience's attention throughout a programme' (ibid.: 153). Hence allowing a story to fizzle out to nothingness can have a negative impact upon the quality of the news programme and ultimately lead to a loss of audience. Examples of effective outros might include:

> As investigators continue to examine the wreckage and try to establish exactly what happened this morning, the school's head teacher has told parents of those involved she will support them in any way she can. A special prayer service has been organized to take place this evening.

> As the jury is adjourned to make its final decision, there is one thing on every celebrity's mind: being in the public eye can certainly have its price to pay.

Task 3.14

Using the same five stories from the exercises above, write an outro for each. Read them aloud to test their effectiveness.

Sports broadcasting

Within the general rubric of broadcast journalism, sports broadcasting is a popular area that many people would like to work in. There are many reasons for this, including the chance that famous sports personalities may be met, opportunities to travel may arise, and fun may be had spending most of the day watching and listening to sport. We would advise those wishing to work in this area, however, to consider that a lot of work goes into producing good sports broadcasting, and that it is not just something of a 'fan' role. In fact, as Schultz tells us, 'sports broadcasting now encompasses a wide variety of topics, including drugs, crime, race, politics, law, and religion. Simply put, sports broadcasters can't write effectively if they don't know anything about other areas' (2002: 61). So sports journalists must demonstrate a wide knowledge of sport-related issues, not just specific knowledge of the sport itself and its star players. A solid background in general broadcast journalism is thus useful for such a role, where sport can be pursued as a pathway to be developed as a specialist area of expertise.

Schultz believes that today's emphasis on entertainment has 'prompted sportscasters to focus more on appearance and presentation. As a result, much modern writing has become redundant, recycled, and riddled with clichés' (ibid.: 57). An example of this might include the much-used play on the expression 'they think it's all over … it is now'. It is, then, the job of the new journalist to ensure that such redundant words and clichéd expressions are replaced with meaningful journalism that focuses specifically on the issues at hand; a 'return to the good fundamentals of writing and broadcast journalism' (ibid. 58). To achieve this, the following ideas, offered by Schultz (ibid.: 61–4) and expanded by us, can be embraced:

- **Creativity and originality:** creative writing does not have to be limited to feature writing in a journalistic context. In sports broadcasting, there may be many opportunities for offering original ways of writing coverage.
- **Rhyme and alliteration:** do not be afraid to experiment with writing techniques such as these. Sports events are often seen as 'shows' and so the language of the journalist can be heightened and made to feel exciting and fresh.

- **Humanize the writing:** sports stories are not just about games, championships or records; they are about the people involved. So, in order to build a strong audience connection, try to emphasize the human qualities of the event.

Radio broadcasting

Some believe that radio is a 'superior medium to television because the pictures are better' (Hudson and Rowlands, 2007: 155). In other words, because the images are conjured-up in the minds of the audience, there is a certain freedom to construct the visual action on a personal level. Spoken words and voices may trigger the imagination, yet the imagination is free to do what it likes, unlike with television. There is a danger with this, however, when it comes to news broadcasting: 'radio paints a picture in someone's mind, but you cannot paint a picture of an idea, a concept or an abstraction. You have to relate to things people are already familiar with, and that means using illustrations' (Boyd *et al.*, 2008: 77). That is, radio news may be wordier because it has to ensure that the audience's imagination does not roam too wildly and that the actual message is understood. For example, in a report detailing tax increases following the chancellor's budget, concrete examples must be given to ensure that the listener knows what this means for him or her. Such examples might include listing how this will affect day-to-day life: two pence extra per litre of petrol; five pence on the price of a bottle of wine; more expensive air travel; etc. This relates to Bell's argument that 'journalists do not write articles. They write stories' (1991: 147). In other words, a radio broadcast must tell its listeners something about *them*; how the news affects their world.

One other specific principle of radio broadcasting is that because visual captions cannot appear like they do on television, fuller narrative sentences may have to be used and names of subjects announced before they speak. For example, whereas visual footage of soldiers firing guns has an obvious meaning, in radio a clarifier such as 'these soldiers are posted in the desert and spend their days practising for attack' may have to be used. Similarly, 'Professor Adams from Cambridge University told us this' would have to be used on radio, instead of television's trick of a simple on-screen caption.

Task 3.15

Listen to a radio news bulletin and watch a television news bulletin. Concentrate on the same stories that are told via each medium, and evaluate how differently they are written. Try replacing one with the other and consider the ways in which they do and do not work.

Online broadcasting

Some of the ways in which broadcast news is being affected by online production and distribution are discussed in the Conclusion to this book. In summary, on-demand and user-generated content is shifting the broadcast news landscape in as much that we as consumers are no longer at the mercy of traditional gatekeepers. Not only that, an increasing familiarity with and ability in using interactive features means that a greater choice of ancillary material available to audiences is almost a given. Effectively, news broadcasters must use convergence techniques to create a 'better' experience for their audiences; ultimately this will also help them to retain their audience share. For example, Wilkinson *et al.* cite the possibilities of covering a sports game (2009: 91–2). Here they suggest that as well as the traditional on-air broadcast, the game may allow for a multitude of interactive, user-friendly additions to be made. These could include interactive polls, evolving pictures of fans, players and their families, real-time updates of game and player statistics, interactive maps, chat rooms and blogs. These additions thus allow the game to be taken away from its traditional on-air (television or radio) setting and be relocated across a multitude of complementary platforms: websites, e-mail, mobile phones, PDAs, etc.

As well as broadcast material transforming between different platforms of delivery, the actual types of broadcast material can also change as technology advances. Wilkinson *et al.* (ibid.: 94–106) suggest the following opportunities for new content, which, although innovative, are not mutually exclusive to traditional content:

- **Material relating to news events:** interactive material, such as additional still photographs, graphics and additional text. This may also include extended interview material (text, online or video).

- **Material reflecting the reporter's or individual's opinion, view, critique or analysis of an issue or topic:** this could take the form of blogging (one's opinions, an expansion of traditional text) or podcasts (one's own views as an audio/video version of the blog).

- **Material primarily geared towards promoting the organization and 'brand' or any of the people working there:** in a competitive marketplace, broadcasters need to 'sell' themselves. As well as on-air promotions of their content (advertising), websites may contain features such as 'meet the newsreader' sections, special 'extra' reports, and even live webcams from the newsroom.

- **Material designed to involve the public in the newsgathering and editing process, such as allowing people to post their own photos during the event:** this consumer empowerment could also include chat rooms, comment links, discussion boards or forums, polls and photo galleries.

What we must consider, however, is how much of the above is actually needed. Although some of the types of content may add to the audience experience, how crucial are they to the event's delivery? Are these really ways of moving broadcasting forward, or are they simply gimmicks?

Task 3.16

Using a website hosted by a traditional television or radio broadcaster, explore the additional content presented. What can you obtain that you cannot in the traditional form? How effective is it? How might such content shape the future of traditional broadcasting?

Career opportunities in broadcast journalism

We have already outlined the qualities required of a broadcast journalist, which should act as a solid starting point if you are considering a career in the field. Overall, you will need a passion for telling stories and finding evidence, and a love of variety, excitement, creativity and the potential for undertaking interesting experiences. Some of these qualities may in fact be tested by a potential employer, who in an interview situation may ask if you have any stories that you would like to pursue, or any experiences that you would like to gain from employment.

Before reaching this stage, however, it is important to demonstrate your skills in broadcast journalism. One useful way of achieving this is by building a portfolio, which may consist of written pieces (to be delivered by a presenter), a 'showreel' (your work presented by you or someone else), or a combination of the two. Work experience is also a very useful thing to have undertaken, and it can make your CV stand out from others. Although gaining work experience in a broadcast environment is not as easy as in a print environment, there are plenty of opportunities out there. For example, apart from the main broadcasting hubs located in London, both BBC and ITV have a plethora of regional news centres. Also, most cities and towns will have at least one local radio station, whether part of a national network (such as Galaxy) or something much smaller like community or hospital radio.

Most students at university or college should also have access to in-house broadcasting initiatives. Most educational institutions have their own student-run radio station, and some even have their own television channel. If these are available, then work placements should certainly be undertaken in order to gain valuable experiences and credits for your CV.

Further reading

Bell, A. (1991) *The Language of News Media*, Oxford: Blackwell.

Boyd, A., Stewart, P. and Alexander, R. (2008) *Broadcast Journalism: Techniques of Radio and Television News*, 6th edn, Oxford: Focal Press.

Franklin, B. (1997) *Newszak and News Media*, London: Arnold.

Harrower, T. (2007) *Inside Reporting: A Practical Guide to the Craft of Journalism*, New York: McGraw-Hill.

Hudson, G. and Rowlands, S. (2007) *The Broadcast Journalism Handbook*, Harlow: Pearson Longman.

Morgan, V. (2008) *Practising Videojournalism*, London: Routledge.

Schultz, B. (2002) *Sports Broadcasting*, Boston: Focal Press.

Wilkinson, J.S., Grant, A.E. and Fisher, D.J. (2009) *Principles of Convergent Journalism,* New York: Oxford University Press.

Web resources

www.bjtc.org.uk
Official website for the Broadcast Journalism Training Council.

www.reuters.com
Official website for Reuters international news and training agency.

www.irn.co.uk
Official website for Independent Radio News, which serves commercial radio stations with national and international news.

Public Relations and Media Relations 4

What is public relations?

Public Relations (PR) is about maintaining and enhancing *reputation*. It is an often misunderstood discipline. An excellent place to start when discussing what exactly PR is and what it is not is to begin with the three definitions offered by the UK's Chartered Institute of Public Relations (CIPR):

> Public relations is the planned and sustained effort to establish and maintain goodwill and mutual understanding between an organisation and its publics.

Central to this definition is the fact that PR is planned and managed. It is not an ad hoc process, but a well thought out activity. This activity also works to maintain mutual understanding between the organization and its consumers, where each seeks to listen and understand what the other is saying. Further definitions from the CIPR are:

> Public relations is about reputation – the result of what you do, what you say and what others say about you.

and:

> Public relations practice is the discipline which looks after reputation with the aim of earning understanding and support and influencing opinion and behaviour.

Perhaps a more comprehensive definition may be that offered by the 1978 World Assembly of Public Relations in Mexico which agreed that:

115

Public relations is the art and social science of analysing trends, predicting their consequences, counselling organisation leaders and implementing planned programmes of action which will serve both the organisation's and the public interest.

Good reputations take time to build and are the foundation stones of organizations. The job of PR is to build, enhance and protect these reputations, ethically and truthfully, whilst listening to their audiences' needs and engaging in a win–win situation. Never before in organizational history has PR been so important, and never before have solid writing skills been so much in demand by those wishing to employ PR professionals.

By the end of this chapter, you should be able to:

- Understand the practical and commercial considerations of writing for PR and media relations.
- Identify Grunig and Hunt's four models of PR.
- Recognize the main activities of writing for PR.
- Understand the importance of persuasion in PR writing.
- Recognize the layout of a news release and be able to imitate it successfully.
- Recognize the importance of the 'backgrounder' and understand its format.
- Be familiar with the different forms of writing for PR and media relations.
- Understand the notion of 'publics' and the importance of crafting individual messages.
- Understand the notion of creativity and functionality within PR writing.

The emergence of public relations

PR may be a relatively 'new' profession, but it has existed for a very long time under different guises. The art of persuasion is deeply rooted in classical civilization. Over four thousand years ago, the philosopher Ptah-Hotep advised Egyptian court orators to link their messages with the concerns of the audience. Socrates of Athens and his student Plato both studied and practised rhetoric, the art of persuasive communication. Later both Aristotle and Cicero developed their ideas of rhetoric and persuasion. PR as we know it today, however, began in 1922 when Edward Bernays wrote a book entitled *Crystallizing Public Opinion* in which he described the new profession of 'public relations counsel'. He suggested that PR practitioners were to be different from the usual publicists and press agents of the day; they were to be professional and socially responsible. They were to use social science techniques to understand public motivations and perceptions. The objective of the 'new, improved' PR practitioner was to interpret the organization to the public and the public to the organization.

Today PR has made organizations more responsive to their publics (their consumers, users and customers) by channelling feedback from them to management. Today PR practitioners increase their publics' knowledge by providing information through the media that the media themselves do not have the manpower nor budget to provide. PR is not marketing, nor is it advertising. Simply put, marketing is about the bottom line. The Institute of Marketing defines 'marketing' as 'the management process responsible for identifying, anticipating and satisfying customer requirements profitably'. Advertising is about persuading people to 'buy' through paid-for media. The Institute of Practitioners in Advertising defines 'advertising' as presenting 'the most persuasive possible selling message to the right prospects for the product or service at the lowest possible cost'. PR, conversely, is about managing reputation. It can work extremely well in conjunction with both the disciplines of advertising and marketing when it then becomes known as 'integrated marketing communications'.

Roles within public relations

Practitioners working in the field of public relations are either employed within the organization itself, a term known as 'in-house', or in consultancies where they will work on various PR projects. Some people also work on their own as freelance practitioners. Whatever role a practitioner chooses to take, the vital skills he or she needs to succeed are the same: the ability to write clearly and succinctly; the ability to think strategically; and the ability to problem solve creatively. These skills demarcate themselves into two distinct, but overlapping, divisions: that of the technician (the writer) and the manager (the problem solver). It is, of course, the role of the technician-as-writer that aligns itself more obviously to the premise of this book.

The main activities of public relations

The principal activities undertaken by a PR practitioner can be summarized as follows:

Activity	Focus	Examples
Internal communications	Communicating with employees	In-house newsletters, suggestion boxes, intranet
Corporate PR	Communicating on behalf of whole organization, not goods or services	Annual reports, conferences, ethical and mission statements, visual identity, logos and images
Media relations	Communicating with journalists, editors from local, national, international and trade media, including newspapers, magazines, radio, TV and web-based communication	Press releases, photocalls, video news releases, blogs, off-the-record briefings, press events, features and articles
Business-to-business	Communicating with other suppliers, e.g. suppliers, retailers, distributors	Exhibitions, trade events, newsletters
Public affairs	Communicating with opinion formers, e.g. local/national politicians, monitoring political environment	Briefings, presentations, private meetings, public speeches
Corporate social responsibility/ community relations	Communicating with local community and elected representatives, schools, etc.	Exhibitions, presentations, letters, sports/arts activities, meetings, sponsorship

Activity	Focus	Examples
Investor relations	Communicating with financial organizations/ individuals	Briefings, events, newsletters
Strategic communication	Analysis of situation, problem and solutions to enhance organizational goals	Researching, planning and executing a campaign to improve the ethical reputation of the organization
Issues and crisis management	Monitoring the macro- and micro-environment and communicating messages in fast changing situations or crises	Dealing with the media after a crisis which could seriously affect the organizations' reputation
Copywriting	Writing copy for different audiences	Press releases, direct mail, newsletters, web pages, annual reports, advertising copy, corporate literature
Events management	Organization of major events and exhibitions	Conferences, trade shows, press launches, receptions, hospitality

As can be seen from this table, all of these activities involve writing to some degree, whether in the planning of an overall campaign or exhibition, or the more technical aspects of writing, such as corporate literature.

Grunig and Hunt's four models of public relations

Prior to any form of PR writing being undertaken, it is necessary to understand the importance of writing for different audiences (publics). James Grunig and Todd Hunt's (1984) four models of PR explain the notion of publics in detail. They can be summarized as:

- Press agentry/publicity model.
- Public information model.

- Two-way asymmetric PR.
- Two-way symmetric PR.

Knowledge of these models enables the PR writer to craft successfully persuasive messages in order to send them to their target audience.

Press agentry/publicity model

Most people probably associate this kind of activity with PR. A press or publicity agent is engaged in order to secure coverage for the client, often someone from the world of showbusiness or a minor 'celebrity' hoping to get media coverage. Absolute truth is not essential, hence the myriad of 'tabloid tales' and salacious gossip in magazines such as *Heat* and *Closer*. The publicist is solely concerned with getting air time or column inches, and is often the individual at the centre of any 'hype'. No wonder PR gets such a bad name! Any research into, or understanding of, the audience is negligible.

Public information model

This model is based on communicating information to people. Unlike the press agentry/publicity model, truth and accuracy are essential. This model does not aim to persuade the audience to change its attitudes; it is concerned only with releasing relevant information to those individuals or groups who need it. Research of the audience is minimal or non-existent and tends to rely on one-way communication: from the sender to the receiver. This model is practised mostly by local and central government, who wish to give the public information about issues which may concern them. A typical tool of public information activity includes the writing of press releases, which give details of local or central government decisions, changes in personnel or budget decisions. The rise of the Internet has helped many larger organizations to communicate these details to the general public faster and more effectively.

Two-way asymmetric PR

This model is based on two-way communication and feedback. However, as the intended change is in the audience's attitude or behaviour rather than in the organization's behaviour and practice, it is considered imbalanced or asymmetrical. It is often described as 'persuasive communication' and is based on the notion of propaganda. Today, propaganda is distrusted; we are suspicious of it, another reason for the general distrust and possible misunderstanding of the true nature of PR. Grunig argues that the asymmetrical model may be considered unethical because it is 'a way of getting what an organization wants without changing behaviour or without compromising' (1984: 39). Examples of two-way asymmetric PR may include government or public health campaigns, and political and not-for-profit campaigns. This model is the most widely used and is not exclusive to the public sector. It is practised by many businesses who wish to convince their publics of the benefits of their products or services.

Two-way symmetric PR

This model describes excellent PR, the ideal, and is rare in reality. It describes a method of communication based on equality and research. It is based on dialogue between an organization and its publics, the result of which is a shift in both the public's attitudes and behaviours and the organization's. The power in the relationship between organization and publics is balanced, and the outcome is a win–win situation. Two-way symmetric PR is strategic; it revolves around negotiation and mutual understanding to the benefit of all. It should be practised by larger organizations such as supermarkets and large retail outlets who behave ethically and have a strong awareness of their corporate social responsibility.

Having briefly discussed what PR is and what it does, it is time to reflect more closely on the media writing elements of PR. Media relations is the PR activity associated with communicating messages to the public via the media, be it press (newspapers and magazines), broadcasting (radio, television, DVD, vlogs) or electronic (the Internet, blogs, mobile phones). Before we explore these ideas further, however, it is important to understand the nature of the relationship between PR practitioners and journalists.

Journalists and public relations writers

The simple fact of the matter is that most PR practitioners and journalists do not trust each other; but they do *need* each other. Their relationship is interdependent, symbiotic and reliant. The PR practitioner provides much of the information the journalist requires to write the story, usually in the form of the news release or briefings, and the journalist provides the means of communication to the mass audience: the newspaper, magazine or whatever the medium happens to be. PR practitioners provide information; journalists provide access. The problem here is that PR practitioners often have their own agenda, and journalists need to see through the spin and hype. The code of practice of the Chartered Institute of Public Relations encourages its members to practice ethical and two-way PR at all times. Unfortunately, in the real world and especially for those publicists practising press agentry, this is not always so. It is vitally important for all media writers to be truthful and have ethical standards if they wish to gain their readers' trust.

What do public relations writers write?

The actual outputs of the PR writer are many and varied. They include the following:

- Corporate literature, including brochures, flyers, leaflets, newsletters and direct mail.
- Annual reports, social responsibility reports and mission statements.
- News releases, press packs, fact sheets and backgrounders.
- Vlogs, blogs, wikis, podcasts and other forms of electronic media.
- Articles, stories and features.
- Opinion pieces.
- Television and radio advertisements.
- Exhibition graphics.
- Web copy.

- Slogans and other advertising copy.
- Speeches.
- Presentations.
- Crisis plans.

Some of these written outputs are explored in other chapters; here we will look at the writing of the PR plan; news releases; press packs; fact sheets and mission statements; online public relations; and speeches and presentations.

Public relations writing

Smith defines PR writing as 'functional writing' (2008: 6). By this he means that the approach to writing emphasizes purpose, format and objective; the writing has a mission to accomplish. He suggests that:

> In the profession of public relations we find virtually every writing purpose (except perhaps self-expression). We write news releases to inform external audiences and newsletters to share information with internal ones. We write brochures to explain our products and services. We write letters and guest editorials to express opinions and public service advertisements to persuade. We prepare scripts for speeches and television programs that we hope will influence our audiences, and we create Web pages to educate and motivate. These are just some of the purposes and some of the formats a public relations writer will use to communicate effectively.

Task 4.1

Find a selection of written PR materials. Try to identify the purpose and objective of each.

The rules for effective writing

The rules for PR writing are: simple words, short sentences, natural writing, active voice. The ultimate goal is to write so the reader can understand. Follow the basic rules of good grammar, word choice and common spelling. Smith (2008) claims that some of the world's most profound ideas have been presented in easy-to-read sentences accessible to any audience. The Gettysburg Address, for example, written by President Abraham Lincoln, averages 1.3 syllables per word. Of 271 words, 202 have only one syllable, yet the address is judged as one of the three greatest speeches in the English language.

The Gunning Readability Formula, also known as the Fog Index, is a good tool for the PR writer. It is a simple formula for assessing the readability of any piece of writing.

1. Select a one-hundred-word passage.
2. Count the number of sentences. If the passage does not end on a sentence break, calculate a percentage of the final sentence in the passage and add this to the count.
3. Divide the number of sentences into 100 to determine the average sentence length.
4. Count the number of long words in the passage. These are words of three or more syllables.
5. Add the average sentence length and the number of long words (totals from steps 3 and 4).
6. Multiply this total by 0.4. This number indicates the approximate grade level (United States) of the passage. You should be aiming for 8/9th grade for general-interest written copy.

Persuasion and public relations

Writing for PR is about writing informative messages. Information can be delivered in a number of ways, from the dissemination of pure information which we call exposition, to entertainment. Narration and description form the basis of exposition. For humans, telling stories is natural; stories tell something of the human condition and abound in every area of our lives. Description is a way of sharing aspects of our surroundings that have an impact on us as human beings. When description and narration are used together, the result is fiction. The two most common forms of description are *technical description* and *suggestive description*. Technical description is mostly found in technical journals and manuals. Its purpose is to instruct. Suggestive description is used mostly to persuade. It is used often in feature and non-fiction writing and particularly in PR writing. Entertainment is also used for disseminating information, but it offers it in a much more palatable way. The purpose of encapsulating information in entertainment is to make it more digestible.

PR writing is about writing persuasively: that is, moving an audience to *act* in a certain way. Benoit and Benoit (cited in Cain, 2009: 156) define 'persuasion' as a process in which a source uses a message to achieve a goal by creating, changing or reinforcing the attitudes of others. Persuasion has four important components: it is goal directed in that it is a means to an end. It is a process in that persuasion starts with the source or persuader who has a goal. The source then creates the message which it is hoped will encourage the audience to accomplish the source's goal. The message must then be delivered, and, if effective, will result in the audience complying with the source's wishes. It involves people, and it can change, create or reinforce attitudes. PR developed as a persuasive communication function, and it is vital that PR writers understand the process of persuasion. Persuasion relies on the notion of 'appeal', rather than the means of 'strength', as can be seen from the following list:

- **Reciprocation:** people tend to return a favour, hence the appeal of free samples in marketing and PR.
- **Commitment and consistency:** once people commit either verbally or in writing, they tend to honour that commitment, even if the price of a product or service is raised at the last moment ('cognitive dissonance').
- **Social proof:** people like to conform and tend to follow the behaviours or purchasing decisions of others.
- **Authority:** people tend to obey authority figures even if they disagree with the action.
- **Liking:** people are usually easily persuaded by people they like.
- **Scarcity:** perceived scarcity can generate demand. Prospects often respond to sales if they are for a 'limited time'.

'Cognitive dissonance' is a psychological term adopted by Festinger (1970) to describe the uncomfortable tension that may result from having two conflicting thoughts at the same time, or from engaging in behaviour which conflicts with one's beliefs. Simply, it can be the filtering of information which conflicts with what one already believes, in an effort to ignore that information and reinforce one's original beliefs. In PR terms, dissonance can take place after a purchase or 'buying into' an organization's message when purchasers are unsure about their purchase and begin to question the wisdom of that purchase. In order to alleviate the dissonance, they will rationalize their buying decision by changing their cognitions and concentrating on the positive aspects and ignoring the negative ones. A common strategy for dealing with dissonant messages is for PR writers to attempt to change a consumer's beliefs about a product or service by communicating its benefits: what it will *do* or *give* him or her.

So what does all of this mean for the PR writer? Writing a persuasive message or communication is not an easy task. Persuasion is generally audience centred. The writer therefore needs to know the desires and needs of his or her targeted audience: how they will react to emotional or rational appeals. The writer's persuasive messages may be more effective by following these simple principles:

- **Identification:** people relate more easily to an idea or message if they can see a direct link to their own hopes, fears or desires.
- **Suggestion of action:** people endorse ideas if they are accompanied by an action from the originator of the idea. This is why people use tear-off coupons. People like action; it gives them a sense of power.
- **Familiarity and trust:** people are unwilling to accept ideas from sources they do not trust. People tend to trust celebrity endorsements more if they like the celebrity.
- **Clarity:** one of the most important jobs of the PR writer is to explain complex issues and ideas simply. Simple messages are far more effective than complicated and convoluted ones.

Compliance strategies

Compliance strategies are persuasive messages designed to gain agreement through enticement. This means that the receiver of the message is invited to change his or her attitudes, opinions or behaviour, and as such the media writer may use some of the following strategies:

- **Sanction:** this uses rewards and punishments. For example, a persuasive message can offer the reward of big gains if the consumer buys a particular brand of product. If they do not buy, they may be losing out.
- **Appeal:** this counts on the prospect's sense of altruism (desire to give or help). Appeal strategies work well when trying to fundraise for a particular charitable cause.
- **Command:** this uses direct requests with often no rationale. An example of a command strategy is the war poster slogan 'Your Country Needs YOU!'.

Argument strategies

Argument strategies are one of the oldest types of persuasion. They are based on rhetoric and reasoned argument. A common tactic used by persuaders is the motivated sequence of argument. Firstly, the persuader must get the attention of the audience, and then establish a need for the product, service or idea. This is often achieved by presenting a problem which the persuader then goes on to solve. This solution is then supported by the persuader pointing out the pitfalls to any alternatives. Finally, the persuader ends with a 'call to action', asking the audience to respond to their message and making it easy for them to buy.

Task 4.2

Find a persuasive public service advertisement in a consumer magazine or newspaper. Assess what persuasive strategy it is using: compliance, command, argument or appeal. Rewrite the original copy using each of the different approaches.

Writing the public relations plan

Writing the PR plan is a key tool for PR writers. The plan sets out the stall for the campaign and highlights where the project is heading. Gregory (2000: 49) claims that planning for any project is vital because it focuses effort, improves effectiveness, encourages the long-term view, helps to demonstrate value for money, minimizes mishaps, reconciles conflicts and facilitates proactivity. She also claims that in reality the planning process is quite simple: the trick is to break things down into a manageable sequence. The PR writer should therefore ask the following basic questions:

- What do I want to achieve? *What are my objectives?*
- Who do I want to talk to? *Who are my publics?*
- What do I want to say? *What are the messages I want to get across?*
- How shall I say it? *What mechanisms shall I use to get my messages across?*
- How do I know I've got it? *How will I evaluate my work?*

There are ten stages in the planning process, and these all need to be communicated in written form in the PR plan. Gregory (2000) sets out the planning process into ten logical steps: project analysis; objectives; publics (audiences); intended messages; strategy; tactics; timescales; necessary resources; project evaluation; project review. Although in this chapter we will take a brief look at these stages, we urge the reader to consult Gregory's book for a much fuller discussion.

Analysis

Analysis is the first step of the planning process and is based on research to identify the issues on which the PR programme will be based. Analysis will include both a PEST and a SWOT. The PEST analysis divides the overall environment into four key areas that can affect an organization: Political, Economic, Social and Technological. The SWOT analysis is more of a microanalysis. The approach here is to explore issues that are internally driven and particular to the organization. The key areas for consideration are: Strengths, Weaknesses, Opportunities and Threats. The analysis of the issues to be explored within the campaign will be driven by other research techniques such as questionnaires, focus groups, interviews, media research and communication audits.

Objectives

Setting realistic objectives is vital if the campaign is to have direction and be achievable. Objectives should be SMART: Specific,

Measurable, Achievable, Realistic and Timely. Examples of workable objectives are:

- **Corporate:** to inform ten targeted investors about the appointment of a new managing director within a fortnight of him or her taking-up the post.
- **Trade:** to ensure thirty top dealers attend the latest trade show one month prior to opening.
- **Consumer:** to increase media coverage of new products by 25 percent within one month of the launch of a new product.
- **Community:** to inform the local community of local charitable giving within one month.

Publics

Research and analysis should have indicated who the target audience is. Each organization will have its own specific audiences or 'publics'. Generally speaking, publics fall under the following groups:

- **'Public':** broad-based groupings, opinion formers, pressure groups, media and the local community.
- **Financial:** financial media, shareholders/owners, financial agents and the City.
- **Internal:** employees, management and directors, potential staff, unions and company pensioners.
- **Commercial:** suppliers, wholesalers, retailers, customers, potential customers and competitors.
- **Government:** MPs, specialist committees, civil service and local government.
- **Overseas:** customers, governments, international banks, international agencies and business partners.

Messages

There are four steps to determining the message that the writer should communicate in the PR plan. These are:

- Decide what the existing perceptions about the products are.
- Define what shifts can be made in those perceptions if necessary.

- Identify the elements of persuasion to be used.
- Ensure the messages are credible and easily delivered through PR.

Once the writer has determined the message, he or she will then have to decide how the message should be presented. Format, tone, context and timing will need to be considered, and whether the message needs to be repeated to become credible.

Strategy

Strategy is the overall approach that is taken to a PR campaign. Gregory calls it 'the co-ordinating theme or factor, the big idea, the rationale behind the tactical programme' (2000: 105). The strategy behind the PR plan should move the organization from where it is now to where it wants to be. Typical examples of PR strategies may be 'to ensure our new product is the most cost-effective the market has to offer' or 'to make our new product the celebrities' first choice'.

Tactics

Tactics are the tools or techniques the writer will use to get his or her message across. Tactics should be related to the strategy which in turn should relate to the overall objectives of the campaign. For a sample of different tactics, refer back to the Main Activities grid on pages 118–19.

Timescales

Timescales are so important because they identify those deadlines which must be met in order to complete the campaign successfully.

Resources

Resources in PR plans fall under three headings:

- Human resources.
- Operating costs.
- Equipment.

Evaluation

Evaluation of the programme should be an on-going process. It helps the writer to focus effort and demonstrate effectiveness and value for money. It also encourages good management and accountability. Evaluation should measure the efficacy of the objectives. If the objectives have been met, the PR campaign has been successfully completed; if not, then more work needs to be done on the plan.

Review

While evaluation is a regular process, the review takes place less often and, as such, is not part of the original written plan. A six-month or annual review should examine the research and analysis undertaken, and check that the strategy for the communications programme is still working.

Positive practices for public relations writers

PR writers should reflect on and practice good relations with the media. There are several things they can do to help this process. They should:

- Rely on news values alone and not mere hype to ensure that their information is used by the media.
- Become familiar with the media and know which journalists are interested in which type of news.
- Build up a level of trust with journalists.
- Look at their organizations objectively and decide what potential audiences would be genuinely interested.
- Generate newsworthy actions for their organization and create opportunities for disseminating their messages.
- Learn media deadlines and respect them.
- Ask journalists how they prefer to receive information: email, mail or telephone?

There are also several things PR writers should not do. The following will severely dent their credibility:

- Spending a lot of time on attention-getting gimmicks. Journalists can see right through these.
- Begging or threatening the journalist to run the story.
- Asking to review the reporter's story before he or she runs it.

Writing the news release

The news release (also known as the press release) is the major vehicle for communicating news about an organization to journalists. It is a test of the PR writer's skill. News releases are not creative works of art; they are formulaic (follow a set pattern). Too often, news releases end up in the bin and the main reason for this is that the news release is not newsworthy, rather it is based on spin or mere hype and publicity. The result is much wasted time and frustration for everybody and, ultimately, damage to the writer's reputation. Remember, effective PR is about establishing and maintaining a good reputation. Smith (2008: 115) provides the following remarks made by established journalists as some of the main reasons why news releases end up in the bin:

- Too commercial and promotional.
- Not news.
- Not for us – out of our interest zone.
- Too general.
- No real hook.
- Boorish self-aggrandizement.
- Routine.

Subsequently, the PR writer crafting the news release should never forget the needs of their customer, which is in this case the media.

Bearing this in mind, then, how does the PR writer craft news releases that will be noticed by journalists? It is important to remember the first two rules: news releases should be newsworthy, and they should be written in journalistic format. They are also short, no more than three hundred words and no more than two pages, double spaced in twelve point Times New Roman or Courier. Every newsworthy story has three vital parts: the headline, the first sentence, and the subsequent body copy. The headline should sum up the story in ten words or less. It should not be too clever nor too obscure, but should be simple and easily understood. The first sentence should summarize all the main points of the story; it should tell the reader who has done what, where and why, when and how. This is known as the '5Ws and H':

- WHO is the story about?
- WHAT happened or is going to happen?
- WHEN did it happen or is going to happen?
- WHERE did it happen or is going to happen?
- WHY did it happen or is going to happen?
- HOW did it come about or is going to come about?

The 'SOLAADS' seven-point model expands on the 5Ws and H:

- <u>S</u>ubject: what is the story about?
- <u>O</u>rganization: what is the name of the organization?
- <u>L</u>ocation: what is the location of the organization?
- <u>A</u>dvantages: what is new, special or beneficial about the product or service?
- <u>A</u>pplications: how and by whom can the product or service be enjoyed?
- <u>D</u>etails: what are the specifications and details with regard to colour, size, price, etc.?
- <u>S</u>ource: what is the source of the product or service if this is different from the location?

The news release should be to the point and should not contain any non-essential information. The body copy should add extra information in order of importance. Editors delete paragraphs from the end of the release to fit the copy boundaries in the newspapers, so vital news should not be left to the end. News releases should be factual and state the benefits of the product or service. Quotations from reputable sources should always be included in the body of the release because they add credibility and allow for observation and point of view. They also allow the writer to make a claim that need not be substantiated, and quotations are free from the rigorous analysis of the ordinary text.

News release format

News releases are typically written on plain, white, bond paper with no decorative or fancy border. Journalists have little time and need to be able to see the point of the release immediately. Margins should be four centimetres on all sides, and the address of the sender should be placed on the upper left-hand corner of the first page. The address should be complete with the name of the contact and telephone numbers. Include a night time telephone number; newspaper offices work through the night and an editor needs to be able to contact the writer whatever the hour should any details need to be clarified. The release date should be written on the right-hand margin. The title should be short and to the point, and the body of the release should begin about one-third of the way down the page. Body copy should be double spaced; this allows the editor to write in comments or notes.

If the release runs to more than one page, the word 'more' should appear within dashes at the bottom left-hand side of the page. Any following pages should be identified with a slug-line (abbreviated title) followed by several dashes and the page number at the top of the page, either flush left or flush right. The end of the release is designated with the word 'END', in capitals, centred on the page.

The best topics for a news release include the following:

- New products.
- An unusual product or company.
- A new factory or investment.
- A new division or restructuring.
- Record sales, exports or financial results.
- New appointments or promotions.
- Charity events, community activities, sponsorship or awards.
- The case study or application story.
- Celebrity visits or endorsements.
- Survey and report findings.

Task 4.3

Google 'press release examples' or 'news release examples'. Choose five releases and check them against the established format, the 5Ws and H, and SOLAADS. Do they conform?

Following this, try writing your own press release for:

1. A new product to be launched.
2. A local charitable event.
3. A new appointment to a national organization.

Media placement

Once the writer has produced well-crafted and newsworthy news releases, he or she needs to decide where to send them. A good media directory is an indispensable tool for the PR writer. Media directories address nearly every industry and range from global checkers that include a variety of sources in every medium, to specialized directories dealing with a single medium. The two most widely used media directories in the UK are BRAD (British Rates and Data) and Willings' Press Guide. BRAD is a resource which provides vital information for the UK media community. With more media entries than any other source, and comprehensive advertising-related information on each one, BRAD is essential for any PR writer who is also involved in planning, buying or researching media. BRAD has around thirteen thousand media entries which detail advertising costs and circulation and audience research figures. The BRADnet system enables users to access data online via multiple search criteria. Willings' Press Guide is a directory in several volumes of press contacts, target audience information, advertising rates, e-zines (online magazines), and contact information in Europe, China, the USA and South America. The three volumes, UK, Western Europe and the World, have clear and easy-to-use referencing, website and broadcast media information.

Task 4.4

Browse the web sites for BRAD (www.brad.co.uk) and Willings' Press Guide (www.willingspress.com). Evaluate the usefulness of these directories for the placement of news releases.

Writing the press pack, the fact sheet and the mission statement

A press pack (sometimes called a media pack) is a collection of background information and key facts on a company, organization, event, service or product which is distributed to journalists and reporters. The press pack can act as an introduction to the organization, informing journalists and editors who the organization is and what it does; or, it can provide information on a specific event, service or product.

Press packs usually contain some or all of the following:

- A news release.
- Background information on the organization, service or product.
- Website details for the organization.
- The purpose/mission statement.
- Relevant position statements.
- Interesting facts and figures.
- Financial information.
- Key dates and events.
- The organizational structure.
- Biographical information about key people.
- Photographs.
- Product samples.

Press packs make the lives of journalists easier by providing all the information they need, and they increase the possibility of media coverage. The main part of the press pack is the 'backgrounder'. These are in-depth information pieces and are often written by the PR writer. In order to make the backgrounder comprehensible, the PR writer must research as many sources as possible, including old articles, brochures, reports, news releases and materials published outside of the organization. A backgrounder should begin with a statement of the issue being addressed. Most follow this basic format as suggested by Bivins (2005: 143):

- Begin with an opening statement on the issue on which the accompanying news release is based.

- Follow with a historical overview of the issue. The writer should trace its evolution: how it came to be, and the major events leading up to it. For example, if writing a backgrounder on a new surgical technique, it would be useful to trace briefly the history of the technique's development and tie this in with current developments. Be sure to name your sources in the body of the text because readers like to know where the information comes from.
- Work from the historical to the present situation. Be factual yet interesting.
- Present the implications of the issue being discussed and point the way for future considerations.
- Use subheadings to promote understanding.
- Most backgrounders are four to five pages in length. The object of them is to provide information, so do not fill them with 'fluff' and padding.

Fact sheets

Fact sheets contain just facts and nothing more. Figures and charts can help to explain the topic more easily, and so have their place in the press pack. A fact sheet should be no more than one side of A4 paper.

Writing the mission statement

An organization's mission statement is usually discussed amongst the management team and then crafted by the PR writer. The mission statement is a written form of intent; it is designed at getting all the members of an organization to pull in the same direction, sharing the same vision of the organization's goals and philosophy. If well crafted, the mission statement will reward the organization by enhancing the company identity and position within the marketplace. A mission statement is not a loose collection of ideas, but a clear, simple, introspective and practical statement of purpose. The mission statement is also the backbone of a strong and credible marketing effort.

A mission statement should be two to three sentences long and between twenty five and a hundred words. There are four basic steps to follow when writing the statement:

1. State who the organization is, including the company's name and the areas it specializes in. Include any highlights of customer service policy and any values that guide the company's daily decisions.
2. State where the organization wants to go. Clarify those markets to be targeted (the market niche). State which individuals or businesses are hoped to be served, and where the markets are located, their nature and geography. State the company goals and where it would like to be in five to ten years' time.
3. State how the organization plans to get there, i.e. what the organization plans to sell or provide. Include the products or services to be offered and which customer needs the organization will meet. The key benefits of using the organization's products or services should be stated, along with the skills and talents the organization has, that makes it superior to the competition, and how it intends to beat the competition.
4. Link the intentions of the mission statement to a compelling reason: why does the organization want to get where it does?

The following is a simple example of a mission statement for a hypothetical organic restaurant called Simply Organic:

State who you are:
Simply Organic Restaurant.

State markets you will serve:
Customers looking to eat superior, fresh, organic produce.

State products you will sell:
Additive and preservative free, fresh, organic products.

State reason why:
To serve healthy, affordable food.

Below are examples of more in-depth, but equally valid, mission statements:

- **The Sturgess Company:** The Sturgess Company of Southampton is dedicated to maintaining its position as a leader in providing quality financial service products to businesses and individual customers through a staff of highly trained advisors sharing a tradition of integrity and service to its clients.

- **Low-Cost Travel:** Low-Cost Travel provides cheaper holiday travel and related services to customers in the UK who expect efficient, problem-free travel arrangements at low cost.
- **IBM:** Our goal is simply stated. We want to be the best service organization in the world.

All these mission statements have one thing in common: they are clear and simple. A mission statement is the foundation upon which all good organizations are built. It does not have to be fanciful but it does have to be solid. A clear mission statement shared with employees and customers creates high employee morale, efficient operations and more loyal customers.

Task 4.5

1. Write a mission statement for a hypothetical national chain of contemporary jewellery shops.
2. Write a mission statement for a hypothetical budget 'pound shop'.

Online public relations

PR is increasingly evident online, whether that be a simple migration of print work into digital formatting or the emergence of new PR platforms (see also the Conclusion). However, writers working in this domain must still understand the basic notion of how the communication process works. Encoding the message, decoding the message, response and feedback are the communicator's main focus, not the mechanics of presentation.

The act of communication is a *process* involving two key players: the sender and the receiver. In its simplest form, communication theory consists of transmitting information from one source to another and is best described by political scientist and communications theorist Harold Lasswell's maxim: 'Who says what to whom, in what channel, to what effect.' It is useful to examine communication theory from one of the following viewpoints:

- **Mechanistic:** this view considers communication to be a perfect transition of a message from the sender to the receiver.
- **Psychological:** this view considers communication as the act of sending a message to a receiver, as well as the impact of the thoughts and feelings of the receiver upon the actual receiving and decoding of the message.
- **Social constructionist:** this view considers communication to be the product of the interactants sharing and creating meaning.
- **Systemic:** this view considers communication to be the new messages created via 'throughput', or what happens as the message is being interpreted as it travels through people.

A basic model of communication was devised by Shannon and Weaver in 1949. In this model (see figure below), the information source, which can be human or technological, produces a message which is transferred into a set of signals by a transmitter. These signals are sent out via a channel to a receiver, who in turn decodes the message. The received message then reaches its destination. A noise element which is outside of the message can interfere with the sender's original intention, which may cause failures in communication.

If we were to apply Shannon and Weaver's model to an instance of PR communication, the information source would be the PR writer, the message would be the news story, the channel would be the news release, and the receiver would be the journalist. One possible example of 'noise' may be the quality of writing of the press release, or the fact that it may not be 'newsworthy'. If we were to

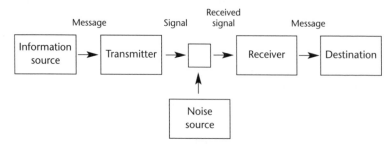

Figure 1   Shannon and Weaver's model of communication

Source: Shannon and Weaver (1949).

apply this model to a magazine article, the information source would be the writer, the message would be the main theme and content of the article (the story), the channel would be the magazine (or e-zine), and the receiver would be the reader.

Bearing in mind the above basic information on the communications process, the writer should be aware of the various technological methods available for putting a PR message online. Bivins (2008: 305–6) offers some simple definitions of such methods:

- An **intranet** is a restricted access network which is owned and managed by an organization. It enables that organization to share information with its employees without confidential information being available to anyone with regular Internet access.
- A **website** is a set of interconnected webpages, usually including a home page, which is prepared and maintained as a collection of information by a person, group or organization.
- A **weblog** or **blog** is a journal that is available on the web. This journal is usually updated daily and contains all the information that the blogger (writer of the blog) wishes to share with the world.
- A **vlog** is a variant of the blog, which uses video to present information. Vlog posts are usually accompanied by text, image, sound and additional metadata to provide a context for the video.
- A **webinar** is an online seminar or type of web conferencing that is conducted over the Internet, and often contains video and audio.
- An **e-zine** is a website that is an online magazine or in magazine format. It is usually updated at least monthly.
- An **online newsletter** is a newsletter delivered via the Internet. These come in various formats, ranging from content that looks like a traditional website to designs available as PDF files. Many online newsletters are delivered via email with links to online content built into them.
- **Podcasting**, a combination of the words 'iPod' and 'broadcasting', is a method of distributing multimedia files such as audio programmes or music videos over the Internet for playback on mobile devices and personal computers.

Evidently the digital revolution has opened up opportunities for media writers working in persuasive communications. Below is a brief exploration of writing for websites with a PR slant. Writing copy for PR is the same whether for online consumption or hard copy; the same rules of good writing as discussed in this book still apply. As before, PR writing is professional writing, whatever the medium. Kilian (cited in Bivins, 2008: 325) suggests that, according to research undertaken by Jacob Nielsen, web readers read 25 percent slower than print readers. Subsequently he concludes that 'if we read 25 percent slower on screen, then perhaps we owe our readers 25 percent less text'. Website writing 'rules' are constantly changing because the medium is constantly changing; however, we optimistically offer the following principles when writing for the online medium:

- Background information and aids to simple navigation must be provided to the reader.
- Website writers should provide a way for the reader to respond easily.
- Web writing should be clear, simple and easy to understand. The KISS principle (see p. 166) applies.
- Deliver the best possible message with the least possible words. Avoid excess words on websites.
- Web writing talks directly to the reader in the personal voice. The writer should avoid sounding 'preachy' and use 'I' and 'we' rather than 'you' and 'your'.
- Web writing should use correct grammar, syntax and punctuation, with clarity and consideration to the reader.

Task 4.6

Locate two websites, one for a retail outlet and the other for a charitable organization. Evaluate their effectiveness in terms of the above principles.

Writing speeches and presentations

Speech-writing is about putting your words into someone else's mouth. This is no easy task, and in order for it to be successful, the speech-writer must know the speech-maker inside out. The speech-writer must study the speech-maker's tone of voice, speech patterns, body language and personality. This is because the audience must believe that the speaker truly believes in what he or she is saying. Consequently, speech-writing becomes a collaborative effort. It is based on rhetoric: the study and art of persuasion. Classical rhetoric goes back over two thousand years to the days of Aristotle. Today, rhetoric is studied in universities around the world. Oral communication is more about making an impression on the audience than it is about imparting information. Consider the rhetorical and powerful speeches given by John F. Kennedy, 'Ask not what your country can do for you', and by Martin Luther King, 'I have a dream'. These speeches were actually written by the speakers, but nowadays most speeches, both political and commercial, are often crafted by the PR writer. A speech is the primary example of interpersonal, face-to-face communication, and is also an excellent way of applying a human dimension to an organization.

Speeches can be classified by purpose:

- A speech to **inform** is written to clarify, instruct or demonstrate.
- A speech to **persuade** is written to influence or convince, and usually carries a 'call to action'.
- A speech to **entertain** is written purely to entertain, and includes celebrations, eulogies and dinner speeches.

There are two basic modes of speech delivery:

- **Extemporaneous and impromptu:** here the PR writer is responsible for researching and compiling the information necessary for the speech. These are given to the speaker in outline form, who will study the notes and then deliver a fluent speech based on the topic.
- **Scripted and memorized:** here the PR writer is entirely responsible for the writing of the speech.

Planning the speech

Planning and preparation are the most important elements of speech-writing. Speech-makers should not be encouraged to 'speak off the cuff'. There are too many examples of politicians and chief executive officers who have famously destroyed their credibility with unwise ad-libs (for example, Gerald Ratner's famous declaration that the reason his products were cheap was because they were 'crap'). The foundations of an effective speech include the following:

- Learning about the speaker.
- Understanding the specific purpose of the speech.
- Knowing the audience.
- Researching the topic.
- Organizing ideas.

Learning about the speaker

Speeches are doubly encoded. First, the writer produces the words that encode the meaning to be shared with the audience. Second, the speaker encodes a second meaning via the tone and pace he or she gives to the words spoken. In other words, speakers can change meaning by their attitude to the words. When PR writers draft speeches, they must give attention to the way the speaker handles various types of written material. It is important for speech-writers to meet the speaker and listen to the way he talks. Considerations would then include: Can he use humour? Is he inspiring? How does he use language?

Understanding the specific purpose of the speech

Speeches are results-driven because, as the writer of the speech, you must be absolutely certain of the purpose of the speech. You should consider if the speech is intended to persuade, to motivate, to entertain or to inform, for example. Or is it a combination of these?

Knowing the audience

Knowing the audience means understanding the context in which the speech is to be delivered. It is important to consider the background and circumstances of the speech. For example, why has the audience gathered together to hear the speech and what do they expect to hear? The speech-writer also needs to consider whether the speech is a one-off or part of a wider set of communications, and whether it is an opening or a closing speech. He or she also needs to think about how long the audience expects the speech to last. We would suggest that twenty minutes be the maximum length of any speech before the audience begins to shuffle in their seats.

Researching the topic

The speech-writer should have total command of the topic in hand. Research should include recent available information from any newspapers or periodicals, as well as any information on the organization given to him or her by the intended speaker.

Organizing ideas

The best way to organize ideas and to plan the speech is to remember its purpose. Use that purpose as the template for the plan.

Below is a typical speech format, as suggested by Bivins (2005: 288):

- **Introduction**
  Attention-getter: tell people why they should listen to the speech.
  Establish rapport: create a bond with the audience. Show them what you have in common.
  Preview: tell people what they are going to hear.

- **Body/discussion**
  Main points arranged logically: in order of importance.
  Data supporting each main point: evidence always reinforces credibility.

- **Conclusion**
  Review: summarize the key points the audience has heard.
  Memorable statement: create a desired state-of-mind that will stay with the audience.
  Call for action: if applicable.

As can be seen from the above format, there tends to be a lot of repetition. Repetition is necessary in a speech because it reinforces the message with maximum impact. The body of the speech can be approached in a number of ways. It can be organized *chronologically* (cover this year's events, then next year's), by *direction* (talk about the organization's development as it moved its headquarters from

London to Manchester), by *topic* (cover one set of related ideas then move onto another set of related ideas), by *need and fulfilment* (describe 'what we need' and then 'how we are going to get it') and/or by *question and answer* (describe the problem and then the solution). Smith (2008: 323) suggests that one of the best ways to organize a speech is to develop a summary sheet which should include the following information:

Preliminary questions

1. What are the expectations of the audience?
   Towards me?
   Towards my topic?
   Towards this specific situation? (Are there any extenuating circumstances that should be considered?)

2. How do I expect the audience to be affected by the speech?
   The general purpose of the speech is to inform/persuade/reinforce certain ideas/entertain.
   The specific thesis: after listening to the speech the audience will …

The Body of the speech

3. What is the best structure to follow given points 1 and 2 above?
   Should the speech be arranged chronologically? Directionally? Topically? By need and fulfilment? By question and answer?
   The structure chosen is the best in this particular situation because …

4. What are the three or four main points suggested by the specific structure?

5. How will I support these main points?
   Will I use statistics, examples, analogies, case studies, direct quotations?

6. How should I adapt my language and word choice to suit audience expectations?
   To what extent should I use jargon and buzzwords?
   To what extent should I be conscious of defining certain words?

7. Should I use any visual aids?
   What should be visualized?
   How should it be visualized?
   Why should it be visualized?

8. How should I introduce the speech?
   Why should my audience listen to this message?
   How will my audience benefit by listening to me?
   How can I make my audience want to listen?
   You should listen to me because …

9. How should I conclude the speech?
   How do I relate the conclusion to the main points I have covered?
   In conclusion …

It is important to remember that a memorable speech is not just based on the quality of the writing but on the impact of the delivery. This is a variable which unfortunately the speech-writer has little control over.

Sound bites

The author Mark Twain described the (as then unrecognized) notion of the sound bite as 'a minimum of sound to a maximum of sense'. The sound bite today is characterized by a short sentence or phrase which deftly captures the essence of what the speaker is trying to say. These sound bites then become powerful media messages because they are easy to memorize. Politicians in the twenty-first century are carefully coached to produce and deliver sound bites that capture the public's imagination. They are often extrapolated from longer speeches, and some famous political sound bites include:

- 'The only thing we have to fear is fear itself' (Franklin D. Roosevelt's first Inaugural Address in 1933).
- 'Ich bin ein Berliner' (John F. Kennedy on 26 June 1963).
- 'Read my lips: no new taxes' (United States presidential candidate George H. W. Bush in 1988).
- 'I feel the hand of history upon our shoulders' (Tony Blair following the 1998 Good Friday Agreement).
- 'Houston, we've had a problem' (James A. Lovell, the Apollo XIII mission in 1970).
- 'Yes, we can' (Barack Obama, Presidential address, January 2009).

Creativity and functionality in public relations writing

Whilst reading this chapter on writing for PR and media relations, it may have been noticed that most of the writing tools and techniques demand a level of functionality. They are written to a formula and are designed primarily to persuade a prospect to 'buy into' a product, idea, service or organization. PR writing follows 'rules', so where is the creativity? Creative writing is artistic, artful, imaginative, innovative and aesthetic. PR writing is purposeful, intentional, functional, rational and objective. So, are the two mutually exclusive? We would argue that all writing is creative because it is about the insight and ownership a writer brings to facts and ideas. A PR writer will think about the ideas and thoughts surrounding a writing project before putting the task in hand. A good (and creative) writer will make observations, link ideas, give birth to stories within stories, gain insights and make connections. PR writers write creatively when they take a thought and skilfully share it with others to serve the original purpose. Creativity and functionality can coexist within PR writing. Andy Green, in his seminal book *Creativity in Public Relations*, argues that:

> creativity is the ability to create something new by bringing together two or more different elements in a new context, in order to provide added value to a task. A creative act consists of not only originating but also evaluating the added value it contributes. It is not novelty for its own sake, but it must produce some form of value. (1999: 8)

PR tells the organization's 'story' but not in the standard format of the novel, script, short story or feature article. The narrative uses different tactics: the news release to inform external audiences; newsletters to share 'story' and information with internal audiences; brochures to explain products and services; letters and editorials to express opinions; public service advertisements to persuade; script copy for television and radio to influence audiences; and web pages to educate and motivate.

Task 4.7

Write five hundred words on how creative and functional writing compare and how you see these definitions coming together to describe PR writing.

Careers opportunities in public relations and media relations

PR presents some excellent career prospects. The profession is healthy, vibrant and growing with an estimated 45,000 people working in PR today in the UK. The Chartered Institute of Public Relations quotes PR as the third most desirable graduate destination. Students can expect entry-level positions to emphasize technical competence in writing, communication and related areas. The skills typically sought include proficiency in preparing brochures, memos and letters, newsletters and articles, news releases, proposals, reports, scripts and speeches. Related skills include conducting research, interviews and editing. You would also be expected to be flexible, have a keen awareness of what is happening in the news, and a passion for finding out new information. The media section in *The Guardian* newspaper on Mondays and the social section on Wednesdays run advertisements for PR writers, some of which are entry-level positions. The trade magazine *PR Week* also runs recruitment advertisements. Many of these will not specifically state the job is for PR writing and so you should look out for openings with job titles such as 'media relations assistant', 'press officer', 'publications editor' or 'account assistant'. The website for the Chartered Institute of Public Relations (www.cipr.co.uk) also holds a great deal of information on finding openings for PR writers.

Further reading

Bartram, P. (2006) *How to Write the Perfect Press Release*, Brighton: New Venture Publishing.

Benoit, W.L and Benoit, P. (2008) *Persuasive Messages: The Process of Influence*, Oxford: Blackwell.

Bivins, T. (2005) *Public Relations Writing: The Essentials of Style and Format*, 5th edn, New York: McGraw-Hill.

Cain, S. (2009) *Key Concepts in Public Relations*, Basingstoke: Palgrave Macmillan.

Cialdini, R. (2007) *Influence: The Psychology of Persuasion*, New York: Harper-Collins.

Cook, J.S. (1996) *The Elements of Speechwriting and Public Speaking*, Harlow: Longman.

Festinger, L. (1970) *Theory of Cognitive Dissonance*, Stanford, CA: Stanford University Press.

Foster, J.L. (2005) *Effective Writing Skills for Public Relations*, London: Kogan Page.

Green, A. (1999) *Creativity in Public Relations*, London: Kogan Page.

Gregory, A. (2000) *Planning and Managing a Public Relations Campaign: A Step-By-Step Guide*, London: Kogan Page.

Grunig, J. and Hunt, T. (1984) *Managing Public Relations*, Toronto: Holt, Rinehart & Winston.

Smith, R.D. (2008) *Becoming a Public Relations Writer: A Writing Process Workbook for the Profession*, 3rd edn, London: Routledge.

Wilcox, D. (2005) *Public Relations Writing and Media Techniques*, 5th edn, Boston, MA: Pearson Education.

Web resources

www.cipr.co.uk
Official website for The Chartered Institute of Public Relations, a British forum for public relations practitioners.

www.brad.co.uk
Official website for the media directory called British Rates and Advertising Directory.

www.willingspress.com
Official website for the media directory called Willings' Press Guide.

Copywriting and Advertising 5

The Institute of Practitioners in Advertising defines advertising as presenting 'the most persuasive possible selling message to the right prospects for the product'. According to Gabay (2000: 2), the world's first-known copywriting agency was based in London in 1786. The first international agency was Gordon and Gatch of Melbourne, Australia, which opened for business in 1855 and had its first overseas branch in London in 1867. Copywriting has a long history and Gettins claims that that by the time the average Brit reaches his or her 35th birthday, she or he will have seen 150,000 commercials (2006: 7). A successful copywriter will make sure that his or her message is the one from amongst this cacophony of 'noise' which catches the attention of the intended audience. Copywriting uses language that is persuasive in nature; ultimately, language that is designed to influence the reader to buy a product, a service or an idea. In order to do this, copywriters craft advertising messages that will resonate with consumers and influence, sell to or educate them. Their main task is to take complex marketing objectives, then distil them down to simple ideas which aim to change attitudes and ultimately buying behaviours. These ideas are then turned into words expressed in print, on the radio, online or on television, including outputs such as direct mail, leaflets, brochures, newsletters, press releases and press packs, posters, radio and TV advertisements, and advertising web copy.

By the end of this chapter, you should be able to:

- Understand the notion of copywriters as communicators who manipulate words and images in order to sell benefits.

- Recognize the role of copywriters in the discipline of advertising.
- Be familiar with the informative and subliminal nature of the creative process, including copywriting techniques and devices.
- Discuss the main fundamentals of persuasive writing, including headlines, strap-lines and body copy.
- Recognize how to structure copy effectively.
- Recognize the different forms of copywriting and their intended audience.
- Understand the creative brief and how it can be interpreted by copywriters.

What is copywriting?

Gabay offers us a comprehensive definition of the copywriter:

> A copywriter is a communicator who manipulates words/images and applies creative strategies within media. Those strategies are balanced to integrate the marketing and sales principles of a specific sector with a literary style that may be informative, persuasive, subliminal or a combination of all three. Through doing this a copywriter communicates product or service benefits. (2000: 5)

Advertising copywriting makes its own rules; redundancy, conjunctions and superlatives abound. Whilst most writers are taught to avoid the one-sentence paragraph, copywriters make a habit of them. However, there is one rule that any aspiring copywriter should follow and that is the rule of the plan. Copywriters should always know their target market, research the product and its users and be aware of which advertising medium will be most appropriate. They should answer the creative brief objectively and simply, and be creative, innovative and ambitious.

Virtually all persuasive copy contains eight elements. Blake and Bly (1997) suggest that successful advertising copy should attract attention, focus on the customer, stress the benefits of the product, differentiate the product from the competition, prove its case, establish its credibility, build value and close with a call to action. Bearing this in mind, the next part of this chapter will explore how to structure advertising copy, beginning with the creative brief.

The creative brief

The creative brief is one of the most important documents for the copywriter. It is a prerequisite plan that enables the copywriter to produce the effective copy that his or her client wants; copy that successfully sells the product, service or idea. Gabay (2000: 51) outlines a working creative brief, suggesting that its components should include:

1. **Who is advertising?** Company name only.
2. **What does this company do?** A general heading like 'Publishing' or 'Pharmaceuticals'.
3. **What is required?** A one-line description such as 'poster' or 'newsletter'. Do not worry about specific media details at this stage.
4. **What is the format?** For example, if having to write a brochure, consider how long it needs to be. Will there be any illustrations? Is it to be in colour? If it is to be a direct mail, how long will it be?
5. **What is the creative work specifically expected to achieve?** Try to be precise; for example to increase website hits by 50 percent.
6. **What are the (a) marketing objectives and (b) corporate objectives?** Try to summarize these in one sentence. For example:

   - To increase market share by 15 percent.
   - To be recognized as a leader in the field.

7. **What is the story so far?** This is the relevant background detail and should include:

   - Where the company stands in its market place.
   - Where it would like to be.
   - Where the creative work will appear.
   - What will support the work, e.g. other advertisements.

8. **Describe the product.** Include any previous leaflets and adverts. What is it? How is it used? How does it work?

9. **Why would someone want it?** List the unique selling points (USPs; see next section). Why buy this one instead of one offered by a competitor?

10. **Who wants it?** Who would want to buy this product or service? Where do they live? How old are they? What is their social economic grouping? What kind of jobs do they have? If the audience is a type of business, what sort of business is it? Who makes the buying decisions? How does the buying process work?

11. **Are there any special offers?** For example, a discount or a gift? What is it? What is its value? What do readers have to do to get it and why would they want it?

12. **Style of copy.** What style should the copy adopt? Caring? Serious? Casual?

13. **What media will be used?** For example, national or local newspapers, trade press, the Web, television, radio?

14. **What is the budget?**

15. **When does the client expect to see the finished copy?**

Defining the unique selling point (USP)

The unique selling point (USP), also known as the unique selling proposition, is the thing that makes the product or service unique and meaningful to the prospective customer. Examples of a USP may be the fact that the company offers a faster service than its main rivals, or that the product is made of locally sourced, sustainable materials. The USP may also be based upon being the oldest or newest, the largest or smallest/most personal, the best value for money, the first, the most advanced, or the only provider of that particular product or service. Whatever the USP, copy should be positive and not negative; text that dwells too much on what will happen if the customer does not buy the product will turn the customer off. Good copy works at a psychological level by using written methods of persuasion and influence. It should illustrate the reward of buying the product by designing the words to appeal to feelings and emotions rather than straightforward, hard-hearted logic. So a copywriter might suggest that a new cashmere scarf offers sophistication and elegance, not just extra warmth. Or, as another example, suppose the product is children's shoes. A promotion that claimed 'if you fail to buy these boots for your children their feet will not develop properly and you will damage your children's feet for life' would cause a great deal of upset. The copywriter needs to be more subtle, and a better idea might be: 'Every parent wants the best for developing young feet. Give yours a head start with our new ergonomically designed boots. They'll set your children on the road to a lifetime of healthy walking.'

Task 5.1

Look around your home or workplace. Choose ten products and try to establish their USPs. Write these down next to the name of the products.

Defining the benefits

Too many promotions stress the *features* of a product or a service. Prospective customers are not interested in buying features alone; they are interested in buying the *benefits* of those features. It is these benefits that the copywriter must stress. So what is the difference between a feature and a benefit? Features are the bare facts about how a product or service works: how it is made, what it is made of, who designed it, where it is manufactured, etc. Benefits are what the product can do for the customer. Benefits are the *reasons* why customers should buy the product. The copywriter should first identify the key features of the product and then make a corresponding list of its benefits. The table below demonstrates how this might be done for a new sofa:

Feature	Benefit
Sturdy wooden frame	Durable
Removable cotton covers	Washable
Feather-filled cushions	Comfortable
High-backed	Neck-supporting

Successful advertisements should appeal to a deep-rooted and emotional need within the audience. Here is a selection of some of the most important ones:

- **Altruism:** we like to help others, to be seen as worthwhile and generous.
- **Association:** we have images of ourselves, as country ladies or squires or sharp business people.
- **Display:** we like to show off our wealth, whether as a faded oriental carpet or a hi-tech television.
- **Efficiency:** anything which simplifies our busy lives is worth having.
- **Elegance, beauty and sophistication:** the promise of health, youth or good looks are powerful motivators.
- **Individuality:** we like to feel we are individual and different.
- **Insurance:** we want security and reliability.
- **Investment:** investment means that a purchase will last a long time and gain in value.
- **Keeping up with the Joneses:** although this is rarely expressed in a blunt fashion, this type of appeal works well when subtle.
- **Knowledge:** we like to buy knowledge in the hope that it will make us wiser, more charismatic or get us a better job.
- **Money saving:** we like a bargain.
- **Novelty:** we like new things.
- **Pampering:** we like to be cosseted and feel relaxed.
- **Toys for the Boys:** many men like machines with dials and knobs.
- **Status:** power is highly sought while status proves our wealth.
- **Style:** we want to be seen to have good taste.

Not every benefit is a concrete one (such as good taste). Often the benefit is abstract, and this is especially true for the products of service companies, where common invisible benefits to business users may include: academic or industry reports being written about the company; introduction of ancillary services; receipt of awards; development of a caring company ethos or corporate culture; increased creativity; installation of a customer hotline; more efficient back-up services; receipt of endorsements; guarantees being offered; becoming more hard-working, honest, innovative; becoming long established; mould breaking; people-orientated; gaining a reputation for research quality/patents; receipt of a royal warrant; improved staff quality; being sympathetic to customer needs; understanding of the market; acquiring well-known customers.

Task 5.2

Using the principles listed above, write a list of features and benefits for a clock radio.

Making the headlines

Successful advertisements follow the AIDA principle, a marketing acronym which stands for Attention, Interest, Desire and Action. The copywriter must first get the prospect's attention, then their interest in the product, then attempt to gain their desire to own the product, and then make it easy for them to action their buying process, i.e. make it easy for them to buy the product by offering solutions such as place of purchase, web addresses and telephone numbers. Ali (1997: 136) suggests there is a definite route or 'eyepath' which we follow on seeing an advert:

1. **Picture:** we look at this first.
2. **Headline:** we look at this second; 80 percent of readers stop there.
3. **Bottom right-hand corner:** those still reading look here next, which is why advertisers place their name and logo here.
4. **Caption:** the reader moves on to the caption on the photo or illustration.
5. **Cross-heading:** this is followed by a scan of the cross-heading, subheadings and other illustrations.
6. **Body text:** only then do people move on to reading the main part of the advertisement.

The lesson here is simple: headlines count, so make them stand out. The headline must not simply state what the picture shows; it should add to the message of the picture. Together, they are more than the sum of their parts. The function of the headline is fourfold: to create immediate impact; to gain attention; to attract the right prospective customers; and to lure prospects into reading the body text. Headlines fall into five main categories: direct; indirect; 'how to'; questions; commands. All of these categories should grab the audience's attention, appeal to the reader's self-interest, deliver a meaningful message and express the sale's proposition in a lively and engaging way.

Direct headlines

Direct headlines get straight to the point. For example: 'Baked Beans – only 25p a Tin at Tesco'. This is not very exciting, but the strength of the direct headline is that it does get the message across, though it does this so effectively that it prevents the potential customer from reading any further body copy.

Indirect headlines

Indirect headlines attract curiosity and interest, but make little sense without the right sort of body copy. For example: 'Pure Comfort'. This headline may be successful in attracting attention, but it is hard to work out what it actually means. The reader would need to read the rest of the advertisement to find out.

'How to' headlines

These headlines are what they appear to be: 'How to Choose a New Car'; 'How to Get Free Insulation'.

Question headlines

With question headlines, the question must be phrased succinctly to elicit an answer: 'Do You Want Your Heating Bills to Cost Less?'

Command headlines

These headlines instruct the reader: 'Cut Out this Coupon and Win a Holiday'; 'Take Care – Fireworks Can Kill'.

Subheadings

Sometimes the main headline is followed by a secondary headline below it. For example: [photo of a motorboat] 'Imagine Owning This … You Could, if You Invest with Dixon Investments'. Subheadings can supplement points made by the headline, but should be kept short and tight so they do not become the headlines themselves. There is no set length for a headline; it can be as long or as short as it needs to be in order to get the message across.

> **Task 5.3**
>
> Think of a set of headlines: direct, indirect, question, command and subheading to communicate your previously chosen ten products.

Writing Body Copy

It will come as no surprise to learn that advertising is most effective when it is easy to understand. The clearer the copy, the more products will be shifted. Lengthy sentences, clichés, big words, lack of specifics, technical jargon and overuse of superlatives will not help the copywriter's cause, and should be avoided at all costs. The following tips will help to create clear and comprehensible body copy that sells.

Always put the reader first

Address the readers as 'you'. Consider if they will understand every word of the copy. If you were the intended audience yourself, would you buy the product? Blake and Bly (1997: 34) offer the following examples of copy written from the advertiser's point of view. The right-hand column shows the copy revised towards a 'you' orientation.

Advertiser-orientated copy	Reader-orientated copy
Bank Plan is the state of the art, user-friendly, sophisticated, financial software for small business accounts receivable, accounts payable and general ledger applications.	Bank Plan can help you balance your books, manage your cash flow and keep track of customers who haven't paid their bills. Best of all, the program is easy to use – no special training required.

Advertiser-orientated copy	Reader-orientated copy
The objective of the daily cash accumulation fund is to seek the maximum current income that is consistent with low capital risk and the maintenance of total liquidity.	The cash fund gives you the maximum return on your investment dollar with the lowest risk. And you can take out as much money as you like – whenever you like.
To cancel an order, return the merchandise to us in its original container. Upon receipt of the book in good condition, we will inform our accounting department that your invoice is cancelled.	If you're not satisfied with the book, simply return it to us and tear up your invoice. You won't owe us a cent. What could be fairer than that?

Organize the unique selling points

The body copy should be well organized. The headline states the main selling point and one or more paragraphs follow and expand on this. Secondary selling points can be covered in the second half of the advertisement. If the copy is long, then each secondary selling point can be given a separate heading or number. Above all, the copy should flow from point to point in order of relative importance.

Divide the copy into short sections

Short sections with plenty of white space make copy easier to read. Long, unbroken sections of type intimidate the reader. Avoid a dense look to the copy.

Use short sentences and short paragraphs

Crisp, short, snappy copy is easiest to read. Linguist Rudolf Flesch suggests that the best average sentence length for business writing is fourteen to sixteen words; twenty to twenty-five words is passable, but above forty words and the writing becomes unreadable (cited in Blake and Bly, 1997: 96). A premium is placed on clarity. Sentence length can be reduced with the use of full stops and punctuation. For example, the sentence

Today, in these cash-strapped times, every penny counts and Solent Business Park wants to offer the best service for money.

works better as

In these cash-strapped times, every penny counts. Solent Business Park wants to offer the best service for money.

To keep the body copy lively, it is important to vary the sentence length. Remember there are no rules in copywriting, so it is perfectly acceptable to use sentence fragments and phrases and clauses that are not grammatically complete.

Use simple words

Simple words communicate better than long and complicated ones. Why say 'facilitate' when you mean 'help'? Why say 'purchase' when you mean 'buy'? Why say 'obtain' when you mean 'get'?

Use jargon sparingly

Jargon can be useful when communicating with technical specialists, but if the intended audience is Joe Public, beware of jargon at all costs; it will only alienate.

Be concise

People today are exposed to more words and messages than ever before. They do not have the time to waste on deciphering 'wordy' communications, so it is vitally important that the body copy is concise and precise. Redundancies, run-on sentences, wordy phrasing, the passive voice and unnecessary adjectives should all be avoided in concise copy. Why write 'can be considered to be' when you can simply write 'is'?

Be specific and get to the point

Specifics sell: getting to the point keeps the reader's attention. The headline may be the most important part of the advertisement, but the lead paragraph lures the reader into the body text by fulfilling the promise of the headline.

Be friendly

A conversational and friendly tone in the body copy is very important because written words are replacing face-to-face interaction. An easy way to write in a conversational tone is to imagine speaking the actual words to a reader, and asking whether the address is appropriate. If not, the copy should be rewritten in a friendlier manner.

Task 5.4

Write the body copy of between fifty and a hundred words for an advertisement to accompany the headlines that you wrote for your chosen ten products.

Writing for specific audiences

We are now living in an era where specialized messages are key. Consumers are looking for products, services and applications which suit their particular needs. So, before writing any copy, it is important to consider the audience of the intended message. Different audiences will have distinct needs, preferences and interests, which is why it is imperative to get into their heads. Consider what will interest them; make them sit up and take notice. What is their situation? How much time do they have to read the advertising message? Think about what they will be doing when they read the copy. Think about how they will be feeling at the time. Copywriters explore such 'psychographic factors' when considering the type of person they will be aiming their messages at. Below is a simple list that identifies some of these segments in more detail:

- **Actualizers** are active, successful and sophisticated. They have plenty of resources at their disposal and possess high esteem. They seek to explore, develop and grow as individuals. Image is important to them, and they seek to express themselves in many different ways. They tend to appreciate the finer things in life.

- **Fulfilleds** are mature and reflective. They value things such as order and responsibility. Most are well educated and many work in professional fields. They are self assured and base their decisions on principles. They avoid societal risks but may take personal risks. They are open to new ideas, but are generally conservative consumers who seek durability and value in their purchases.

- **Believers** are conventional and conservative. They believe in family, the nation and the church. They prefer well-known brands, have a modest education and income, and prefer regular routines.

- **Achievers** are in control of their lives, committed to their families and successful in their careers. They enjoy their jobs and value structure and stability. They are conservative and respect the status quo. They prefer major brand products and services that represent their success.

- **Strivers** have less economic and social resources. They desire approval from others and believe that money signifies success. They try to emulate others who have more material goods, and tend to be impulsive and unsure of themselves.

- **Experiencers** are usually young, impulsive and enthusiastic. They are action-orientated and seek excitement. They enjoy sports, exercise and social activities. They are usually uninformed and politically uncommitted.

- **Makers** are self-sufficient and are practical. They enjoy raising children, DIY and working on their cars. They buy products that have a functional purpose such as tools and fishing equipment. They are conservative and respect authority, although they resent personal intrusion on their individual rights.

- **Strugglers** have limited economic, social and psychological resources and often suffer from ill-health. Many believe the world is a difficult place. They focus on the present rather than thinking about the future, and are cautious when buying goods or services. They are concerned about feeling safe and secure.

Writing slogans and straplines

Slogans, also known as straplines, are advertising one-liners, designed to sell a specific product or service. In essence, they tell a *highly condensed* story about the values of the brand being advertised. Words or phrases are used to sum up and express the spirit or aim of a company, and their strength is that they can be changed to reflect new marketing strategies. The Advertising Slogan Hall of Fame (www.adslogans.co.uk) quotes the memorable and rhythmic 'Beanz Meanz Heinz' as one of the most successful slogans of all time. Although this slogan is memorable because of its use of assonance and rhyme, the brand message is clear: when it comes to baked beans, there is simply no choice but Heinz.

Task 5.5

Visit The Advertising Slogan Hall of Fame and evaluate the effectiveness of the slogans for some of your favourite brands. Ones we recommend include: Mars, Orange, Coca-Cola, McDonald's, Nike and HSBC.

Hopefully you have found that all of the slogans have one thing in common: their simplicity. Great slogans should resonate with the audience and should be difficult to forget. They should not be forced, artificial or contrived. Great slogans should beg to be chanted or sung by others; they should create vivid pictures in the audience's mind; they should get advertised free by word of mouth; they should provide identity and uniqueness. Most of all, they should use as few words as possible. Ideally they should also appeal to people's emotions or sense of pride in a positive manner. Writing effective slogans is not as easy as it looks. Consider the following slogan for the pain relieving tablets, Anadin: 'Nothing works faster than Anadin'. Although on the surface this may seem like a positive endorsement, a deeper reading of the slogan in fact suggests that it is better to take *nothing* to cure a headache! Ali (1997: 61–6) offers eight time-tested copywriting devices, all of which are powerful techniques in the design of copy for straplines or slogans:

1. **Alliteration** is the use of similar sounding words at the beginning of neighbouring words, for example:
   Katy's cakes are creamy yet crunchy.

2. **Puns** are common devices in marketing copy. They should be witty and memorable, but not so obscure that people fail to 'get them'. Consider the following:

    - *Hurry overture nearest phone.* (Telephone booking service for an orchestra's winter season.)
    - *Dramatic savings bard none.* (Half-price ticket offer by the Royal Shakespeare Company.)
    - *Stick a tenor in someone's card this Christmas.* (Advertisement for theatre gift vouchers.)
    - *A bank for people with very little interest in banks.* (Advertisement for a high-interest bank account.)

    Bear in mind that, like the Anadin example, puns can go horribly wrong if unintentional. Consider:
    NEW! Crash course in driving or the howler *We dispense with accuracy*, a genuine advert for a pharmacy!

3. **Assonance** is the repetition of vowel sounds to form an incomplete rhyme. It works only with vowels in stressed syllables. Consider the slogan for the American president Ike Eisenhower: *I like Ike.*

4. **Rhyme** in slogans is very popular but is about *sound* rather than *spelling*. Therefore they are more successful in radio than written advertisements. Consider this rhyme offered by the Government's clampdown on benefits fraud:
    Know of a benefit rip-off? Give us a telephone tip-off. Call the Beat-A-Cheat Line.

5. **Ellipsis** is the omission of a word or words in a piece of copy which readers must supply themselves. The missing words must be obvious or the resulting copy will not make sense. Consider the following example for a smart restaurant. The photograph shows a table laid with a starched linen tablecloth. The copy reads: *This is starched ... our service isn't.*

6. **Homonyms** are words than can be spelt the same as another but have a different meaning. Consider the following radio advertisement for the London Dungeon. The voiceover is provided by actor Vincent Price, famous for playing vampire roles: *You'll love the London Dungeon. I'll **stake** my heart on it.*

7. **Antonyms** are words that mean the opposite. They are different from synonyms, which are words that have the same meaning. Antonyms work well in marketing slogans. Consider:

- *A little car with a big personality.*
- *Overspill your trolley, underspend your budget.* (Advertisement for a supermarket.)
- *High in taste, low in fat.*
- *A big newspaper for a small coin.* (Used when *The Sun* reduced its price to 20p.)
- *Before you check-in, check-out our prices.* (Advertisement for duty-free airport shopping.)

8. **Unexpected deviance** is literally what it says: where the last line of copy deviates from a list or series of sentences. Consider:
100% customer service ... 100% quality ... 100% choice ... 0% finance.
Or consider the real-life example from Virgin Direct Personal Financial Service:
Good quality, good value, good service and good riddance to salesmen!

Task 5.6

Write a series of slogans for some of your previously chosen products using the devices of alliteration, pun, assonance, rhyme, ellipsis, homonym, antonym and unexpected deviance.

The KISS principle

Keep it Simple, Stupid! The KISS principle is the number one rule for all copywriters, but it is far harder to achieve than expected. Keeping it simple means more than cutting back on any extraneous copy; it means paring down to the bare bones. The need for simplicity is part of the craft of copywriting. Do not make the mistake of believing that because the intended audience is intelligent, they require complicated communications. Or, as Mark Twain asserted: 'Eschew surplusage'. This tells us everything we need to know about the art of copywriting in the shortest possible number of words.

The KISS principle is supported by clarity; that is, ensuring that advertising messages are easily absorbed and remembered by the audience. In order to achieve maximum clarity, the copywriter should:

1. **Put important words at the end of the sentence.** Consider the following inefficient and badly written copy:

   The planet needs taking care of. So when you're at your office supplier next, Opti is the product to ask for. It is one of the most environmentally friendly correction fluids you can get. Opti is non-polluting because we don't use chlorinated hydrocarbons in the ingredients. On paper Opti quickly dries out and it doesn't need thinners so every last drop can be used up.

   Important words should be given greater emphasis by placing them at the end of each sentence or before a punctuation mark. Consider the above rewritten using the KISS principle. The result is efficient, readable copy:

   Do your bit for planet Earth. Ask your office supplier for Opti, the environment-friendly correction fluid. Non-polluting Opti does not contain damaging chlorinated hydrocarbons. The fluid dries on paper in seconds and can be used down to the last drop without thinners.

2. **Use headings.** Avoid acres of continuous text. Break up the text with headings that tell the reader what is coming next. The headings should list benefits in their order of importance.

3. **Number the points.** If reader see there are ten points to absorb, rather than a continuous stream of text, they will absorb the information more easily. This technique encourages the copywriter to ask him or herself: 'What points am I trying to communicate?'

4. **Summarize the issues.** Benefits can be summarized in a coupon, in the postscript (PS) section of a letter, or on the back page of a brochure. Think of the summary as saying to a friend at the end of a discussion: 'The point I'm making is this ...'

5. **Phrase it from the customer's point of view.** Ensure that sentences focus on the customer's needs and interests. Do not

sell them the products, but solve their problems instead. Use the word 'you' to address the reader directly.

6. **Avoid starting a sentence with the word 'and'.** 'But' is acceptable; 'and' is not.

7. **Be bold.** Be confident about the products or services on offer. Avoid saying things like 'We think you'll enjoy this holiday'. Be braver than this; anything less will raise doubts in the customer's mind.

8. **Write factually.** A single fact is worth several generalizations. Consider this fact:

   '80% of all our reservations come from past clients or recommendations'. This acts as an instant endorsement to the organization and is sure to tempt the prospective customer.

9. **Give the writing the overnight test.** Leave the copy overnight; the morning light may shine on all sorts of errors.

10. **Show the draft to someone else.** Find someone whose opinion you trust; someone who will be honest about the copy. Ask him or her to comment on the simplicity of the copy, the clarity of points made, and whether it holds his or her interest.

Copywriting assignments

The chapter so far has explored *how* writing should be effective and clear in order to communicate messages intended to sell products or services to targeted audiences. The remainder of the chapter will now concentrate on *what* type of copy should be produced. It will explore some of the different copywriting assignments given to copywriters, and offer various tasks to undertake.

Copywriters may produce glossy press advertisements, corporate slogans and television advertisements, but the range of materials they produce is wide. Copywriting assignments or tasks can be broken into four distinct types:

- **Written communications**, which include direct mail letters, press releases and press packs (see pp. 169–75), press advertisements, brochure and leaflet copy, and newsletters.
- **Audio-visual promotions**, which include radio and television advertisements.

- **Online communications**, which include web-based copy and the use of social networking sites (to be explored in the Conclusion).
- **Ambient copy**, which is more 'miscellaneous' copy such as that found on van sides, street furniture and exhibition graphics.

Direct mail

Direct mail belongs to that annoying family we know as 'junk mail'; junk because it is unsolicited and usually badly written. However, it has one redeeming feature and that is the fact that it is easily targeted and its success rate is easily tested and measurable. The writing of direct mail packages is subject to strict rules, based on in-depth research into what works and what does not. Most mailings comprise a covering letter and one or more enclosures such as a mail order catalogue, an order form, a reply card, a leaflet, a questionnaire, a newsletter, a product sample, a brochure, a money-off voucher or a pre-paid envelope. The covering letter is important as it acts as a navigator, explaining to the reader what else is enclosed and why. It should not be too long; no more than two pages of text. The aim is to capture the reader's interest immediately. Remember the majority of direct mail communications end up in the bin. Before starting to write the covering letter, decide on its purpose: is it to sell, to generate a lead, to offer information, or to steer the reader through the enclosures? Like other narratives, the covering letter should have its own 'three act structure': a beginning (the hook), a middle (facts/details/propositions), and an end (what action is required/a response device).

Ali (1997: 127) suggests that when crafting the covering letter, the copywriter should include the 'Five Ps' in order to keep it:

- **Punchy:** preferably on one side only. If covering two sides, end page one with a split sentence to encourage the reader to turn the page.
- **Personal:** write in the first person. Be natural and use everyday words. Use a writing style appropriate to the audience and the subject matter.
- **Persuasive:** put forward powerful reasons why they should buy the product.

- **Pulling:** make sure everything about the package has pulling power, attracting the reader and keeping him or her.
- **Pushing:** gently push the reader in the right direction, enabling him or her to place an order or return a coupon for more information.

Other principles to consider when crafting the direct mail letter are to:

1. **Offer a friendly greeting.** The worst type of salutation is 'Dear Sir/Madam'. This tells the reader they are one among many. Ideally address letters to a named individual as this will increase the response rate.

2. **Use a strong headline.** Remember the KISS principle. The reader must be able to grasp the central message of the headline with one scan.

3. **Use subheadings.** Subheadings are smaller headlines that guide the reader onto a new subject. They also break up dense text on the page and make the reading process easier on the eye.

4. **Make the opening powerful.** Give your letter a dramatic start. The following are a selection of 'openers' that sell:

   - Challenge: 'Do you know how many days your company loses through sickness?'
   - Impressive fact: 'We spend £25 million a year on gritting roads ...'
   - Personal experience: 'When recovering from a car accident, I ...'
   - Knowledge of your interest: 'As a keen gardener ...'
   - A story or case study: 'When Romance Riviera Holidays needed extra office space ...'
   - Warning: 'Your company can be closed down tomorrow if you don't ...'
   - A special offer: 'We'll give you free gym membership for three months ...'
   - A problem shared: 'Do your gutters leak?'
   - Trial: 'Try this test. Apply this cream to your hands every day for a month.'

- Pose a question to which the answer is 'yes': 'Would you like to own a brand new car?'
- Personal appeal: 'You can lose one stone a month with our new healthy eating plan.'
- Dramatic statement: 'This letter could save your life.'
- Financial benefit: 'A set of cutlery for just £2.'

5. **Sell the benefits.** Remember, the benefits are what people buy, not the features.

6. **Emphasize important words.** Use a legible format. On A4 paper, text should be 150 mm wide, with a 30 mm margin on either side. Use twelve point text or bigger.

7. **Let the story unfold.** Sentences should be linked and ideas should develop in logical order. The letter should move from simple ideas to more complex ones. It can also move from benefits that affect everyone to those that affect fewer people.

8. **Make the reader act.** The end of the letter, when the reader has digested all the benefits, is the time to make him or her act. This is called the 'call to action'. A simple paragraph should tell the reader to do one of the following:

- Ring now for a demonstration.
- Fill in the reply-paid card.
- Send £20 to the address below.
- Ask for a technical representative to call.
- Contact a web address for further information.
- Phone a telephone number for further information.

9. **Add an incentive.** This will sometimes overcome a reader's inbuilt inertia. An example of an incentive is 'Reply by the 1st January and we'll give you two free cinema tickets'.

10. **Sign off in a friendly way.** Sign off using your given name and surname, and your position in the company.

11. **Use a PS.** The PS should be reserved for a just-remembered benefit. The PS is artful because it demands to be read and often serves to summarize a sales point that has already been made.

12. **Offer a reply device.** These boost responses and make it simpler for the reader to act.

13. **Overcoming objections.** Readers will look for any excuse not to respond to direct mail.

The following are examples of how to overcome these objections:

Objection	Response
Cannot afford it now	Easy payment plan
Need to compare it with others	Provide a comparison chart
Do not want to pay this month	Pay nothing for 30 days
Not sure whether colour would match furnishings	Try it in your home for a week
It looks complicated	Customer helpline
It may break down	Nationwide chain of service agents
I do not know anything about your company	Celebrity endorsement

An example of a successful and persuasive direct mail letter, aimed at a bank's existing credit card holder, is shown opposite.

Task 5.7

Find several more examples of professionally produced direct mail. Consider all the direct mail copy devices used and evaluate their effectiveness.

Writing leaflets and brochures

Nearly every kind of organization has a leaflet or brochure of some kind. They are essential and powerful selling tools. They may be something as simple as an A5 flyer or they may be a more substantial ten-page full-colour brochure. Whatever the format, they must start selling on the front cover. The remainder of the brochure should answer any questions prospective buyers may have. It is important, however, that the copywriter does not overload the leaflet or brochure with text. In today's visual age, people tend to concentrate less on copy and more on 'style': pictures, and overall design perhaps, used to illustrate key points. It is also advisable not to include any dates. Brochures are expensive to produce and any indication of date will immediately limit their shelf-life.

Premier UK Bank Ltd
www.premierukbank.co.uk

Mr J Smith
12 Gateways,
Long Treach,
Willingborough.
WI6 T45

August 2010

**Would you like to save money by transferring balances to your
Premier UK Bank Credit Card?**

Dear Mr Smith

We know you wouldn't turn down the chance to save some money. So we are
pleased to be able to offer you a special low rate for balance transfers from other
credit or store cards – **just 1.9% per annum (0.16% per month)** for six months
from the date of transfer.*

You can make as many transfers as you like up to your credit limit. Since it will
cost you absolutely nothing to make this transfer, why go on paying more
interest than you need to?

It's easy to request balance transfers – just complete the form attached or
alternatively call us on 08456 678 443** and we'll arrange it over the phone.

Making the most of your Premier UK Bank Credit Card

As one of our credit card holders, you can take advantage of the following great deals:

- membership of the Premier UK Bank Travel Club, entitling you to an extra
  discount of 10% on holidays booked with Astral Travel Direct.
- Special offers and great discounts that appear regularly in your monthly statements.
- 10% discount on comprehensive car insurance for the over-fifties.

Don't forget ... you can always check your account details whenever and
wherever you are: via your branch, by phone, or over the internet.

Be good to yourself and take this opportunity to save money with our special low
rate offer on balance transfers.

Yours sincerely,

Richas Croesus
Head of Cardholder Services

P.S. Don't forget to check our website for more incredible money-saving offers.

Premier UK Bank Ltd, St Peter's Way, Heaven's Gate, London. SW1 7RR
www.premierukbank.co.uk
Registered in England number 123123123, Registered Office: 9 America Square, London. E15 6JJ
Regulated by the Financial Services Authority

Important Notes
*The special transfer rate lasts for six months from the date of the balance transfer, at the end of which time the rates will
revert to the variable standard rates then applicable to your standard balance. Please allow around 10 working days between
us receiving your instruction and the date by which any repayment is due on the balance to be transferred. We accept no
liability for any interest or charges incurred if the transfer is not made by the date you anticipate. The closing date for this
offer is 1st December 2010.
**Lines are open 8am to 10pm everyday (except Christmas Day, Boxing Day and New Year's Day).

It is important to review copy before it goes to the printer; any errors or omissions will be costly. We encourage that, where appropriate, writers check that some or all of the following essential elements have been included:

- Company name.
- Logo.
- Address.
- Phone numbers and extensions.
- Hours to call.
- Email address.
- Website address.
- Store hours, locations and directions.
- Credit cards accepted.
- Branch offices, including addresses and directions.
- Guarantees.
- Disclaimers.
- Other required legal wording.
- Brochure date and code number.
- Permissions and acknowledgements.
- Trademarks and registration marks.
- Copyright notice.
- Product codes and other official emblems.
- Call to action.
- Price list and order form.

Task 5.8

Imagine you are writing a brochure for a new car. Write down the questions a purchaser might have and the answers a brochure might supply. When you have done this, go to a car showroom and take a few brochures. Has the company followed this process or not?

Writing newsworthy newsletters

Staff and customer newsletters are often seen as pure marketing tools, mostly unread and usually discarded. There are, however, a few simple rules to making newsletters 'newsworthy', interesting and effective.

Firstly, the copywriter must consider the *purpose* of the newsletter. Is it to produce extra sales, to gain corporate awareness, to persuade opinion formers, or to keep staff informed? Secondly, the copywriter should consider *who* the newsletter is aimed at. Those aimed at both staff *and* customers will not be effective because they will often mix messages. Other points to consider are where the information itself will come from and how the copywriter will select pertinent stories. A wide range of stories will be needed to keep the newsletter interesting: an average of three to five stories per page which should include a combination of serious and light-hearted news. Always put the most important story first and ensure that this is not one that readers are already familiar with. Newsletters benefit from regular features because they give it consistency and aid branding.

It is useful to gather regular feedback from readers; this will ensure that the newsletter is giving them what they want and not what the copywriter thinks they want. A 'Letters to the Editor' page is a useful way of achieving this, and some organizations encourage contributions by offering a prize for the best letter. Humorous articles certainly have their place in a newsletter, but humour does need to be controlled and it takes a talented writer to craft genuinely funny articles or snippets of copy. Competitions, quizzes, editorials and interviews also have their place in a newsletter.

Common errors that copywriters make when crafting newsletters include: un-newsworthy stories; complexity which baffles the reader; weak headlines; an emphasis on the trivial; and writing a newsletter that is perceived simply as a company 'mouthpiece'.

Task 5.9

Design the outline for a newsletter for a local charity. Devise a title and the format. Decide which articles you will place and where.

Writing the television advertisement

Television is a persuasive medium. The combination of sight, sound, motion and colour enables television to demonstrate a product, engage viewers' emotions, and show, not tell, product features. Television is also credible; consumers believe television advertising more than advertisements in any other medium. White states that 'the television commercial [is] a combination of sight and sound that moves to impart fact or evoke emotion … [it] is one of the most potent selling tools ever forged' (1994: 41). One drawback, however, is that it is a very expensive medium: placing advertisements adjacent to popular TV shows (soap operas, national sporting events, etc.) is available to only the largest advertisers. However, advertisers can buy time on cable television as an alternative to over-the-air television. It is much less expensive than advertising on broadcast television, and cable can be narrowcast and niche, allowing advertisements to be focussed towards defined audience segments. Increasingly television stations are using the Internet to expand their services and reach new audiences. It is the job of advertising copywriters to write copy for television advertisements. This is usually done in-house by large advertising agencies, and is rarely a job for a novice copywriter.

Television advertisement formats

Television advertisements are generally thirty seconds in length, but can also be bought in slots of ninety, sixty, twenty, fifteen and ten seconds. The last two are known as 'cut downs': shorter versions of a longer advertisements, designed to boost frequency of showing. The shorter the advert, the more times it can afford to be screened; this does, however, reduce impact. Some television advertisements are word-led: they have extensive dialogue and the pictures play a supporting role. Others are primarily visual exercises and have less dialogue. It is often the case that products which appeal to the head (financial services, home improvements, etc.) are word-led, while those that appeal to the heart (fashion, cars, etc.) are more visually orientated. Television advertisements notably fall into two distinct types: live action, which uses real people, and animation, which includes cartoons, slide sequences and computer-generated imagery.

Most advertisements use a similar format. They start with a proposition, such as 'New Whiter than White washing powder gets your clothes super clean'. This is followed by a section which adds proof or a demonstration of the proposition. The final section summarizes the benefits. In a variant on this theme, the advertisement identifies a problem (hair is dry and fly-away); it then offers a solution (improved conditioner); and finally it shows the result (glossy, manageable hair). This type will usually also end with a picture of the product in its packaging – known as a 'pack shot'.

Television advertisements usually fall into distinct themes, each having their own story type and plot. These include:

- **Appetite appeal.** 'Sell the sausage, not the sizzle.' Food advertisements should make the viewer drool at the mouth.
- **Clown.** These advertisements feature an idiot juxtaposed with a clever person. The clever person gives the idiot a lesson, such as which car insurance to take out. The clown makes the lesson memorable and saves it from becoming pompous.
- **Cartoons.** Cartoons endow the brand with personality and let the product speak for itself. They are also amusing.
- **Demonstration.** Demo advertisements are ideal for products that 'do' something, such as lawnmowers or cars. They are usually action based.
- **Drama 'stories'.** Will the business executive be able to deliver successfully his or her presentation despite travelling such a long way? Answer: yes, because he or she has chosen such a comfortable airline.
- **Endorsement.** A celebrity tells the audience why they use a particular product or service. This type of advertisement transfers in some people's minds the respect the viewer feels for the celebrity to the product.
- **Exaggeration.** Exaggeration relies on humour and is often used to advertise children's products.
- **The expert.** The Managing Director tells the audience why his double-glazed windows are the best. Some experts speak directly to the viewer whilst others are seen dispensing advice to others.
- **Fantasy.** Fantasy can be fun: a girl travels all over the world in her tiny car; a man parachutes a bunch of roses to his girlfriend.
- **Lifestyle.** Aspirational advertisements show beautiful people doing exciting things.
- **Mood.** Shampoo, perfume and other products with no unique or discernible benefits are products for which an atmosphere is

created through photography alone. Some advertisements do away with words and rely on mood entirely.

- **News advertisements.** Non-food brands such as toothpaste rely on the news advertisement to tell the viewer that a product is new and improved.
- **Musical heritage.** Advertisements can use well-known records to reinforce image. The effect is to link brands to a nostalgic era.
- **Problem–solution.** A car driver is stranded at night; a rugby shirt is soiled; a child is hungry in the morning. These problems are solved with the help of a motoring organization; a washing powder; a breakfast cereal.
- **Proof.** Crops are harvested day or night and the advertisement shows this. A 'proof advertisement' takes the product's USP and dramatizes it.
- **Sex.** Never overdo the sex in an advertisement: use it sparingly, or the result will be that the viewer remembers the sex but forgets the product.
- **Slice of life.** Two children argue at the dinner table before eating fish fingers. This tells the viewer that boisterous children should be fed a particular brand of fish fingers.
- **Soap.** In thirty to sixty seconds, the viewer is given a glimpse of a relationship developing. A man borrows coffee from his next-door neighbour, and the viewer is left to wonder what will happen next.
- **Talking head.** One person talks directly to camera – simple but effective.
- **Two women talking in a kitchen.** Or, as in a recent advertisement for a brand of kitchen towels, two men pretending to be two women talking in a kitchen.

Task 5.10

Watch a number of television advertisements. Identify which of the above themes they fall into.

A television advertisement can be presented as a script or a storyboard. A script is divided into two columns, the left column being for visual instructions and the right column for audio instructions, including music and sound effects.

Tips for writing television advertisements

When writing a television advertisement, it is necessary to make the dialogue as natural sounding as possible; if not, the audience may feel that they are being 'preached' to. Avoid also trying to make too many points as this can lead to confusion and a muddying of the intended message. The benefits of the product should always be summarized, whilst keeping the message clear and simple. Finally, it is good practice to end the advertisement with a picture of the product, ensuring that the audience can visualize it for future purchase.

Although copywriters need to be aware of script jargon, they need only incorporate the basics into their script. The production company will add the detail at a later date. However, the copywriter should be aware of the following jargon:

Photography
WA: wide-angle shot; sets the scene.
MS: medium shot; can show two people together.
MCU: medium close-up.
CU: close-up; shows a face or a plate of food.
ECU: extreme close-up; shows detail; lips, for example.
POV: point of view; where the camera looks at the scene through the eyes of one of the characters.
Eyeline: the position of a subject's eyes on screen.

Sound
Lead-in: initial words spoken by the voice-over at the start of the action.
DV: direct voice; coming from a character on stage.
FVO: female voice-over.
MVO: make voice-over.
SFX: sound effects.
Ad lib: spontaneous dialogue, not scripted.

Scene changing
Mix: one image fading into another.
Cut: change abruptly from one scene to another.
Super: superimpose.
Editpoint: the point at which a scene change is planned.

Below is an example of the layout for a simple thirty-second television advertisement for a second-hand furniture shop:

Title: Buy Second-hand Length: 30 seconds	
VIDEO	**AUDIO**
EXT shot of shop.	SFX: smooth, calming music. FVO: Times are hard, so why not turn your trash into cash?
CU of frontage. (5 seconds)	
CUT TO: inside shop.	FVO: From jewellery to furniture … paintings to crockery … *The Alchemist's Daughter* can offer you great value on your second-hand goods.
Pan over goods. (7 seconds)	
CUT TO: shop assistant serving a Customer. (9 seconds)	Why not try our new swap service? You never know what surprises you might find …
End title: *The Alchemist's Daughter*	*The Alchemist's Daughter*. Get a good deal … today.
Address. Web address. (9 seconds)	

Task 5.11

Choose a television advert that interests you. Write the script as the agency might have done. Determine who the target audience is.

Writing the radio advertisement

Radio advertisements are far easier and much cheaper to produce than television advertisements; they rely on sound only and airtime is relatively cheap. They are made by local media production agencies for clients and the majority of them are aired on local, commercial radio. Like all advertisements, radio needs to attract the listener's attention, create desire and encourage them to act. Here, however, the similarities end; radio is a medium with few restraints and offers greater creative opportunity. The copywriter can set the advertisement in any location and in any era he or she wishes. Radio advertisements use approximately two words per second, and the majority of words should be no more than one or two syllables, easy to pronounce and easy to understand. Tongue twisters and excessive alliteration should be avoided and a call to action should be inserted at the end.

Radio advertisements fall into two types of 'story': the straightforward announcement and the plot. Below is an example of a straightforward announcement. It is simple, to the point and brief.

Client: **One Acre Garden Centre**
Title: **Standard**
Length: **30 seconds**

Great news for gardeners! Yes, One Acre Garden Centre is open all day Sunday. There's everything you need for the garden under one roof. We've shrubs, conifers, bulbs, plants and trees, plus the biggest selection of pots ever.

We're open on Sunday from 9 'til 6. So don't miss out. Come along to One Acre Garden Centre, Dorchester, this Sunday. You're in for a great deal.
(END)

The example below is for the same client, but uses real people with a real plot. Inside twenty seconds, the listener gets a glimpse into the lives of Joe, Jack and Emma. It may not be Shakespeare, but it works well for radio.

Client: **One Acre Garden Centre**
Title: **Pub**
Length: **20 seconds**

Jack:	See you down the pub on Sunday, Joe?
Joe:	No, sorry Jack, I've got to do the gardening.
Jack:	But it's Sunday!

Joe:	Yes, Emma's found out that One Acre is open all day Sunday.
Jack:	That's a shame … I just tell my wife it's shut.
Emma:	Not any more you don't, Jack
Voice-over:	One Acre Garden Centre, Dorchester. Open 'til 8 p.m. each week day and all day Sunday 'til 6. Sorry about that, Jack.

Task 5.12

Listen to a set of radio advertisements. Categorize them into either announcement or plot. Assess how much use each advert makes of the medium's creative potential.

Having read and digested the information on copywriting and completed the tasks, let us consider again how copywriting uses *story with purpose* to communicate messages. For some of the copywriting assignments, notably the crafting of television and radio advertisements, this is obvious. Here there is a need to shape and plot narrative carefully in such a way that it is both accessible to audiences whilst relaying a pertinent message. Other copywriting assignments, such as the writing of direct mail, newsletters and slogans, certainly define the need for persuasion and conviction, and direct mail letters use the three-act structure device; but do they necessarily rely on the notion of *story* within their narrative to relay their marketing messages? Some would argue that narrative needs to contain more than a swift and clever marketing message to carry the label of 'story'. We would argue that it is clever and skilful indeed to be able to condense an idea or 'story' into as few words as possible.

Task 5.13

Refer back to the Introduction of this book. Re-read the definitions of communication and consider in what ways the craft of copywriting meets these definitions.

Career opportunities in copywriting

There are certainly job opportunities available for aspiring copywriters, either as freelancers or attached to advertising or public relations agencies. To work in an advertising agency, you would normally need a degree in Advertising, Marketing or Communications. To work as a copywriter in a public relations consultancy, it is preferable to have a degree in Public Relations, Media Writing or Communications.

It is easier now than ever to set up as a freelance copywriter. Developments in technology and the online revolution have paved the way for aspiring copywriters. There are advantages: you can fit your work around other commitments; you can work from home; and you can slowly build your own client base. There are obvious disadvantages, too: your income can be unreliable. Read the job advertisements in magazines such as *Campaign*, *Marketing*, *Marketing Week* and *PR Week*. Look in *The Guardian*'s job advertisements on Mondays when they publish the media section.

Further reading

Ali, M. (1997) *Copywriting*, Oxford: Butterworth-Heinemann.

Blake, G. and Bly, R. (1997) *The Elements of Copywriting: The Essential Guide to Creating Copy that Gets the Results You Want*, New York: Macmillan.

Cutts, M. (1999) *The Quick Reference Plain English Guide*, Oxford: Oxford University Press.

Gabay, J. (2000) *Teach Yourself Copywriting*, 2nd edn, London: Hodder & Stoughton.

Gettins, D. (2006) *How to Write Great Copy: Learn the Unwritten Rules of Copywriting*, 2nd edn, London: Kogan Page.

Goddard, A. (2002) *The Language of Advertising: Written Texts*, London: Routledge.

Meeske, M. (2003) *Copywriting for the Electronic Media: A Practical Guide*, 4th edn, London: Thomson Wadsworth.

Rosen, E. (2000) *Net Words: Creating High-Impact Online Copy*, London: McGraw-Hill Education.

Veloso, M. (2004) *Web Copy that Sells: The Revolutionary Formula for Creating Killer Copy Every Time*, New York: Amacom.

White, H. (1994) *How to Produce Effective TV Commercials*, 3rd edn, New York: McGraw-Hill.

Web resources

www.adslogans.co.uk

The Advertising Hall of Fame, home to great advertising slogans that have achieved international recognition.

www.asa.org.uk

Official website for the Advertising Standards Authority, the independent regulator for advertising, sales promotion and direct mail in the UK.

Screenwriting: Fiction **6**

The term 'screenwriting' is relatively new to the UK; it has been adopted from American culture, where it has been used for many more decades. In contrast to the more commonly heard term 'scriptwriting', screenwriting is concerned purely with the art and craft of writing for the screen. For most, this means writing fictional drama for film and television, although as explored in Chapter 7 this can also mean writing factual or 'real life' film and television. Recently screenwriting has also come to include the writing of narratives for computer and video games, also known as 'scripting'. Like film and television, this is concerned with creating interesting characters and appealing storylines, albeit for players to immerse themselves in, not viewers to merely watch. Although there is a growing market for screenwriters to cross over into forms such as computer and video games, this chapter will focus upon the traditional form of screenwriting: film and television drama.

By the end of this chapter, you should be able to:

- Understand the practical and commercial considerations of screenwriting.
- Recognize the layout of a screenplay and be able to imitate it successfully.
- Become familiar with the fundamental elements of narrative structure and the relationship between story (emotion) and plot (action).
- Understand the difference between character and characterization, and how each can be approached in a practical, developmental way.

- Become familiar with the tools of genre and use them to build a screenplay.
- Understand the foundations of writing screen dialogue and use them effectively in writing practice.
- Recognize the fabric and function of a scene and be able to write a series of scenes, each one having its own function and style.

What is a screenplay?

In practical terms, a screenplay is the written text of the drama: the guide, or map, of how the story on the page will be realized into the story on the screen. It is written in a specific way and to a specific style, carefully guiding the reader through the unfolding narrative. Through written action and dialogue, and through a process of imagination, screenplay readers can 'see' the drama unfolding before them. This is crucial in commercial terms because those who commission scripts want to know that the proposed drama will work on the screen and will, of course, attract an audience. As such, the film or television drama commissioner is looking for scripts that quickly and effectively stand out from the rest: the jewel in the slush pile.

Thinking about the screenplay in practical terms brings to the fore a number of important issues. These are especially pertinent when screenwriting is compared to other forms of creative and media writing, as shown below:

- **A screenplay is only ever the blueprint for production.** Unlike a novel, a newspaper article or advertising copy, which is published in its written form and then consumed by an audience, the screenplay is only the end product of pre-production. The screenplay may take two or more years to develop and write, but it only takes shape as a consumable through its production: casting, rehearsal, shooting, editing, distribution, etc.
- **Screenwriting is heavily reliant upon planning.** Screenplays can sell solely on their treatment (a prose version of the story) or their step-outline (a scene-by-scene synopsis); the script does not even have to be written. This means that the screenwriter must

be dedicated to developing the story and characters in a very 'embryonic' way, potentially for a very long time, before a word of dialogue is even written. In fact, some screenwriters earn a living from selling story ideas ('optioning'): they may never sell an actual screenplay, let alone have one made.

- **Screenwriting is seen as very business orientated.** Most screenplays are written with a particular genre and/or market in mind, meaning that the writing can feel like it is packaged and shaped according to how the industry operates. As such, successful screenwriters need to be market savvy, aware of current trends and patterns in the drama market. They must also be good networkers, not afraid of speaking to people and being prepared to pitch an idea in any given situation.

- **Screenwriting is extremely collaborative.** The screenwriter will work in collaboration, and often at odds, with various personnel during the development of a commissioned screenplay. These collaborations depend upon the script being written, but can include: development producer; executive producer; script consultant; script editor; director; and actors. Not only that, the act of screenwriting itself is not as individual as it may seem. As well as co-writing and team-writing (common practice in America), screenwriters can often be hired and fired from a project. In these cases, several writers may be paid to write and rewrite the same script, with possibly only one or two of them being named ('credited') in the final production.

As we can see, screenwriting is a very special and often misunderstood form of writing. Although it shares common patterns and principles with other forms of media writing in terms of content, it varies widely in terms of its practical processes.

A screenplay, however, is more than this; it is more than a mere technical document, written in a mechanical way for a commercial cause. Screenwriting often takes place from a very personal experience and viewpoint, and can be written with a unique voice. How original this voice is will depend upon the writer himself and also the context of the production: Hollywood 'vs' independent outfit; mainstream TV series 'vs' first-time independent director; etc. A screenplay driven from passion and experience can be an emotionally powerful text, drawing an audience into its narrative and taking them on a journey that mirrors that of the characters. In this sense, the screenplay becomes more than the sum of its parts: it becomes an *experience*, felt within the cinema or domestic sphere, and beyond. Torben Grodal writes:

> The film [and television] experience is made up of many activities: our eyes and ears pick up and analyze image and sound, our minds apprehend the story, which resonates on our memory; furthermore, our stomach, heart, and skin are activated in empathy with the story situations and the protagonists' ability to cope. (1997: 1)

As this shows, screenwriting is not merely an individual venture which may turn into a collaborative business project, but an attempt to reach out to the potential audience and make them *feel* something. Kristyn Gorton writes about television emotion, arguing that it 'allows for a way of seeing that is different from other viewing. It allows viewers a chance to acknowledge their neediness whilst also feeling connected to something outside themselves' (2006: 78). Here we could go as far as reconfiguring this to include the word 'feeling': the difference in this 'way of seeing' is that it also offers a 'way of feeling'. Similarly, Luke Hockley writes that the emotional connection between screen character and audience is one rooted in psychological attachment, and a way of interpreting narrative space is 'as an expression of the inner state of the central identification figure ... inner psychological concerns and attitudes take on a visual form within the film – story space becomes psychological space, if you will' (2007: 43).

How, then, does this relate to screenwriting practice? The guiding principle that stems from these ideas is simple: when writing a screenplay, consider how the story you tell can evoke meaning in the audience. 'Meaning' is often understood as 'theme' and in simple terms translates as: what is this story really about? The plot may see a family being forced out of their home and having to settle in a nearby town, but that is not what the film is about; this is merely what happens. What the film is about, its meaning, may be concerned with love, or loss, or guilt, or greed. As Robert McKee writes: 'a storyteller is a life poet, an artist who transforms day-to-day living, inner life and outer life, dream and actuality into a poem whose rhyme scheme is events rather than words – a two-hour metaphor that says: life is like *this!*' (1999: 25).

As this suggests, screenwriters should be concerned with creating screenplays that touch an audience, reminding them that 'life is like this'. This is not to say that films and television dramas must be serious or deeply reflective, but should at the very least have some hidden meaning that connects with the audience. Think about this: how many comedy films have you seen that purely make you laugh? How many can you really say do not have an underlying meaning that you are supposed to empathize with? Even films such as *There's Something About Mary*, *Knocked Up* and the *American Pie* franchise have deeper themes that at some point in the narrative surface above the hilarious comedy: love; friendship; growth; 'coming of age'; etc. This is an example of the skill possessed by what McKee calls 'master storytellers', those who 'know how to squeeze life out of the least of things' (ibid.: 28). In other words, the situation does not have to be emotionally grand or even emotionally obvious, but within it there is an element of emotion that can be squeezed out and played upon. In sum, emotion plays an integral part to the screenplay because it creates a connection between writer and reader, character and audience, one that even in a moment of gross-out comedy ensures that the heart is touched or the nerve is tickled.

Task 6.1

Make a list of five films that made you feel something whilst watching them. What did you feel? How did these feelings come about? Now choose a film that did not make you feel anything; one that did not connect with you. Why did you not feel anything? Watch the film again and try to uncover what the intended feeling might have been.

Screenplay layout

There is only one way to lay out a screenplay – correctly. Failure to do this not only looks unprofessional, it can jeopardize the chances of the script being read by the appropriate person in the first place. In today's culture, there is no excuse for poor screenplay formatting because so many packages exist to do the job. The most well known of these is Final Draft, readily available and easy to operate on a computer. It can be costly, however, and numerous updated versions can make you feel that you always need to upgrade. An alternative to Final Draft is the BBC's free software ScriptSmart, again easy to operate on a computer. The advantage of ScriptSmart is that, as well as being free, it has multifunctions so that you can choose between formatting screenplays, theatre plays, radio plays, and even novels. It is available from the BBC Writersroom website, which has a whole host of other resources for writers (www.bbc.co.uk/writersroom).

The key points of a screenplay layout are:

- The **slugline** is another word for 'scene heading', indicating where a scene is set ('INT.' means 'interior', 'EXT.' means 'exterior'), along with an idea of time.
- **Scene action**, or screen direction, details what is actually happening on the screen. It is used to describe visual action and sounds.
- The **character name** indicates who is speaking at any one time, and appearing underneath this is the actual **dialogue**. Sometimes voice-over is used by a character, but this is still written as dialogue, with the addition of 'voice-over' or 'V/O' in parentheses underneath the character name.
- **Parentheses** are also used when the writer wishes to indicate how something is said, or when a minor form of action takes place between the dialogue.
- Occasionally **scene transitions** are given at the end of a scene, but this is usually only when a specific effect is desired. Otherwise a simple 'cut to' is implied by the ending of one scene and the beginning of another.

Here is an example of a standard screenplay layout, from the film *Almost Famous*:

```
INT. BACKSTAGE HALLWAY - NIGHT

The band moves quickly down the hallway, with William
moving to keep up. A young and grizzled red-haired
roadie, RED DOG, catches them on the way. The band
swarms around him.

                        RUSSELL
          Red Dog!

                        RED DOG
          We're playing here tomorrow night.

                         JEFF
               (aside, to the kid)
          This is Red Dog, the Allman Brothers
          Band's number one roadie.

Russell clamps an arm around Red Dog's neck.

                        RUSSELL
          How're the guys?

                        RED DOG
          Havin' a ball, man. When we have a
          party, we have an Allman Brothers
          Band party. Everybody boogies.
          Everybody gets off. It's family,
          man. We all got these now.
               (flashes new mushroom
                tattoo on forearm)
          We'll see you guys in Boston, right?
               (specifically to Russell)
          Dicky and Gregg send you their love.

Camera catches flash of envy on the face of Jeff
Bebe, as Stillwater sweeps forward into a small
dressing room.
```

The most effective way to learn how to format a screenplay is to read
a variety of them. As well as becoming more familiar with the layout,
techniques will be picked up as to how to write in the style of a
screenplay – the specific 'voice' that it has.

Narrative structure

Screenplays are built around a narrative, which in short means a sequence of events made up of various constituents that come together to create the whole. In screenwriting, the constituents include character, dialogue and action, and when put into a sequence of events they cumulatively produce the complete screenplay experience. Arguably there are two levels to narrative structure: *story* and *plot*. As with the above discussion of emotion and action, these two 'DNA strands' (Batty and Waldeback, 2008: 29) work symbiotically to create the complete narrative experience that an audience expects. Using the terms 'character' and 'structure' to mean 'story' and 'plot', Robert McKee writes that:

> Structure and character are interlocked. The event structure of a story is created out of the choices that characters make under pressure and the actions they choose to take, while characters are the creatures who are revealed and changed by how they choose to act under pressure. If you change one, you change the other. (1999: 106)

Although we can see two levels of narrative structure working in a screenplay, 'order of events (plot); emotional character arc (story)' (Waldeback, 2006: 21), the success of the screenplay lies in these two working together. The term 'journey' is often used in screenwriting, meaning the road that the character(s) travels from start to finish. Also known as the 'character arc' (see, for example, Gulino, 2004: 136), this general notion of a journey is useful because it allows the screenwriter to map the movement his or her character(s) will make across the narrative, both in terms of action and emotion. In this way, the terms 'physical journey' and 'emotional journey' give weight to the dual threaded nature of the screenplay narrative. The following sets this out in more detail:

Physical journeys are concerned with what characters literally *want*. The audience sees them trying to achieve a physical goal (plot) that might include:

- Getting to a particular place, often by a particular time.
- Finding a way home or out of an unfamiliar situation.

- Rescuing someone in danger, often also stopping the cause of the danger.
- Making someone fall 'head over heels' for them, sometimes ending with a marriage.

Emotional journeys are concerned with what the characters really *need*. The audience sees them develop emotionally (story) in tandem with their physical goal, and examples might include:

- Realizing who they really are, or what makes them tick.
- Learning to love again, perhaps after a bad experience that has left them feeling empty.
- Finding inner happiness, which may have been haunting them for years.
- Sparking their imagination and breathing a sense of new life into them.

Task 6.2

Choose a protagonist that you are familiar with and make notes about the journey they take. What is their physical want, and their journey to gaining it? What is their emotional need, and their journey to embracing it? How do they combine to create the complete narrative?

Once the overall intention of a screenplay has been developed, the most difficult part of the process begins: creating a narrative structure. Structure is one of the most important elements of a screenplay because it shapes the viewing experience; it enables connections to be made between audience and character through scene order and point of view, and allows situations to be understood and felt as intended. As such, structure can make or break the film or television drama. There are numerous ways of dealing with narrative structure and many 'models' exist for writers to work with. The best advice we can give here is to read and explore the various models available (almost every screenwriting book has a 'unique' approach), and then use the one that feels the most comfortable. Different models resonate with different writers, and it is down to the individual to use (or reject!) accordingly.

Sequences

One way of approaching screenplay structure is through the use of *sequences*. This is a model that sees screenplays comprised of a set number of 'mini narratives', usually eight, which when put together create the master structure. Paul Joseph Gulino (2004) and David Howard (2004) write about this method, advising writers to use sequences from the outset in order to gain an overall sense of the screenplay's structure and to identify and resolve narrative problems. Briefly, sequences work as follows:

- **Sequence 1** establishes the story world and the 'normality' of the protagonist (who also has a problem). A disturbance to the normality, the *inciting incident*, raises the central dramatic question (usually related to the plot goal).
- **Sequence 2** shows the protagonist struggling with this new problem, leading to a decision to deal with it. This turning point becomes the end of Act 1.
- **Sequence 3** sees the protagonist trying to solve the problem with a 'plan of action', doing first what seems easiest. Often more effort is needed (rising action) as the problem refuses to go away.
- **Sequence 4** shows the protagonist trying harder, often applying more serious tactics. Obstacles increase, requiring more effort; the stakes are raised. The *midpoint* usually comes here, spinning the action in a new direction (or with new focus; sometimes emotion prevails over action).
- **Sequence 5** sees the protagonist reacting to the midpoint change. He or she may be re-inspired by what has happened, leading to a new plan to achieve the goal.
- **Sequence 6** shows that although the protagonist is working hard he or she is still unsuccessful. This culminates in a new decision, which marks the end of Act 2. In stories with a happy ending, this is usually the 'lowest point'. In stories with a tragic ending, things seem hopeful at last.
- **Sequence 7** sees the climax or 'biggest battle', incorporating the protagonist's 'hardest choice'. Most often this is where the goal is achieved (or not). Occasionally there is a false resolution, and sometimes there is a twist or unexpected event.

- **Sequence 8** shows the final resolution, both of action and emotion. Depending on the type of story, this can also be the climax scene – the final showdown. Sometimes there is an 'epilogue' tying the ends together once and for all.

Sequences are interesting from a historical point of view, as Gulino outlines, because in the early days of film it was necessary to separate them into 'mini films', purely because there was only one projector and the spool would need to be changed (2004: 3). During the late 1920s, features became the more dominant form of film, and as such most cinemas invested in an extra projector to make the viewing experience seamless. Interestingly, 'formal and rigorous adherence to writing for each reel became unnecessary, but the structure persisted, evidenced by the organization of screenplays into sequences identified by letter, ... a practice that lasted into the 1950s' (ibid.: 3–4). Even when talking pictures arrived, and Broadway playwrights used to the 'three act structure' model were drafted in to write screenplays, the sequence approach remained: 'the result was an eight-sequence structure married to three acts' (ibid.: 4). Gulino's book *Screenwriting: The Sequence Approach* offers an array of useful film analyses and is highly recommended for a deeper understanding of how sequences work.

Three act structure

By far the most understood and practised model of screenwriting narrative, *three act structure* is a base for all screenwriting models. Whether using sequences (as above) or mapping out the 'hero's journey' (see Campbell, 1993; Vogler, 1999), three act structure is a solid 'container' that divides a narrative into beginning (Act 1), middle (Act 2) and end (Act 3). Three act structure has its roots in Greek tragedy, as written about by Aristotle, who saw that plays of the time could easily be identified as having a beginning, middle and end:

> a thing is whole if it has a beginning, a middle, and an end ... A well constructed plot, therefore, will neither begin at some chance point nor end at some chance point, but will observe the principles here stated. (1982: 52)

A useful book for contemporary screenwriters is Ari Hiltunen's *Aristotle in Hollywood: The Anatomy of Successful Storytelling* (2002). As the title suggests, this book offers some useful insights into how Aristotle's *Poetics* can be applied directly to screenwriting, demystifying what can potentially be seen as a difficult text and giving it contemporary practical application.

The author most commonly associated with three act structure is Syd Field, whose books have become seminal for beginner screenwriters. Adopting a very 'how to' approach, Field's books are useful for grounding writers with the basic principles of screenwriting and offering detailed film analyses to illustrate them. Field's model of the three act structure (2003) is used as a basis for the following summary:

- **Act 1: setup (¼).** This act introduces the protagonist and other central characters, the story world or setting, and establishes the underlying theme that will drive the narrative. Through the *inciting incident*, the goal of the protagonist is identified: what he wants to achieve by the end of the narrative. This act should also identify what the protagonist has at stake: what he stands to lose if the goal is not achieved. It also identifies the potential antagonistic forces (people or things) that will pose problems and obstacles for the protagonist to overcome in pursuit of the goal.
- **Act 2: confrontation (½).** This act is where the story truly starts. Having decided to undertake the challenge of achieving the goal, the protagonist's journey begins and progresses at speed. Obstacles and hurdles are met and overcome, testing the protagonist's will and asking whether he really is up to the challenge. Conflict is crucial. New situations are met and experienced, developing the protagonist's knowledge and awareness of things unfamiliar, and new friends (and enemies) are made. Important to this act is the protagonist beginning to learn internal lessons: his character 'grows'.
- **Act 3: resolution (¼).** The narrative begins to wind down or change direction when the protagonist gets or does not get what he has come looking for – the goal. In most films the goal is achieved, although sometimes in a different way than expected, and sometimes not at all. The protagonist then goes back to the beginning, to his ordinary world. However, now he has gained new knowledge

and insights of himself and of the world: he has changed. Usually the protagonist has eliminated the problem he had at the start and as such can move forward to a 'better' way of life.

Drawing from the above, here is a short summary of a classical narrative pattern using the three act structure:

> The *disturbance* in a character's life sets him or her on a *journey* to achieve a *goal*, which incorporates a *physical want* and an *emotional need*. *Obstacles* stand in the character's way, creating *dramatic conflict* which must be *overcome* before the goal can be achieved and *resolution* found.

The 'inciting incident', referred to above, is a term which means a 'disturbance' or a 'call to adventure' (Vogler, 1999: 99–101). It disturbs the protagonist's normal world, acting as a wake-up call which propels him or her on the journey undertaken. It most often comes in the form of a problem posed or a challenge set, and because it disturbs the normality seen so far it is the point where the dramatic story is truly set into motion. *Motivation* is crucial in screenwriting, and here it connects especially well with the inciting incident. Quite simply, if the protagonist has no impetus to undertake the challenge then the story lacks conviction and the audience will not care if he or she achieves the goal or not. Rather the inciting incident should offer a moment of crisis where the protagonist must make a decision to undertake the challenge – he or she is literally incited to make the journey.

The inciting incident can come in an array of forms, but common ones are:

- **Someone sets a literal challenge**, where the task is to complete it by a given deadline. If there is no challenge, there is no story. Example: in *How to Lose a Guy in 10 Days*, magazine feature writer Andie sets herself the challenge of finding a boyfriend and then making him dump her in ten days. At the same time, ironically, advertising-guy Ben is set the challenge of making a girl fall in love with him in ten days.

- **Boy meets girl** (or variation) for the first time, where one realizes the other must be chased or wooed in order to earn the other's love. If there is no meeting, there is no chase, and subsequently no story.

Example: in *My Big Fat Greek Wedding*, Toula serves 'hot guy' Gus in her family-run restaurant; she believes that he is the man for her, even though he does not notice her. This ignites in her a commitment to change (physically and emotionally), and the romantic chase soon ensues.

- **Someone sees something they really want** and the goal is to try and get it; often by whatever means possible. Nothing seen means nothing sought.
  Example: in *There Will Be Blood*, Daniel has already begun his successful oil empire when Paul pays him a visit to tell him about the presence of oil in Little Boston. Daniel cannot resist the temptation of this venture and so sets off to try and make even more money.

- **Something is stolen** and the goal is to recover it, often by a given deadline. If nothing is stolen, then there is no reason for someone to try and find it.
  Example: in *Catch Me If You Can*, Frank's lifestyle and happiness are taken away from him; the family has to give up their house, and mum and dad file for divorce. When asked where he wants to live, Frank runs away, and in an attempt to regain the lost money (and subsequently the depleted family), he embarks upon a journey of con-artistry. At the same time, he is chased by FBI agent Carl.

- **Someone dies or is injured**, triggering a goal of revenge and affirmation. No death or injury means no impetus to seek revenge.
  Example: in *Kill Bill*, 'The Bride' comes out of a coma and remembers how she got there: she was gunned down at her wedding by former lover Bill and his assassin assailants. Realizing that her husband-to-be and then unborn child are dead, she undertakes a dark mission fuelled by revenge.

Narrative structure case study: *The Wizard of Oz*

Much has been written about *The Wizard of Oz* and its use of narrative, and even today it remains one of the most useful case studies for demonstrating how writers can create well-structured stories. Quite simply, the film employs such a well-defined classical three act narrative structure that it is essential viewing for any budding screenwriter (or, indeed, storyteller).

The film begins by depicting protagonist Dorothy Gale's unhappy life: she lives on a farm with her family but craves a better life, somewhere 'over the rainbow'. Dorothy feels that she is not wanted by her family and that others see her as the silly little girl who just gets in the way; so, she decides to run away. This plan is scuppered, however, when fake fortune teller Professor Marvel tells her that she must go back home to tend to a sick and worried Aunt Em. In this, Act 1, we see quite clearly Dorothy's want: to run away. Scenes depicting why she feels so are essential in providing the necessary motivation for her want, and as such we as viewers empathize with her goal. The inciting incident of the film literally spins the action in another direction when a storm lifts Dorothy's house from the ground and blows it away. Interestingly, the reason that Dorothy is in the house, alone, is because as she was running away she missed the opportunity of entering the storm shelter with the rest of her family. Thus, this narrative moment is not only credible, it symbolically depicts the need for Dorothy to 'learn a lesson', which will be revealed once the house settles again.

Now 'over the rainbow', Dorothy hesitantly leaves the house and finds herself in the land of Oz. Here she is faced with a world totally different to the one she left behind (Kansas): one full of colour, strange objects and, of course, Munchkins. Thus, Dorothy is positioned into a new world that is bound to offer her new experiences. The Good Witch, Glinda, tells Dorothy that in order to return to Kansas she must find the Wizard of Oz; but that will mean undertaking a long journey down the yellow brick road. Instantly the narrative sets up the proposition that Dorothy must travel a physical journey, and we can sense that in some way she will also experience an emotional transformation. The journey is not proper, of course, unless it is laden with conflict and obstacles. Unbeknown to Dorothy, her house landed on and killed the Wicked Witch of the East, and now her sister, the Wicked Witch of the West, is out to get her. Furthermore, Dorothy has taken possession of the magical ruby slippers that the Wicked Witch desperately wants, giving her a physical motivation too. The Wicked Witch, then, is set up as the antagonist of the narrative, pitted against an innocent Dorothy.

The turning point of Act 1 into Act 2 occurs when Dorothy literally steps onto the yellow brick road and decides to follow it. Fuelled by the song of the Munchkins, she commits to the journey with the goal of getting to the Wizard. Along her long journey, basically Act 2, she meets new friends: Scarecrow, Tin Man and Cowardly Lion. These characters are instrumental in helping her along her journey, and in fact later become the means by which she finally achieves her goal, but in terms of emotional transformation they function purely for Dorothy's character. Each one represents a 'quality' that Dorothy needs, identified by passing references at the start (in Kansas): a brain, a heart and courage. Thus, as well as physical manifestations that provide help, guidance and humour, the Scarecrow, Tin Man and Cowardly Lion function as emotional signifiers of what Dorothy lacks and what she will learn to embrace by the end of the narrative.

Conflict is encountered along the yellow brick road, some of it initiated by the Wicked Witch: multiple paths to follow; apple-throwing trees; scary woods; poisonous poppies; flying monkeys. These obstacles are essential to the narrative because they stall the happy ending and teach Dorothy valuable lessons about life. Without these obstacles the meeting with the Wizard would be all too easy, and Dorothy would not earn her reward. The reward itself is stalled, however, when the Wizard is found out to be a fake. Dorothy is distressed, feeling like she will never get back home, but the Wizard sets her one final test: kill the Wicked Witch and bring back her broom. This represents the turning point of Act 2 into Act 3, where the dramatic stakes are raised.

The Wicked Witch captures Dorothy who has to be rescued by her new found friends. During the time she is held captive, Dorothy sees a vision of her Aunt Em and realizes that she was a fool to have run away in the first place. In narrative terms, this is Dorothy's 'lowest point' because she fears that she will die, and die alone. We see her regret that she wanted to leave Kansas in the first place, which functions to highlight her emotional journey: to be happy with her family and content in Kansas. Finally, Dorothy is saved; but the chase is not over yet. The Wicked Witch sets out to kill Dorothy and all of her friends, and so throws a fireball. This sets the Scarecrow alight, so Dorothy quickly throws a bucket of water over him to extinguish the fire. Unknown to her, however, is that the Wicked Witch cannot touch water; and so, as the water also hits the Wicked Witch, she melts. This is a very interesting narrative moment because Dorothy has not purposely killed the witch; rather, she has inadvertently killed her as a result of trying to save her friend. This symbolizes Dorothy's growth, thinking of others first, and thus signifies the true turning point in her character development: she has learnt a major life lesson.

It is with this that Dorothy returns to the Wizard and is promised her return home. She says goodbye to her friends and they all remind her of what they have acquired from the Wizard: a brain, a heart and courage. She too, of course, has acquired all of these things. The balloon is about to go up when her dog Toto climbs out, and as she goes to get him, the balloon sails off. Dorothy thinks that now she will have no way of getting home, but Glinda the Good Witch reappears. She informs Dorothy that she has had the ability to go home all along; she just did not realize it. She tells her to repeat the mantra 'there's no place like home' and she will get there; and she does. Dorothy then wakes up from this 'dream' to find herself back in Kansas, and back at the farm. She tells the story to her family but they just laugh. To Dorothy, however, it does not matter; what matters is that she has learnt her lesson. She looks at her family and tells them that she loves them dearly, and that she will never run away again; after all, 'there's no place like home'. And so, as the narrative comes to its completion, we can see that Dorothy has undertaken a journey over three acts that has not only developed her physically, but mentally and emotionally. She has 'arced' from an unhappy girl with a want to run away, into a happy, more mature girl who has learnt the value of family and never wants to leave home again.

Narrative structure: key questions

Robert McKee (1999: 19) offers six key questions which are useful for the screenwriter to test the narrative 'skeleton' of his or her screenplay. Being able to answer each question means that there is the germ of an idea; not being able to answer all of them means that there is still work to be done. The six questions are:

- Who are the characters?
- What do they want?
- Why do they want it?
- How do they go about getting it?
- What stops them?
- What are the consequences?

Task 6.3

Spend some time developing an idea that you think would work well as a film or television drama, and then apply these questions to see whether there is enough mileage in the idea yet. With a partner, use the questions as a basis for a conversation about the idea and see whether you can elaborate upon them to give the idea even more detail.

Breaking narrative rules

Although 'classical' forms of storytelling are by far the most common, even in today's culture, some screenwriters choose to break the rules; or so they think. Rather than being constrained to 'rigid' frameworks and the inevitable 'happy ending', experimental narratives offer some of the following: anti-heroes; open endings; parallel stories; multiple protagonists; backwards stories; chaos narratives. Although these types of narratives are emerging more, and are appealing to many screenwriters, we feel that there are two distinct considerations here:

1. Of course you can break the rules; rules are there to be broken. However, it is still imperative that the audience and their experience is considered. If you change the shape of a story, or decide to 'rip it to shreds' and put it back together in a more random form, will the audience still want to watch? Indeed, will they be able to follow what is going on? If nothing happens in a narrative, where characters do not actively pursue a goal of some sort, then there is a real chance that audiences will actually turn off.

2. Even if you think you are breaking the rules, the chances are that you are not *really* doing so. You may be using screenwriting

principles in a more creative way, or perhaps adopting the narra-tive framework in a more subtle way, but it is likely that the core of your screenplay is informed in some way by classical struc-ture. For example, a backwards-and-forwards narrative structure like that seen in *Click* may at first seem innovative and ground breaking, but in fact its guiding principles are still drawn from the three act structure; the overall shape of achieving a goal, with both physical and emotional gains.

A useful book to consult on alternative narrative structures is Linda Aronson's *Screenwriting Updated: New (and Conventional) Ways of Writing for the Screen* (2001). This book examines various forms of 'new' storytelling, such as parallel stories and sequential narratives, but the overall premise is as we have outlined: they are ways of *adapting* and *reworking* traditional structures. Further detailed work on alternative structures also appears in Chapter 10 of Craig Batty and Zara Waldeback's *Writing for the Screen: Creative and Critical Approaches* (2008).

Task 6.4

Choose a film that you think defies the rules of traditional storytelling; write why you think this is so. Now watch the film again and identify elements which can be seen as stemming from more traditional story-telling. Is the film really *that* different?

Some useful examples are: *Babel, Brick, Donnie Darko, Hidden, Lost in Translation, Me and You and Everyone We Know, Mysterious Skin, Paris Je T'aime, Requiem for a Dream, Wolf Creek.*

Character

Character is sometimes a misunderstood concept in screenwriting. The term 'character' is often used to mean everything that relates to fictional persons featuring in the story: appearance, dialogue, back-story, narrative drive, psychology, physiology, etc. What is perhaps more useful is to approach character in two ways: *character* and *characterization*. In this approach, 'character' relates to the inner workings of fictional persons, and 'characterization' to their outer appearance. As such, 'character' is used to discuss character psychology and the development of character drive and motivation, whereas 'characterization' is used to discuss physical appearance and voice. The two are related – for example how a character looks may affect how he or she feels – but the two distinctions are useful for screenplay development purposes.

Character, then, is tightly linked to story and narrative structure; it is very difficult to look at the screenplay's plot and its underlying theme without looking at the essence of character. As McKee postulates, 'structure *is* character. Character *is* structure' (1999: 100); they work symbiotically and inform each other's shape and structure. For example, if we were to look at the journey Character X takes through a foreign land, meeting new people and encountering new experiences, can we really believe that he will have learnt nothing (emotionally) from this? Similarly, if Character X held strong views about a particular subject or a type of person, and met them on his journey, can we really expect that his views would not inform the way in which he deals with this subject or person? Character and structure (plot) are thus resultants of one another, each growing and developing because of the other. McKee makes the point:

> Structure and character are interlocked. The event structure of a story is created out of the choices that characters make under pressure and the actions they choose to take, while characters are the creatures who are revealed and changed by how they choose to act under pressure. If you change one, you change the other. (ibid.: 105–6)

As this highlights, because character is so strongly linked to structure, the screenwriter must undertake much preparatory work in developing the inner substance of characters. It is one thing to map out a plot and then try to fit characters into it; it is another to allow the plot to emerge from the characters. Using the latter, the story will always feel like it is telling itself, not forced into action by the writer. When considering physical and emotional journeys (as detailed above), we can see that emotion shapes drama whilst the physicality of action frames it. As such, we can begin to understand characters as *tools* of story, used in ways to live out the plot, create audience connection and 'persuade' them of the story being told. A range of characters operate in a screenplay, namely the *protagonist, main characters, secondary characters* and *minor characters*.

The protagonist is the central driving force of the screenplay in traditional narratives. Also known as the *hero*, he or she is the one the audience is vying for to succeed; it is *his* or her story. More often than not, a protagonist should be likeable so that the audience can connect to him or her and offer empathy. Indeed, sometimes audiences project themselves onto the protagonist, almost living the story as if it were their own. The protagonist must be active, not passive, driving the story forward through making choices and decisions. Because he or she occupies the majority of screen time, the protagonist is the one whose point-of-view the narrative is experienced from. Of course, the key to any protagonist is that he or she changes throughout the course of the narrative, emotionally as well as physically, this transformation eventually bestowing him or her with the 'heroic' title he or she deserves.

Task 6.5

Choose one of your favourite films and decide who the protagonist is. Make a list of reasons why this character is so likeable. What makes him or her unique? Why do we want to spend time with him or her?

The *antagonist* is also a main character in the screenplay. Sometimes antagonism comes from sources such as nature and ideology (rules), but in most cases it is manifested into an actual person. The role of the antagonist is to challenge the protagonist and stop him from getting what he or she wants, often down to a 'final battle' or 'life-or-death fight'. Another function of the antagonist is to clarify the role of the protagonist, shining light upon him or her and what he or she stands for. This is important for audiences because if the protagonist is weak and there is no other character to show him or her in a positive light, the narrative might fail. Sometimes the protagonist and antagonist are at such odds because they are both after the same thing. Using this technique in a drama is useful because it 'proves' to the audience who really deserves the reward and heightens the stakes for the protagonist so that, when it is claimed, it is seen as a more satisfying event. There are many famous antagonists in film and television, perhaps as many as protagonists. Examples include: Norman Bates (*Psycho*), Hannibal Lecter (*The Silence of the Lambs*), Cruella De Vil (*One Hundred and One Dalmatians*) and The Joker (*Batman*). Most television soap operas also use the antagonist to great effect, having the typical 'bad boy' and 'bitch'. Across the decades and across continents, these characters are a staple of the soap opera because they remind us that in whatever domestic setting we belong, there is always someone who is out to cause trouble for the good folk.

Task 6.6

Identify at least five antagonist characters from as many soap operas as you know. Try this for a range of British, Australian and American soaps. Now look across the list and try to identify the essential traits of a 'bad boy' and a 'bitch'.

Secondary and minor characters are used in a multitude of ways, not least to consolidate the overall narrative shape of the drama and feed into the prevailing theme. *Secondary characters* often have their own journey in the drama, albeit of a miniature nature compared to the protagonist's. Secondary characters are often agents of *subplots*: the storylines that, although not at the forefront of the drama, are an integral part of the overall narrative shape. Subplots can work alongside the main plot, shedding light on it or perhaps reinforcing its theme. On other occasions, subplots work against the main plot, challenging the overall journey and, inevitably, its protagonist. Either way, the secondary character is an inferior agent to the protagonist (and antagonist) in terms of screen time and plot importance, but he or she has a big part to play in terms of reinforcing themes and supporting (either explicitly or implicitly) the protagonist. *Minor characters* can easily be confused with secondary characters, but the real essence of minor characters is that they are often merely in a scene or two, or appear throughout the drama but with very little or no journey of their own. Minor characters can serve several purposes: they help or hinder other characters, sometimes in as simple a manner as blocking a path or doorway; they illuminate the theme of the drama, their physical or verbal presence adding weight to issues that are running through the narrative; they add colour and texture, sometimes providing light relief from more serious scenes. Sometimes minor characters appear subconsciously from the writer's mind, perhaps as a mere instrument of the plot, but if they are carefully considered and developed, they can really bring a script to life. Dramas are sometimes memorable for the rich tapestry of minor characters on board, 'enabling [them] to entertain, enliven, relieve and refresh an audience' (Batty and Waldeback, 2008: 28).

Characterization

Characterization is concerned with bringing character to life; the inner fabric of character has been developed, and now their on-screen execution takes shape. Screenwriting as a visual medium requires careful attention being paid to the audience's experience of seeing as well as hearing, and this should not be forgotten in character execution. As such, here are some key considerations for bringing characters to life:

1. **Action and behaviour** are key techniques for displaying character. The way that a character acts and reacts tells us not only what he or she does or does not like to do, but how he or she feels about a situation. 'Actions speak louder than words' may be a cliché, but in screenwriting it is an essential working tool. Examples include:

    - How would a character behave in a situation alien to him?
    - What would a character do if told that he had to take off all of his clothes?
    - How would a kind and modest character react to people who think they are superior to him?
    - How would an arrogant and inconsiderate character react to people who think they are superior to him?
    - What would a straight-laced, model citizen do when, after losing his job, he finds a bag of counterfeit money?

2. Working with **physical appearance** is useful in visually expressing character identity. Images are instant and audiences will be able to decode such signs easily. Examples include:

- What does a character wear?
- What does a character not wear?
- How does a character carry himself, and is it always in the same way?
- What is a character's home like (size, location, style, tidiness, etc.)?
- Does a character have body art or piercings?

3. **Lifestyle** is similar to physical appearance because it is also an outward expression of identity, albeit linked to consumption and patronage. How a character lives, whether through choice or default, can speak volumes about who he or she is. Examples include:

- What kind of car does she drive?
- What does she do in the evenings?
- Where does she like to holiday?
- What is her favourite meal when eating out at a restaurant?

4. A character's **job**, again whether through choice or default, can tell us much about him or her. Whether denoting qualifications or skills, capability or ambition, jobs are part and parcel of the 'profiling' of characters and are much used in screenplays (especially during openings) to establish characters quickly. Examples include:

- Where in the job hierarchy is a character?
- Where in the hierarchy would he like to be?
- Where, realistically, could he be one day?
- Does a character have a specific role within his organization, such as first aid officer, fire marshal or union representative?
- Does a character take work home in the evenings?

5. If appearance is a visual expression of identity, then character **voice and language** is a vocal expression of identity. Sometimes characters have particular ways of speaking which suit their personality, such as mumbling or stumbling through sentences. Vocabulary used can also be highly evocative of personality and attitude. Examples include:

- Does a character speak clearly and eloquently, or quickly and incoherently?

- How does a character speak when in the presence of someone of a higher social order?
- How does a character speak when in the presence of younger, less experienced people?
- What is a character's level of vocabulary?
- Does a character use convoluted yet incorrect words in an attempt to impress?

Task 6.7

The following exercises are designed to bring together character and characterization, asking you to consider both the internal and psychological elements of character with those of visual and verbal expression.

1. Write a monologue from the point of view of a character you are developing, asking the question, what am I doing here?! Allow the writing to be organic and continuous, not forced. Read the monologue back and note any interesting insights or discoveries you make about the character; it could be something that you had not thought of before.

2. Collect images (magazines, newspapers, catalogues, etc.) which you think represent your character well, and make a visual portrait. From this, write a character profile. Use these artefacts to remind yourself of the character once you begin to write the screenplay; the visual reminder should help you to stay true to his or her essential nature.

3. Choose one or two adjectives from the character profile and write a scene that depicts him or her using action only. It is important to put the character into a given situation and then let the adjectives dictate the action. Repeat this several times so that you have a bank of potential scenes which can be incorporated into the screenplay.

Genre

McKee rightly notes that 'the audience is already a genre expert. It enters each film armed with a complex set of anticipations learned through a lifetime of moviegoing' (1999: 80). From Western to gangster to sports, films, and increasingly television dramas, are structured and styled according to a set of principles that have become embedded in their audiences' expectations. As such, a need has been created for familiar story patterns, stylistic tones and even archetypal characters. Dancyger and Rush usefully refer to genre as 'story forms' (2007: 76), which places emphasis upon the creation of the drama and its narrative shape, as opposed to stylistic interventions and end-user result. This is important because it brings genre back around to the screenwriter: a genre is written, not merely consumed. Although audience expectation and appeal is a predominant driving force of genre, giving heed to notions of restriction and conformation, for the writer it is more useful to think of genre as something that can breed opportunity. Dancyger and Rush go on to state that genre offers 'a type of story that has a visceral appeal to its audience' (ibid.), which again places emphasis upon the writing and not the consumption because it encourages the consideration of story values and theme – genre is used to make an audience *feel*. So genre must work within the text of the screenplay, and it is the writer's job to ensure this is successful.

Detailed analyses of working with and against genre are available in Dancyger and Rush (2007: 76–153) and Batty and Waldeback (2008: 82–8). Here we will raise some key points as to how the principles of genre influence the building of screenplay.

Genre and narrative structure

Different genres have different demands upon the type and shape of a story. All screenplays are about a journey and a character transformation, but genre shapes this in its own particular way. For example:

- A **romantic comedy** is always about the comedic chase between two lovers. The inciting incident is the meeting of the two, and the subsequent narrative is driven by the conflict of the pursuit. The story of a romantic comedy develops until the lovers do eventually get on and the climax comes when they are united in some way.
- In **horror**, the inciting incident usually occurs early – a 'hook' – and is usually a death of some gruesome sort. The narrative is

driven towards finding the killer, all the while other victims falling foul of the maniac. The climax of horror comes when the killer is revealed, which is often accompanied by an explanation of why the crimes were committed.

- In a **sports** story, the narrative drive is usually a protagonist who needs to prove something to himself or to others, using the playing of sport as a symbol of this plight. Being in a team is crucial to sports narratives, where friends and enemies are made and then used to prove worthiness. A typical sports climax sees an important match where the protagonist will get his chance to show who he is and overcome his inner issues.

Genre and character

Genre places similar demands on character: protagonist, antagonist and often secondary (supporting) characters. We can say that genre dictates a need for a certain ensemble of characters that are used to bring familiarity and cohesion. For example:

- In a **detective** story, the audience expects some kind of renegade cop who, as well as trying to put the world to rights, may overcome his own inner problem. A sidekick invariably also features, who is less experienced but often brings a special quality to the story (attitude, experience, skill), helping in not only the solving of the crime but the lead detective's personal journey.
- The lone hero is the driving force of a **Western** story, with ideals drawn from nature, history and tradition. He may have a personal dilemma, such as the struggle of survival with 'old ideals' when faced with a fast-changing world. As such, the Western hero sets out to overcome the evil of a town, embodied in an antagonist whose 'new' ideals draw from wealth and greed.
- **Science fiction** stories employ a similar lone hero protagonist, and his battle with 'aliens' represents a fear of the future and a technologically changing world. The protagonist may be emotionally wounded too, where the action of battle is a symbol of internal turmoil. Like the Western, science fiction stories usually climax with a showdown between protagonist and major (alien) antagonist who is out to destroy the world as we know it.

Genre and visual style

Visual style is the element of screenwriting most commonly thought of when genre is mentioned; however, as we have seen, it forms only a fraction of what is a multifaceted process. Nevertheless, visual style is an important part of genre construction and is used to give a story a particular look or feel. For example:

- **Colour**: a dark, eerie thriller? A light, bright comedy? Colour used in set design, costume and filmic tone can evoke a strong sense of genre.
- **Objects**: knives, scissors and boiling pans in a 'slasher'? Flying horses and hidden chests of treasure in a fantasy? Objects carry symbolic meaning of genre, providing a currency which the audience understands.
- **Costume**: linked to colour, costume is a visual signifier of genre and can evoke period, class, status and mood. When constructing a genre, clothes can be used to tell a story in themselves.
- **Tone**: primarily a directorial concern, scenes can be filmed with a certain hue or a specific lighting effect to evoke a sense of genre. Writers can suggest these in the screenplay, however, by carefully written screen directions.

Task 6.8

Compare two films or television dramas, each of a different genre. Use the three headings above to make notes about how each genre achieves its result, and how it is different to the other.

Writing dialogue

Dialogue is perhaps the most underestimated element of screenwriting. Contrary to belief, dialogue is not simply 'how people speak': in fact it is where most amateur scripts fall down. Badly written dialogue can sound wooden, clunky and almost certainly superfluous to requirement. Rather, it must be carefully thought through and well polished to avoid it sounding like it is trying too hard. As Aronson points out, 'dialogue is not like real life conversation at all. It is a very tightly and carefully structured illusion of conversation' (2001: 256). As part of the overall dramatic structure of the screenplay, dialogue too must be structured. In a scene, for example, characters usually speak in a way that is directed towards the function of the scene, teasing it out carefully and with conviction. 'Illusion' is useful to highlight because, although the dialogue is structured, it has to sound like it is not structured – that it is real. So, even though read or heard dialogue may sound 'normal' or 'easy', in actual fact it has been carefully crafted and probably rewritten a dozen or more times.

Here are some basic foundations of writing screen dialogue:

- **Every word counts.** There is little time for random chatter in a screenplay, unless for a specific reason; all the while story and character revelation should be 'turning'.
- **Dialogue should be directed at the function, transaction or heart of a scene** (see below). As well as literally pulling the scene along, spoken words express feeling and attitude towards the scene's function. Dialogue should therefore be used to build the scene, keeping the audience aware of its function and feelings towards it.
- **Expressive words can be replaced with looks and gestures:** 'oh!', 'what?', 'really?', etc. This makes the screenplay sound less wooden and also helps to build pace. Not only this, it can be far more interesting to *see* characters' reactions rather than hearing them.
- **Redundant words can be cut away:** 'well', 'so', 'ok', 'umm', 'but', 'yes', etc. Unless for a specific character or story purpose, these reactive words slow down pace and make the screenplay sound amateurish. The general rule of writing screen dialogue is to be sharp and to the point, spending more time on words that actually matter.

Dialogue flow is also important when writing a scene. Rather than banal lines in the form of question/answer/question/answer, dialogue should be layered and textured. People in real life talk at cross-purposes, interrupt each other, or even deliberately avoid what someone else is saying – this is even more important in a screenplay. This way, what people do not say, or what they prefer to say instead of what is desired, reveals true character feeling and attitude towards story. Tension is built by layering dialogue, which the audience can understand on a deeper, subtextual level. The same rules apply to comedy: humour often comes out of cross-purposes, irony and innuendo, and if the characters' lines were merely reactive, the comedy value would suffer greatly.

It is vitally important to remember that the audience can see what is going on at the same time as hearing dialogue. It can be difficult coming to terms with writing for a medium which at the time of writing does not exist (i.e. the drama is not on screen yet), but if things that are intended to be seen are referred to in dialogue, the result can be somewhat unrealistic and very clunky. Take this example:

```
INT. BEDROOM - MORNING

TINA looks at the clock: it's 9:30. Her eyes widen.

                         TINA
        Damn! I'm late for work.

She jumps out of bed and frantically tries to get
dressed.
```

Here the audience can see that it is 9.30 and would probably guess that she is late for something by the fact that her eyes widen. This, followed by her jumping out of bed, is more than enough to suggest that she is late and angry at being so. To then deliver the line 'Damn! I'm late for work' is not only unnecessary, but wooden and somewhat unrealistic.

Writing scenes

A scene is a moment of action, contained within one location and one time frame. The function of a scene is to drive the narrative forward, using characters, setting, action, dialogue and visual grammar to do so. Usually a scene should contain at least one beat of action; that is to say, a fragment of story that drives the plot. A story beat can be simple, such as 'Steve tells John that they must leave'; or it can be more complex, such as 'Anna gives Rachel a present, leaving

Sarah feeling jealous and unsure of how their friendship fares'. When writing a scene it is important to know its function, its beat, so that the scene can be structured effectively. Failing to do this can leave a scene feeling lost, where the writing has little direction and becomes difficult to write. As Charlie Moritz writes: 'if you cut to the heart of what the scene you're dreaming up is about, reduce this to a one-liner, note this down and then build the rest of the scene up around it, you won't miss the scene's meaning or leave it unfocussed' (2001: 98). Knowing the function of each scene, even in one line, can thus save a lot of heartache later in the development process, when the overall screenplay somehow just does not work. Many screenwriters produce what is called a *step-outline*, a document which provides a scene-by-scene running order of the screenplay, where each scene's function is mapped out (usually in terms of action and emotion).

The general principle in writing scenes is that they should start as late as they possibly can, and end as early as they possibly can. In other words, rather than stringing out the action and losing valuable pace, the writer should aim to jump straight into the action or conversation and then leave it when the function of the scene has been achieved. Like the screenplay as a whole, with a function to 'hook in' its audience from the first page, the scene should pull in the audience and not allow any time for loss of interest. In reality, 'formalities' may precede a scene (entering buildings, greetings, etc.), but in a screenplay such formalities are not necessary. Rather, it can be a useful technique for the audience to play 'catch up', where they have to work out what has happened between scenes. For example, if a scene starts in the middle of a conversation, the audience has to work out what has been said prior to the scene's start, and in fact why the conversation is happening in the first place. Similarly, leaving a scene on a punctuated moment, such as a specific word or a look, gives power to the scene and enables a swift drive into the next. Leaving a scene 'formally' (leaving buildings, goodbyes, etc.) can slow pace and waste valuable screen time.

Screen direction, or scene action, should be written in present tense, giving the illusion that the action is unfolding here and now. The writer should be careful to include only things that the audience can see and hear, not superfluous detail such as a character's back-story. The directions should be tight, snappy and fluid, and longer descriptions can be split into smaller paragraphs. The principle here is that if the focus shifts from one character to another, or if the camera's focus should change, then another paragraph should be started.

Task 6.9

Watch the opening five minutes of a film or television drama. Make a note of every scene that takes place and, in a line or two, the function of each. Put these lines together and summarize the function of the opening: what is the overall intention being displayed to the audience? Once this has been completed, work on the opening five minutes of your own screen drama. Plan what you want your audience to know/see/feel, and then write a series of scenes that fulfil this. Test it out on a friend.

Career opportunities in screenwriting: fiction

There is no denying that forging a career as a screenwriter can be extremely difficult; there are many more aspiring writers than there are commercially viable projects. Nevertheless, screenwriting avenues do exist as well as a whole range of affiliated jobs. Many screenwriters have experience of writing for other mediums, namely radio and theatre. This is a useful 'career path' to consider because credits can be achieved in these other forms and, through credits and industry networking, screenwriting commissions can be earned. Others have found their way as a screenwriter by working their way up through the industry, proving themselves in other roles first. In the feature film market, this can include being a script reader (for a film production company, film council, agent, etc.), a script developer, a script producer, or even an affiliated role such as directorial assistant. In television, a common path is working in television series, perhaps starting as a script assistant or script researcher, then moving up to a script editor or a storyliner, and potentially a writer. Producing is another role to be considered in film and television because it has at its core a strong emphasis upon creating, developing and telling stories, albeit in a more 'managerial' way. In either film or television, however, it is an absolute necessity to possess strong networking skills and a passion to work hard in order to achieve your desired job.

With developments in technology and the online revolution, opportunities do exist for aspiring screenwriters to have their scripts made independently. Although there is a lot less money involved and distribution exposure is not guaranteed, some writers have found success in this way. Many groups of like-minded people collaborate, using their own time, equipment and money, to make screen fiction. Digital cameras and editing facilities are relatively cheap and easy to use today, making this process much more accessible. Internet networking sites such as *Shooting People* are also leading the way in independent production, where literally thousands of people post ideas, gather crews and eventually get together to make films and television pilots. For the aspiring screenwriter this is an extremely valuable resource, and we would recommend trying to become involved in as many projects as you can; after all, industry employees are always looking for those who have demonstrated a true passion for what they do.

Further reading

Aronson, L. (2001) *Screenwriting Updated: New (and Conventional) Ways of Writing for the Screen*, California: Silman-James.

Batty, C. and Waldeback, Z. (2008) *Writing for the Screen: Creative and Critical Approaches*, Basingstoke: Palgrave Macmillan.

Dancyger, K. and Rush, J. (2007) *Alternative Scriptwriting: Successfully Breaking the Rules*, 4th edn, Oxford: Focal Press.

Field, S. (2003) *The Definitive Guide to Screenwriting*, London: Ebury Press.

Gulino, P.J. (2004) *Screenwriting: The Sequence Approach*, New York: Continuum.

Howard, D. (2004) *How to Build a Great Screenplay*, London: Souvenir Press.

Indick, W. (2004) *Psychology for Screenwriters: Building Conflict in Your Script*, California: Michael Wiese.

Maras, S. (2008) *Screenwriting: History, Theory and Practice*, London: Wallflower.

McKee, R. (1999) *Story: Substance, Structure, Style and the Principles of Screenwriting*, Methuen: London.

Moritz, C. (2001) *Scriptwriting for the Screen*, London: Routledge.

Seger, L. (1994) *Making a Good Script Great*, 2nd edn, California: Samuel French.

Truby, J. (2007) *The Anatomy of Story: 22 Steps to Becoming a Master Storyteller*, New York: Faber & Faber.

Web resources

www.bbc.co.uk/writersroom
Highly recommended, with insights into writing, guidelines on formatting, tips on submitting scripts and ongoing competitions.

www.scriptfactory.co.uk
UK-based script training organization, offering year-round workshops and special writers' events.

www.script-o-rama.com
Extensive database of downloadable film and television scripts, all for free.

www.twelvepoint.com
Highly useful resource, with articles, blogs and user forums dedicated to the scriptwriting industry.

Screenwriting: Fact **7**

Writing factual material for the screen has both similarities and differences with writing fiction for the screen. On the one hand, the approach is markedly different: factual stories require much more research and particular attention to detail when it comes to historical facts and figures. On the other hand, the approach is much the same: what is being told is a story, and that requires compelling characters, a central theme or premise, and an effective narrative structure. As such, although some of the specific practicalities of writing fact are very different from writing fiction, many of the aesthetics are the same. Factual material written for the screen can be included in a range of forms, from the corporate film to the TV magazine show. For this chapter, however, although we discuss the corporate film to some extent, we focus specifically upon the creation of the film and television documentary.

By the end of this chapter, you should be able to:

- Understand the nature of a documentary and how it differs/does not differ from that of fiction storytelling.
- Recognize the various stages involved in planning a documentary and be able to undertake them accordingly on a given project.
- Appreciate the value that research plays in planning a documentary.
- Become familiar with narrative construction techniques and apply them effectively to a potential project.
- Recognize the differences between a proposal, a treatment and a script, and write each one effectively.

- Understand the opportunities and limitations of interviewing subjects and the techniques of interviewing that can be used to gain maximum potential.
- Appreciate some of the key principles of writing good voice-over narration.

What is a documentary?

A common perception is that a documentary is a true account of fact or reality; that the documentary maker produces a film or television programme based purely upon recorded actualities. Although this has some truth to it, namely that the material used is 'recorded' and (usually) not 'staged', there are many more complexities to the definition of 'documentary'. For example, according to Jarl, 'there is no difference between a documentary and a feature film. However, the nature of each is different. They both came into being so that film-makers could express themselves' (1998: 150). In other words, whether fact or fiction, what lies at the core of a narrative is the same: a story; an exploration of an issue; an expression of a theme. Just like fictional screenwriting, factual screenwriting also intends to make an audience feel something about the subject matter being explored. Whether an investigation into the injustices of the legal system, or an exploration of what happens when someone achieves his or her goal of being crowned world champion, 'many documentaries bear all the hallmarks of a gripping story or a well-wrought drama' (Kilborn and Izod, 1997: 9).

According to Young (2002: 6), the intention of a documentary usually falls into a category of promotion, propaganda, investigation, education, entertainment or dissemination of information. From this, we may assume that from the outset a documentary maker's intentions are prescribed, perhaps institutionalized, where a clear function of the production exists. This is common in many television documentaries which, for example, seek to expose people for their misdoings (*Rogue Traders, The Cook Report, Border Security: Australia's Front Line*) or educate an audience about a current social, political or economic issue (*Panorama, Dispatches, Frontline*). However, 'with the advents of affordable digital technology, the concept of producing non-fiction film as a form of creative self-expression is becoming much more of a reality' (ibid.). In other words, we are now seeing more 'personal' documentaries which, rather than being driven by events or issues of interest to the broadcaster, are driven by the individual and his or her need to express.

Broadly speaking, as outlined by Kilborn and Izod (1997: 58–76), there are three main types of documentary. These are:

- **Expository.** This is the most 'scripted' type of documentary, which sees a compilation of footage (live action, library images, interviews, re-enactments, etc.), often complemented by voice-over narration. Like a fictional film, it has a strong sense of narrative logic with a problem and a solution. Documentary films serve this type well, examples including *Touching the Void*, *An Inconvenient Truth* and *Man on Wire*.
- **Observational.** This is more 'fly-on-the-wall' in style, where the documentary maker enters the subjects' lives and constructs a narrative from the raw footage that is recorded over a given period of time. Paul Watson has made a name for himself here, with documentaries such as *The Family*, *Malcolm and Barbara: A Love Story* and *Malcolm and Barbara: Love's Farewell*.
- **Reflective.** In this type, the documentary maker is seen as obviously involved in the production. Seeing him or her in action, the making process becomes an actual part of the documentary. Nick Broomfield is a useful example here, with documentaries such as *Kurt and Courtney*, *Aileen: Life and Death of a Serial Killer* and *Ghosts*.

Task 7.1

Identify one documentary that you have seen recently for each of the above types. Think about what makes them different from an audience point of view. How do you relate to each type? Do you get a different feeling from each type? Which do you prefer, and why?

The expository type of documentary is perhaps the most commonly seen and, because of its 'scripted' nature and relationship with fictional modes of screenwriting, is the type that will be explored more fully in this chapter.

The fact/fiction divide

Before detailing the processes involved in developing a documentary, we think it necessary to once more reinforce the idea that writing fact is not always that different from writing fiction. The story being told in a documentary is of course always one based upon real life, not as in a film where the imagination can go anywhere; but does that mean that the two forms of writing are different? On the contrary, fact and fiction collide; there is as much creativity in planning and writing a documentary as there is in planning and writing a feature film, for example. To clarify:

> The task of the documentarist is not only to record reality but also to give the recorded material a form that allows the resultant film or programme to speak to its audience in a language that can be readily understood. In other words, the production of a documentary is not simply an act of chronicling; it is just as much an act of transformation. (Kilborn and Izod, 1997: 4)

This tells us that a documentary is never as 'raw' as it may seem; like fictional screenwriting, it also goes through a development process that is intended to make the story as appealing as possible, told in the best way possible, and using subjects (characters) that an audience can connect with. From facts and figures to live footage and interviews, the 'transformation' of material is a creative process that contravenes any notion of the documentary as purely an act of 'chronicling'. A documentary is still a story; it still uses a plot shape to best tell this story; and it still employs narrative techniques to give the story the most impact. It should be no surprise, then, that documentaries 'make use of structuring devices that were developed in narrative fiction', and, because they are made by people not robots, 'the account offered is one that is seen from a particular perspective' (ibid.: 5). We all have personal tastes and we all have an axe to grind; therefore, when we are commissioned to write something from fact, can we ever stop ourselves from resorting to nuances of fiction?

Planning a documentary

Commonly, documentary producers or directors also act as documentary writers. As Hampe tells us, 'unless the writer is a hyphenate – a producer-writer or director-writer – his or her role in a documentary production often ranges from ambiguous to non-existent' (1997: 120). Individual writers can be brought in to help develop the project in its early stages, and sometimes writers will even be commissioned to write the actual script (if there is one); moreover, though, they are used in the planning, researching and developing stage. As such, the role of the media writer in a documentary may differ from project to project: as writer, researcher, development personnel. Whatever the project, however, one key aptitude remains for any media writer: a keen interest in the story idea and a need continually to find out more about it. If this can be achieved, then what appears in the final documentary will in fact mirror this enthusiasm, creating a greater appeal to the audience. As Kriwaczek suggests: 'the driving force of the story is the question: what happens next? What keeps them watching is the desire to know how things turn out. The documentary maker must find in his or her subject those story elements which keep that question uppermost in the viewers' minds' (1997: 24).

Not only does this tell us that the narrative must be structured in order to keep the audience hooked (see below), it tells us that the only way to achieve this is by having found out enough interesting and exciting information about the idea in the first place. Thus, the media writer must feel compelled to explore the subject in a variety of forms, from a variety of perspectives, culminating in a package of work which asks the very question: what happens next?

That said, it must be highlighted that the eventual produced documentary may be different from the one actually intended. Unless the documentary is made purely for a competition or for internet exhibition, the reality is that the broadcaster or film distributor will have its own idea of what works and what does not. So, creative decisions made early in the development process may have to be sacrificed for more commercial, social or even political reasons. As outlined by Kilborn and Izod, 'the attempt on the part of the institutions to exercise control over both form and content of documentary programming has inevitably led to strains and stresses in the relationship between documentarists and broadcasters' (1997: 171). Thus, although documentary makers may have a clear drive and vision for their projects, the fact remains that they will only be commissioned and broadcast if someone within the institution they are making it for likes the idea, trusts it and believes that it suits the ethos that the institution is promoting. There is sometimes, then, a fine line between creativity and commercial viability, and so it is the job of the media writer to understand the possible constraints and work around them.

> **Task 7.2**
>
> Choose a television broadcaster and conduct some research into its ethos or programme remit. What kind of programming does it strive for? What defines its identity? What might work and not work as a documentary idea for the broadcaster?

Sourcing ideas

Most documentary makers have a passion. They want to tell an audience about something they know; something they care about that they want others to care about too. The 9/11 terrorist attacks, for example, ignited a passion in both Michael Moore and Dylan Avery to explore what they considered the 'real truth' of the events: *Fahrenheit 9/11* and *Loose Change* emerged, respectively, and both were deemed as groundbreaking and received global critical acclaim. Others, especially student documentary makers, may not have such a passion; instead, they want to tell a good story and spend time investigating something worthwhile. The latter can work, but what is essential is the need to think constantly about the given topic, asking a multitude of questions about it in order to generate a multitude of answers. Through this, material naturally comes together and provides a rich source for the documentary maker to draw from. If the documentary maker does not care about the topic, then it will be blatantly clear to an audience that this is the case. Audiences want to be engaged, surprised, shocked and intrigued about a topic; it is the duty of the documentary maker to provide this, through the results of his or her own inquiring mind.

Rabiger (2004: 129–31) outlines some useful sources of inspiration for those who want to make a documentary. These sources, some of which are listed below, are not only useful for those new to documentary making and exploring what they want to investigate, but are useful creative tools for seasoned documentary makers too. By using the sources, the mind is kept in a mode of critical thinking and meaning making.

- **Journal or diary.** A good way to get the mind thinking is to make daily notes about your thoughts and feelings, especially in relation to current events or issues, both personal and social. This documenting of self-expression allows the mind to roam further than it would normally, and it may spark a passion in you to explore more about a topic that interests you.
- **Newspapers and magazines.** The world is full of interesting stories, and if people enjoy reading about them, the chances are that the same people enjoy seeing them on screen. Sometimes serious stories can spark an idea about issues, such as the 'credit crunch', knife crime or a natural disaster; at other times, it is the 'quirky' or unbelievable stories that capture people's attention.
- **History.** Similarly, history presents us with a multitude of interesting people and events from which we can draw inspiration. Reading about the past can also have uncanny connections with the present, and the documentary maker can find a common thread to connect the two. Anniversaries of historical events also provide useful documentary material.
- **Family stories.** Does someone in your family have a good story to tell? Is he or she doing something at the minute that would interest an audience? Has something happened in the family's past that an audience would be interested in hearing about? This is the basis for the television series *Who Do You Think You Are?* A valuable documentary topic can lie on your own doorstep, so do not be afraid to use it. After all, you have access to the people who know this story better than anyone else.
- **Fiction.** Sometimes reading or viewing fiction can inspire the documentary maker: does this kind of person exist in reality? What would it be like to actually be in that situation? Many documentaries take characters and situations from fiction and

find their real-life counterparts, presenting audiences with an intriguing insight of: what if that really does happen?

'The documentary idea may begin with nothing more than a vague urge in some direction' (Hampe, 1997: 103); and it is from sources like these that such a vague urge starts to emerge. Interacting with news, history, people, places and even oneself enables ideas to surface, be explored and assessed for potential development. It is important to test ideas thoroughly before commitment is made to developing them into a documentary, otherwise they may fall flat very quickly. As Rabiger states: 'good documentaries go beyond factual exposition or celebration: they tackle areas of life that are complex, ambiguous, and morally taxing' (2004: 132). In other words, what may seem a good idea on the surface is not always one that will provide enough depth or magnitude to develop into a full project. The documentary maker must ensure that the idea is interrogated fully, pursuing all avenues of exploration so that something important can be presented, not merely a series of facts. Thus, when a vague urge presents itself as an idea to be explored, the documentary maker can start the development process rolling: research.

Task 7.3

Using two of the sources of inspiration above, think of three ideas from each that could be used as a potential documentary project. Ask yourself: why is this idea interesting? Would anybody want to know about it? Why? Where could I take the idea from here, in research terms?

Research

It cannot be stressed enough how important research is to the creation of a documentary. During the early stages, when a mere idea is being developed into something more fully formed and workable, research is the one thing that can make or break a project. Initial research into an idea not only provides the documentary maker with facts and evidence that can be used in the finished product, but actually helps to define the documentary's core story and the shape by which it will be told. In fact, the length that a documentary maker is willing to go to in order to conduct research 'can be the factor which separates the ground-breaking documentary from the merely run-of-the-mill' (Kilborn and Izod, 1997: 194). The more research undertaken, and the longest metaphorical distance travelled to obtain that material, the more likely there is to be better quality, original material suitable for final presentation. By researching, 'you are going to try and turn up everything that looks dramatic, compelling, or interesting' (Rosenthal, 1996: 37). The key words here, 'dramatic', 'compelling' and 'interesting', tell us that research is not merely an exercise in finding facts and evidence that 'fit' the project, but an exercise in uncovering interesting, intriguing, perhaps surprising material. To interest an audience and provide them with a compelling, dramatic story, something different must be found; something original. Thus, research is as much about creative avenues of exploration as it is fact-finding.

Kriwaczek (1997: 187–8) suggests that there are two stages of research involved in the creation of a documentary. These are:

- **Stage 1: theoretical or content research.** This is where the media writer takes hold of an idea and interrogates it for maximum effect. Some of this research will be 'desk based', such as reading books, newspapers, magazines and websites to find out as much as possible about the subject. Some of it will be 'active', primary research, such as talking to historians, lecturers, experts and witnesses. The point of this is to absorb the topic fully in order to become an expert, which then allows the creation of a survey, history or digest of the topic that can be used as a backdrop to all further work on the project.
- **Stage 2: practical, production research.** Most of this will be left mainly to the producer or director, considering elements such as shooting locations, budgets, potential people to pitch to, and eventual production schedules. However, some of the writer's research may be crucial here. For example, are there specific locations found in the research that are essential to the documentary? Are there certain people (subjects) who would almost certainly have to be interviewed? Crucially, have any other documentaries been made about this topic before? If so, what is different about this one?

It is easy to settle upon research uncovered quite early on, thinking that nothing more important will be found and that this research is enough. This, however, should be avoided at all costs. Although something found may seem like a definitive answer, or may appear to be the most compelling account of the topic in existence, the chances are that there is something better than this. Even if the further research does not find anything as compelling, or does not seem quite as dramatic compared to what has already been found, such research has been necessary in order to confirm those initial thoughts. Not only that, there will almost certainly have been something found along the way that has aided the documentary and given it further shape and direction. The writer thus has to embrace the role of researcher, constantly striving to find out more and bringing it all together to make greater conclusions. As Rosenthal reminds us:

> You must be observer, analyst, student, and note taker. Over a period that can be as short as a few days or as long as a few months, you must become an expert on the subject of the film, a subject you may never even have known existed a few weeks before – not easy, but always fascinating. (1996: 37)

According to Croton, 'it is only when an idea has been pondered and subjected to critical analysis that it becomes truly viable' (1986: 8). In other words, an idea must become an informed idea before it can begin to develop; it must be fully researched and considered within a philosophical, artistic and practical context. Once such an idea has been fully researched and considered, what is then required is a much clearer and more defined overall concept: the *premise*.

Defining the premise

The initial idea of a documentary maker may be something like 'I want to follow the life of a street cleaner' or 'I know someone who is going to compete in the Olympics'. Although these ideas are good starting points, they are just starting points. There is no story; no idea of what the documentary will be about. The life of a street cleaner is not a story: it is a subject and a situation, from which a story has to emerge. Knowing someone who will compete in the Olympics is a great contact, but what about it? Who cares if you know that person? The key lies in finding out something about him or her that generates a story. As Kopple states, 'documentary film-making has always been about taking the time to go beneath the surface and find the heart of the story' (2005: viii). In developing the documentary idea, then, going beneath the surface is a crucial requirement. Deep and extensive research into a person, fact, event or issue will unearth a series of interesting 'points of attack' from which the documentary can begin to take shape and focus. This gives the documentary an angle, a purpose, a dramatic question or a 'working hypothesis' (Rabiger, cited in Young, 2002: 6): basically, the documentary begins to find its premise, what it is really about.

If we take the idea of knowing someone who will compete in the Olympics, some avenues of research which would help to define the premise could be:

- How old is this person? Are they the youngest to compete? Are they the oldest to compete?
- Have they competed before? Have they come close to competing before? Why is competing important to them now?
- What sport are they competing in? Is it an unusual sport? Has the country ever won a medal in this sport before?
- Where do they come from? Have there ever been other Olympians from the same area? Are there any connections with place?
- How have they got to be in their current position? Have they had to battle against the odds to train? Have they been sponsored by anyone interesting?
- How will they cope with the lead-up to the Olympics? Do they have any particular strategies? Is there something that is really holding them back?

As these questions suggest, the avenues of research are endless. Sometimes the angle to be taken emerges quickly once the research has begun: they had a famous father; they were bullied at school and so undertook the sport as a means of escape; they have had to work night shifts in a factory in order to make enough money for training.

Sometimes, however, the angle is not so apparent, and it may become difficult to envisage how a story will ever emerge from mere fact. Although this may be disheartening, it does signal early on whether an idea has enough potential to be converted into something much more meaningful.

Once an idea has been probed and substantially developed through research, the documentary's premise can begin to be defined. For Kriwaczek, 'a documentary film's most important weapon is simplicity and clarity of concept' (1997: 25). In other words, if the documentary can be summarized in a simple and effective premise, then the essence exists and it can be used to drive the project forward. A premise is usually expressed in no more than a few sentences and boils the whole documentary down into one core idea. The exact format of a premise may vary, but usually it 'tells you why you want to make the documentary, what it will be about, and what effect you hope it will have on an audience' (Hampe, 1997: 94). If we continue the Olympic competitor example, one possible premise might be:

> With the Olympic Games just around the corner, a sense of excitement is filling the nation. However, for one competitor, this excitement has turned into anxiety as he faces the possibility of swimming his last race and walking away empty-handed – again. *On Your Marks* follows John Smith's final, desperate attempt to win a medal for his country and the people who have supported him so emphatically over the last twelve years.

The reason that this is a premise and not just a vague idea is simple: there is clearly a story present within the situation. We can deduce that John Smith is desperate to win; he has missed out on a medal for twelve years now (so, three Olympic Games), and because this is his final race, the stakes are raised and the situation is 'make or break'. We get a sense that the desperation to succeed not only resides in him, but also in his country. The premise also offers a promise of emotional drama: will we see John Smith becoming upset about his situation? Will he pour his heart out to the audience about his desperation? If he does win, how will he respond? If he does not win, how will he respond? All of this is important in turning a simple urge into a workable premise, the germ of an idea into the formulation of a story. As

Young outlines: 'without clearly defined themes, there is a real danger that the film will be no more than a montage of "look at life" images glued together either by music or voice-over narration – visual wallpaper with nothing particular to say and no story to tell' (2002: 7–8).

Therefore, developing the idea into a premise is important in helping to identify the project's appeal and its 'bite' on the audience: 'the best documentary stories, like memorable literary novels or thought-provoking dramatic features, not only engage the audience with an immediate story ... but with themes that resonate beyond the particularity of the event being told' (Bernard, 2007: 19). Once the story and its associated themes have been identified, it is easier for the writer to then flesh out the documentary into a longer working outline and, eventually, a narrative structure.

Task 7.4

Think about a person you know. Make a list of all the interesting facts you know about this person and decide whether any of them would make an interesting idea for a documentary. Conduct more research into this, perhaps by interviewing the person, and formulate a premise for a documentary about him or her.

Constructing a narrative

A documentary does not fall into place by itself; the results of research do not simply connect with each other and create a coherent pattern of storytelling. 'Although by definition non-fiction filmmaking deals with existing material, there still needs to be a narrative structure' (Young, 2002: 5). So, much like writing a film or television drama, the documentary maker must spend time constructing a narrative that best tells his or her story. Documentary maker John Grierson sees narrative construction as a 'creative interpretation of reality' (cited in Wolper, 1998: 285); similarly, Kilborn and Izod view it as 'creative treatment of actuality' (1997: 12). As such, narrative construction is clearly seen as a creative tool in the documentary maker's armoury, giving at least some sense of freedom and personal control over what is, by definition, a factual account of reality.

When structuring a documentary, 'evidence will tend to be presented in such a way as to increase the likelihood of the audience falling in line with the filmmaker's argument' (ibid.: 6). Through the research undertaken, it is likely that the documentary maker will have developed a passion for the topic and even the people (subjects) who have been worked with in gathering the necessary information. As such, it should come as no surprise that the documentary will be structured in order to 'fit' his or her viewpoints and intentions. The way this is achieved is by carefully piecing together the argument, constructing a narrative that is not only coherent, but contains meaning. Thus, when faced with real-life facts and evidence that potentially bear no meaning at all, 'the documentarist has no choice but to make the succession a meaningful one – that is, to find a way through the material that tells a story' (Kriwaczek, 1997: 24). This 'way through' the story, essentially the narrative drive, is analogized by Bernard (2007: 17) as a train: moving a story forward and, concurrently, carrying an audience along with it. The idea of a train works because it suggests a journey to somewhere, from start to finish, just like the story structure; not only that, calling at various places on the way in order to collect passengers is like the documentary narrative picking up evidence as it goes along, adding to the overall argument being made. The train track, then, is the narrative structure provided by the documentary maker; the train is the central argument, moving forward and progressing towards its destination. Bernard tells us: 'get a good train going, and you can make detours as needed for exposition, complex theory, additional characters – whatever you need' (ibid.). In other words, as long as the central premise of the documentary works and has a general structure to follow, the narrative can 'collect' evidence as it progresses, in any way suitable to the whole. If the premise is not fixed and a structure not planned, then 'your train will be derailed' (ibid.).

Wolper writes: 'I always try to tell a story dramatically with a beginning, middle and end, using all the tools at my command: music, narration, interviews, stock footage, stills, etc.' (1998: 285). This reminds us that, like fiction screenwriting, the documentary narrative follows a universal pattern which starts with some kind of introduction and ends with some kind of resolution. Chapter 6 outlined the three act structure, which for fiction relates to 'setup', 'confrontation' and 'resolution'. Within this paradigm, a protagonist is seen trying to achieve a goal that has been set by someone or something, and overcoming obstacles is a key creation of dramatic conflict on this journey. In many ways, the structure of a documentary is not too dissimilar: the protagonist may be a subject who is trying to achieve something, or it might be the narrator trying to find something out; dramatic conflict might be encountered by the subject as he or she tries to achieve the goal, or it might simply be a collection of evidence that supports what the narrator is trying to find out. Clearly, then, three act structure can also be applied to documentary storytelling. The main difference is that rather than a quest to obtain something material, the goal may be to find the answer to a question. The narrative paradigm might look something like this:

- **Act 1: question (¼).** This act sets the central question of the documentary. It starts by positioning the audience in the desired frame of mind so that they want to know the answer to the question that has been set by the documentary maker. Exposition is used to establish why the question is being asked in the first place: facts, figures, voice-over narration, snatches of interview, etc. Key subjects of the story are introduced, offering a sense of character identification (and antagonism) to the audience. Often, intriguing and dramatic elements that feature later in the documentary are used here to tease the audience into wanting to know more, essentially making them stay tuned in.
- **Act 2: exploration (½).** This act explores the central question, using a multitude of positions and viewpoints in order to best provide a pathway to the eventual answer. Here is where the majority of the research undertaken comes into play: historical facts, expert advice, witness reports, reconstruction, interviews, etc. The narrative develops progressively in this act, taking the audience deeper into the question and connecting them more to the central situation and subjects. Often, this act ends with a 'cliffhanger' question that pulls the audience even deeper into the story or presents something that changes the feel or tone: a twist; a revelation; a hidden truth; a surprise.
- **Act 3: answer (¼).** This act pulls all of the threads of exploration together, often recapping the main ideas, and offers an answer to

the question posed at the start. Sometimes there is no definitive answer; so instead a feeling of resolution is created but with a sense that the issue is still ongoing. This act also has to work hard in giving the audience meaning: it should have a feeling of resonance that can be carried forward once the viewing has ended. Thus, documentaries ask further questions which an audience can relate to, and almost always revisit the universal themes and issues presented.

What is important to remember when constructing a narrative is that the process provides a way of shaping meaning, not merely providing a structure to house one-dimensional facts and figures. Like a film or television screenplay, the narrative must have a story at its core, whether that of a person or an issue that we can all relate to. This is why the notion of the *journey* is important to the documentary maker; as with the analogy of the train, where is this story going? Where does the evidence lead us? For Young: 'it is relatively easy to put together a feature showing what somebody is like – it is much harder to get the audience to follow them in a journey through time, where there will be some sort of change and/or resolution' (2002: 10–11).

Thus, narrative structure should be used to maximum effect to create a compelling story about a person or an issue that we care about. It should have 'a logical and emotional whole' (Rosenthal, 1996: 45), meaning that, as well as telling a story in an order that is effective, it should tell a story in an order that is affective. Without this consideration, documentaries can lose focus and drive, and have absolutely no impact upon their audience. Rosenthal notes: 'one sees too many films that are structureless, that amble along, showing an occasionally interesting interview or compelling incident, but with no spine' (ibid.: 48). It is this *spine*, the central drive, that distinguishes a good documentary from a bad documentary – the difference between one that we watch and one that we connect with. Executed well, the narrative can, moment by moment, build a strong sense of emotion to the subject matter. In doing so, the documentary maker enables us to believe in the idea and share his or her passion for the question being explored.

Task 7.5

Taking the person researched for the task above, consider how you might structure a ten-minute documentary about him or her. Use the following questions to guide the construction of the narrative:

- What is the premise? How might you use the opening minute or two to suggest this?
- Will you use a narrator or presenter to guide the overall story?
- Is there a chronological thread that the story could follow? If so, where will it start and where will it end?
- What would be the foreground story (anchoring the narrative), and what would be the background story (weaving into the narrative)? For example, is it based in the past and interwoven with interviews from the present, or vice versa?
- Which sources (research) could you insert throughout the narrative? What would they add to the overall story?
- Are there any elements that would create drama and conflict throughout the narrative, perhaps challenging the perception of the person in question?
- How do you want the audience to feel about the person at the end of the documentary? What techniques could you use to achieve that feeling?

Proposals, outlines, treatments and scripts

Once the documentary has been developed through research, from initial idea to premise, and then the narrative structure carefully constructed, the next stage is to write a *proposal*, or as some people prefer to call it, an *outline*. The proposal has two benefits: firstly, it helps to clarify the intentions of the documentary, consolidating the documentary maker's thoughts and directions on the project; secondly, it is used to pitch an idea to a potential broadcaster or sponsor who it is hoped will fund the project. In both senses, the proposal is an effective document used as a means of pitching: pitching an idea to someone else, and pitching the idea to yourself.

The style and format of a proposal varies between individuals, broadcasters and sponsors, but usually it is a one- or two-page document that summarizes the documentary project in a 'selling' manner, written in a way to grab the reader's attention and convince him or her that the project is worthy of being made. According to Hampe, 'in a few pages the proposal has to engage the fantasy life of the sponsor, stress the benefits of making the documentary, and shake loose the money' (1997: 126). This may be a crude way of putting it, but it does stress the need to produce a document that sells a visual idea from a mere printed page. The reader must be able to 'see' the project, and 'feel' it, knowing how an audience would respond to it both intellectually and emotionally. As Bernard (2007: 137) tells us, ineffective proposals outline the topic but do not give a sense of the story. So a proposal must capture the heart of the documentary as well as its facts; the premise as well as the particularities. As such, the words used must be alluring and convincing, not apologetic.

As stated, there are various ways of formatting a proposal. For Rosenthal (1996: 26), whose experience is particularly in American documentary production, the content should look something like this:

- An overall statement about the film.
- Background to the project.
- Approach, form and style to be taken.
- A potential shooting schedule.
- A budget.
- Intended audience.
- Marketing and distribution considerations.
- The filmmaker's biography and any supporting letters.

For Croton (1986: 9), whose particular experience is with the BBC, a proposal should look something like this:

- The overall idea of the programme and its proposed content.
- Its means of production.
- Target audience and a possible broadcast slot.
- The timescale of the production.
- An idea of the desired budget.

Although the specific formatting guidelines are different, much of the content is the same: idea; style; audience; production; budget. Nevertheless, it is important to research the person or institution that the proposal will be sent to, so that the correct formatting can be used. Although the media writer is unlikely to be involved in budgetary or production consideration of the documentary, he or she may be asked to assist the producer or director in writing the proposal. Usually, the media writer will focus more upon presenting the actual idea of the documentary, so a high level of skill in storytelling and summary writing is essential.

Task 7.6

Using the results from the two tasks above, write a one-page proposal for a documentary. For now, just concentrate on the actual subject matter and story, and potential audience demographic and reach.

The next stage in planning and packaging a documentary is to write a *treatment*. This is basically a prose version of the documentary, much in the style of a short story, and guides the reader through how the documentary will run, from beginning to end. A treatment 'should be thought of as an explanation of the documentary you intend to make. It tells you what is to be shot and why, and how the documentary will be organized to make a statement to an audience' (Hampe, 1997: 94). Like a fiction film treatment, a documentary treatment should tell the reader everything that will be shown on the screen, from action and dialogue to specific shots and sounds. It should be written in the present tense, evoking a sense that the documentary is playing on screen, right now. The layout of the treatment can either be in continuous prose or split into scenes (like the step-outline used in fiction screenwriting). For example, the opening of *On Your Marks* could be presented this way:

We're by the side of an Olympic-sized swimming pool. The water is calm. Music begins to play as a row of swimmers walk to their markers. We focus upon one swimmer: he looks determined as he focuses ahead, carefully putting on his goggles. This is John Smith. As he begins to take his mark, we intercut with shots of real Olympic champion swimmers from Games gone-by, collecting their medals, singing the national anthem, crying with pride, etc. As the music swells, a starter gun is fired and John Smith and the other swimmers dive into the water. The race is on.

Or it could be presented this way:

```
1. INT. OLYMPIC-SIZED SWIMMING POOL - DAY
The water is calm. Music begins to play as a row of
swimmers walk to their markers.

We focus upon one swimmer: he looks determined as he
focuses ahead, carefully putting on his goggles. This
is JOHN SMITH. As he begins to take his mark, we
intercut with:

2. INT. OLYMPIC GAMES CEREMONY - DAY (FOOTAGE)
Real Olympic champion swimmers from Games gone-by
collect their medals, sing the national anthem, cry
with pride, etc.

3. INT. SWIMMING POOL - DAY
The music swells. A starter gun is fired and John
Smith and the other swimmers dive into the water. The
race is on.
```

The length of a treatment depends upon the length of the documentary, personal style and taste, and, again, any requirements set by production companies or sponsors. Usually, however, a treatment can expect to run between four and eight pages, and can only be properly written once a structure has been designed and research has taken place (Young, 2002: 17). In some ways, the treatment can be the definitive document of a documentary because a script is not always written. Instead, the treatment is as near to a script as some projects will come, and from it the documentary maker can plan, shoot and edit the material as desired. 'Key characters, activities, the handling of time and place, and metaphoric devices should all be covered in a complete treatment' (ibid.: 20), and so, even without a script, there should be a strong sense of exactly what is desired to appear on the screen at any one time. The key advice to the media writer, then, is to ensure that the treatment encompasses everything that is wanted from the documentary and all that can be known beforehand and planned. That said, however, it is important to remember one thing: 'never write anything that the reader will think you cannot produce' (Rabiger, 2004: 218).

Task 7.7

Watch the first ten minutes of a documentary and write what you think the treatment for it might have looked like. Try to generate a sense of the documentary's tone and style by using words and expressions that evoke how it is hoped the audience will feel when watching.

How much a documentary script can be written depends upon the proposed narrative events and their predictability. Sometimes the documentary maker can plan his or her footage in a specific way, making decisions about the ordering of events and the flow of an interview. Other times, however, things can happen out of the blue that force a new way of telling the story from the original intention: the footage does not go to plan; an interviewee begins to reveal other information; something important related to the topic develops mid-shoot; etc. As such, a script is more of a planning document in documentary than it is in writing fiction screenplays for film or television. Whereas in the latter the script is the finalized blueprint for production to take place, in the former it is merely a hoped-for format, developed with perhaps more depth than the treatment, but very open to change. Depending upon the type of treatment written, the script will add detail by specifically charting the scene-by-scene development of the story and adding to it the narration, either as voice-over or to-camera. For example:

```
EXT. TOWN CENTRE - DAY
A sea of shoppers, all carrying bags with 'sale',
'clearance', etc. written on them.

                    NARRATOR (v/o)
        When was the last time you paid full
        price for a new pair of jeans? When was
        the last time you bought a CD that
        didn't have a few pounds knocked off?
```

Scripting the results of planned interviews is impossible to do. However, what can be included in a pre-production script is a suggestion of the kinds of thing that people will talk about. Rather than guessing word-for-word what someone might say, the writer can simply indicate content with directions such as 'Interviewee talks about how he was affected by the recession: how he lost his home; how he was under pressure to earn extra money'. What this usefully does is help the writer to position the proposed content of the interview into the overall narrative structure, and, although specific words and expressions cannot be second-guessed, an overall feel for the fit of the content can be achieved: 'you can't know where real life will take you, but you can certainly anticipate a range of outcomes and determine whether or not the story holds sufficient promise' (Bernard, 2007: 35–6).

Working with subjects

Most documentaries rely upon the use of interviews, mostly from key subjects related to the topic but also with other subjects, such as experts or witnesses. Although questions can be set prior to conducting an interview, and possible outcomes determined, no one can ever predict what exactly will be said. So it is crucial that the documentary maker enters the interview with an open mind and is ready to explore territory that has not even been considered. As Gray tells us, 'capturing unique moments of human encounter is a highly challenging and developed skill' (1998: 91). Therefore, interviewing is not something that can just happen naturally; rather, it should be suitably planned and considered beforehand, and skilfully handled during.

There are a number of considerations to broach when planning an interview, especially if the interviewee is likely to raise something that the documentary really relies upon for its telling. For example, if the issue being explored is highly sensitive to an individual, risking the integrity of the interview may result in the interview being cancelled, meaning that new material would then have to be sought. Although the format and approach of an interview is particular to the style of the documentary maker, Kilborn and Izod (1997: 200) offer some initial considerations that may be useful in planning an interview:

- To what extent should the interviewer alert subjects beforehand to the type of question to be asked?

- Should the interviewer be seen in the frame with the subject?
- What level of formality should the filmmaker adopt in conducting the interview?
- How far can the documentarist go in teasing out responses from subjects, where the pain of remembering may be almost too much to bear?

These are considerations, and there are not necessarily any answers. However, the point is that documentary makers must think very carefully about who they are interviewing, what they want to get out of the interview, and how the questions will (or will not) be structured in order to achieve that desired outcome. Hampe's advice is this: 'find out what you can about your subject ahead of time. Most important, find out what you don't know. That's the basis for your questions' (1997: 265). This suggests that interviewing is not simply a process of reaffirming ideas already held, but rather a process of revelation. The interviewee tells you something that you did not already know, and in doing so adds shape, direction and deeper texture to the evolving project. This is also the opinion of Rosenthal: 'I like to outline the project to them in general terms, but I rarely go into too many details. I want to intrigue them into helping me, and try to tell them honestly why obtaining their cooperation and making the film is important' (1996: 40). Here, as well as suggesting that an interview should be allowed to flow naturally and not be overly prescribed, Rosenthal outlines another key feature of an interview: honesty. By explaining to the interviewee the rationale behind the documentary, whatever that position may be, a level of trust is created. Thus, the interviewee will feel comfortable when being asked the questions because he or she knows why the documentary maker is asking them. If an interview is based upon false assumptions, the interviewee may become very uncomfortable and, inevitably, will leave.

The following suggestions are useful not only for planning an interview, but for undertaking one:

- Make a plan of what you want to know. What is the core idea or essence of the situation that you would like the subject to discuss?

- Devise a rough structure for the questions, firstly easing the subject into the interview, and eventually tackling the 'big' issues that you wish to extract the most from.
- Prepare a list of back-up questions. Sometimes the interview will go off-track or become somewhat uncomfortable. Having back-up questions can be useful in calming the situation down or making the subject feel at ease again.
- Avoid closed questions. You are aiming to tease out a story, not reaffirm one you have already created, so allow the subject to say what he wants to say and in a way that he wants to.
- Try to vary the pace and tone of the interview. Different parts of the interview may create different moods or atmospheres, so it is useful to mix them up a little so that the subject is not too strained.
- 'Don't be embarrassed to say "I don't know about that" or "I don't understand", even if you do, it's a good way to get more information' (Hampe, 1997: 270).

Hampe (ibid.: 271) proposes two important questions that a documentary maker should not be afraid to ask at the end of an interview:

- Is there anything I should have asked you that I just didn't know to ask?
- Is there anything else that you'd like to say that you haven't had a chance to?

After all, interviewing can be a draining and emotional experience and sometimes the most obvious of things can easily be missed. These two questions thus help to rectify such a situation and once more put the focus back on the subject who may indeed have something more enlightening to say.

Task 7.8

Choose a subject who appears in a story in today's newspaper. Read the story and write a list of at least fifteen questions that you would ask this person if you had the opportunity. Think carefully about how these questions would relate to a potential documentary made about him or her in the context of the story.

Dialogue and narration

As already highlighted, not all documentaries have a fully written script. However, if dialogue of any sort is to be used, then at some point this will have to be written – either as a script or as an accompaniment to the treatment. In documentaries that use reconstructions, dialogue will be written into a properly formatted scene, as in fiction screenwriting. The scene contains characters who speak as well as act, and so the actors playing these parts will require a recognizably formatted script. This is also often the case when a presenter is used, who may speak to-camera at various points throughout the documentary. More common, however, is the simple use of voice-over narration, recorded before or after the documentary has been assembled and then layered over the unfolding imagery.

'The broad function of narration is to amplify and clarify the picture' (Rosenthal, 1996: 182), giving an audience key details that may not be obvious from the screen. At the start of a documentary, for example, the narrator may need to outline briefly the who, what, when, where and why, just as in a news story. Not only does this set the scene of the topic to be discussed, written well it can hook an audience into the documentary and command their attention. Throughout the rest of the documentary, narration can be used for various effects. For example:

> Narration can quickly and easily set up the factual background of a film, providing simple or complex information that does not arise easily or naturally from the casual conversation of the film participants. It can complement the mood of the film, and above all it can provide focus and emphasis. (Ibid.: 181)

As such, narration is as much about creating meaning as it is relaying factual information. Rosenthal's use of 'focus' and 'emphasis' reminds us that the documentary is made by a person; this person has a particular point of view that he or she wishes to promote, and so narration is an effective way to accomplish this. So, narration 'can be one of the best and most efficient ways to move your story along, not because it *tells* the story but because it draws the audience into and through it' (Bernard, 2007: 211), guiding them to the intended feelings and emotions.

When writing voice-over narration, there are various key principles to consider. These include:

- **Think carefully about the voice you use.** In order to connect an audience with the documentary narrative, the tone of voice has to be right. In most cases, the voice will be authoritative yet not overly bearing or patronizing. It should be clear and simple, yet written down with confidence and credibility. A voice that does not match the subject matter (such as colloquialism use in a serious documentary) can make the audience feel uncomfortable and probably put them off watching further.
- **Consider the style of narration.** Sometimes documentaries use a 'quirky' style of narration that, for example, juxtaposes with the on-screen imagery in an ironic way. Other times, for example, the style is enticing and gripping, using adjectives that put the audience on the edge of their seats. The point here is that the style of narration must match the style of the documentary; after all, voice achieves a feeling in the audience as much as imagery does.
- **Think about the address used.** Should you speak directly to the audience? Should you use the 'we' approach? Is it more effective to write in the third person? How the audience is addressed influences how they connect with the documentary and thus how much they are moved by the topic. It is crucial to get this right, especially for use in the opening minutes when the audience decides whether to continue watching or not.
- **Do not write too much.** It is easy to write 'everything' in narration, the writer thinking that the audience needs to know every detail about the topic. However, with imagery playing underneath the voice-over, it is common that very little actually needs to be said. Voice-over should complement images, not overburden them; it should be peppered over the unfolding action sparingly.
- **Avoid repetition.** Again, it is easy to think that repeating facts will make the audience understand the documentary topic more and follow the intended feeling towards it. On the contrary, too much repetition shows unprofessional writing skills and can make the documentary sound desperate. Therefore, only repeat key facts or phrases if absolutely necessary and, even then, probably no more than three times.

Task 7.9

Rewrite the following passage as voice-over narration, considering the points made above. Remember that visual imagery would be played underneath these words.

> The date was December the 31st. The year was 1999. People from all over the country were getting ready for the biggest and most anticipated celebration in memory: the Millennium. Crowds were heading into towns and cities to celebrate. Bars were cram packed with partygoers. The people of Great Britain had only one thing in mind: to have lots of fun. However, not everybody shared this view of the Millennium. In one particular dark suburb of London, one person had a different idea for the Millennium. He wanted to celebrate the Millennium in his own way. He wanted to let the New Year go out with a bang of a different kind; his own kind. Leaving with nothing but his bullet-filled gun, this man set out for his own party that night. What was to come was truly horrendous.

Writing corporate films

The principles and techniques of planning and making a documentary can be effectively transferred into another form of factual storytelling: the corporate film. In today's world, corporate films are not just found in traditional film or video format; instead, they are found in a range of multimedia formats, such as CD-ROMS, DVDs and Internet streaming. As such, the all-embracing term 'corporate film' is here meant to indicate any form of moving image material that is made for a specific client need, where footage is constructed as a story and, commonly, layered with voice-over. Like a documentary, corporate films have the duty of presenting information to a given audience in a clear and convincing way that promotes the intentions of the creator (as commissioned by the client). Whether a plea to donate money to a charity, a marketing-led 'brochure' for an organization or a training guide for employees, corporate films draw heavily upon the documentary form in order to achieve success. However, as Rosenthal writes, whereas the narrative drive of a documentary is often social or political, 'the ultimate purpose of an industrial or public relations film is to do a good sales job. Such films want you to buy something, to support something, or to participate in something' (1996: 259). The documentary is thus brought together with public relations and advertising in the corporate film, demanding that the media writer demonstrates strong skill in telling a story with purpose.

It can be surprising when considering how much corporate film exists in today's media-saturated world. Traditional types of corporate film, as highlighted, include in-house training films and commercial information about an organization. Today, however, there are more and more opportunities for corporate film to be used. For example, many company websites now stream digital videos that introduce the history of the organization and explore the nature of their business. This is becoming increasingly popular with universities and colleges: a recognition of the need to 'brand' and 'sell' in today's culture. As another example, think about places you have recently visited where a plasma screen has been on display in the reception area. Plasma screens are increasingly becoming the norm in such locations and are used to let the public know about the organization and, moreover, sell their brand image and services. Other common spaces for the use of corporate film material include: music videos (especially aspiring musicians); museum installations; conferences and exhibitions; airline safety demonstrations; press events; pubs, bars and restaurants.

When writing a corporate film, then, the following considerations should be made:

- *Who wants this film to be made?*
  Understanding the nature of the commissioning organization plays a major part in creating the film. For example, is it an international charity with a particular ethos? If so, then the style of the film has to match its vision. Or is it a commercial company with a well-known brand image? If so, then the film has to match this brand image, even if it is a training video for existing staff.
- *Why do they want this film to be made?*
  Although this seems an obvious question, it cannot be underestimated. The rationale for the film defines the approach to be

taken by the writer. For example, how would an educational information film about a charity look if it appeared to be asking for donations? How would a health and safety training video for a creative media company look if it spent more time gloating about the company's brand image?

- *What have they already made?*
  Research into already-existing corporate films will give a good insight into the style, tone and 'safety zone' of the commissioning organization. From viewing such films, it may become apparent that particular narrative styles are preferred or types of expression used in voice-over narration.

- *Are there any style guidelines to follow?*
  Many major companies have branding guidelines that they always conduct their work by; this is their 'house style', which should be followed at all times. Even though such guidelines may be written specifically for public-facing materials (including their actual product), they are extremely useful for all types of communication to be made for the company.

- *Are there any advisers or experts to work with?*
  In some cases, the material presented in a corporate film must be extremely precise; it may be a legal stance on an issue or a health and safety procedure. In such cases, working with advisers or experts in the field is essential for maintaining an accurate film. Companies may supply such people from their in-house team or it may be down to the writer to find someone suitably qualified to assist in writing the script.

Although working in the corporate film market may be more 'bureaucratic, political, and conservative' (DiZazzo, 2004: 10) than the documentary filmmaking market, it can nevertheless be rewarding in its own way. Not only that, it can be a useful way of learning the craft of factual screenwriting, which may then lead to work in other more desired areas. As DiZazzo writes: 'corporate scriptwriting is a creative and exciting way to earn a living ... Once writers become aware that they can earn good money, flex their creative muscles, and see their work produced intact, they quickly become corporate film believers' (ibid.).

Career opportunities in screenwriting: fact

As with fiction screenwriting, it must be highlighted that a career in documentary making is no easy task. There are many people aspiring to work in this field, but not enough projects to house them all. However, with less at stake in financial terms than film and television drama, a greater number of documentaries (and their hybrids, such as docu-soaps and reality TV) are made, offering a good deal of opportunities for the aspiring documentary maker. A common way into documentary making, particularly from a writing perspective, is a job as a researcher or research assistant. Here you are able to consolidate any skills that you have achieved through study by applying them to real-life projects. Although the work may be hard and occasionally mundane, the development of your skills from amateur to professional is far outweighed. If research-based opportunities do not exist, then undertaking a role such as a runner or a production assistant can also be useful; once in, it is easier to move around roles according to your competencies.

As stated, corporate film is a useful way into documentary making. Although the material of a corporate film may be far less interesting than a documentary (though there are exceptions), the experience gained will be much valued. You may work on short-term contracts or you may be employed in-house for an organization; either way, making a variety of films for a living will absolutely strengthen your skills in research, narrative construction and dialogue writing. If you are fortunate enough to gain full-time employment in a media production company that makes corporate films, you may find that documentary making opportunities come about anyway, as such companies often wish to branch out and explore more creative project ideas.

Finally, entering competitions should not be underestimated. A range of competition opportunities exist each year to find new talent and showcase new voices. For example, The Documentary Filmmakers Group, ShootingPeople and BritFilms list major national and international documentary competitions and festivals on their respective websites, giving specific details about the competitions and how to enter them. For British students specifically, The Royal Television Society hosts an annual student competition in each of its regional centres, the winners then progressing to a national final. Such competitions and festivals are not only a valuable outlet to have work showcased, but offer excellent opportunities for networking.

Further reading

Bernard, S.C. (2007) *Documentary Storytelling: Making Stronger and More Dramatic Nonfiction Films*, 2nd edn, Oxford: Focal Press.

Hampe, B. (1997) *Making Documentary Films and Reality Videos: A Practical Guide to Planning, Filming and Editing Documentaries of Real Events*, New York: Henry Holt & Company.

Kilborn, R. and Izod, J. (1997) *An Introduction to Television Documentary: Confronting Reality*, Manchester: Manchester University Press.

Kochberg, S. (ed.) (2002) *Introduction to Documentary Production: A Guide for Media Students*, London: Wallflower.

Kriwaczek, P. (1997) *Documentary for the Small Screen*, Oxford: Focal Press.

Rabiger, M. (2004) *Directing the Documentary*, 4th edn, Oxford: Focal Press.

Rosenthal, A. (1996) *Writing, Directing, and Producing Documentary Films and Videos*, rev. edn, Illinois: Southern Illinois University Press.

Tobias, M. (ed.) (1998) *The Search for Reality: The Art of Documentary Filmmaking*, California: Michael Wiese.

Web resources

www.britfilms.com
A division of The British Council, dedicated to the moving image.

www.dfgdocs.com
Official website for The Documentary Filmmakers Group.

www.shootingpeople.org
Filmmakers' website where members can subscribe to a variety of forums in order to discuss projects and find work.

Conclusion: Media Writing and Digital Technology

The future of media writing is constantly evolving. No sooner do we have a new way of working with a message than it is replaced by an even newer one. Technology is the primary reason for this, habitually providing both new means of creating media writing messages and platforms for exchanging them. By 'future', then, what we really mean is 'digital': more specifically, the development of digital technology in order to change the way that media writing is both produced and consumed. As stated in the Introduction, although the majority of the practical tools detailed in the main chapters may seemingly relate to more traditional forms of media writing, they inherently relate to digital forms too. For example, writing a press release requires the same skill for both paper and electronic release; angling a news story is the same for both print and web news. As such, many of the changes in media writing are more a matter of medium, not message. For Ryan, 'texts supported by digital media may satisfy to various degrees the universal cognitive model, or they may produce creative alternatives to a narrative experience, but they do not and cannot change the basic conditions of narrativity' (2004: 354). In other words, although the way that a message is presented may be different in shape, form or style than its traditional predecessor, the actual message itself is no different. News stories, for example, may now be available to be read via text message, but apart from the fact that they are shorter and contain less detail, they are still news stories designed to have the same effect upon the reader. Where we are not truly positioned yet is a place where new *types* of media writing have emerged specifically from the digital revolution, ones which use the structure of the mode of delivery to alter radically how a message is generated. Public relations is still public relations, however delivered; screenwriting is still screenwriting, however presented. 'The most urgent of the issues that faces developers of new media narrative', perhaps, 'is to find what themes and what kinds of plots take proper advantage of the built-in properties of the medium' (ibid.: 356). Only when this has been achieved can we truly begin to think about forms of media writing that are radically different; forms that promise to change the future.

In this Conclusion, then, we will reflect upon some of the ways in which forms of media writing have changed, or are changing, as a result of digital technology. In doing so, we also want to recognize that there are some interesting contextual, perhaps more philosophical, debates surrounding the practice of writing for the media. To achieve this, instead of approaching each of the forms as already written about in isolation, we will combine them into four general themes: print journalism; broadcast journalism; marketing communications; screenwriting. These themes allow us to consider wider, less localized ideas about the changing nature of media writing, notably the cross-over that can appear between forms.

Print journalism

For Schiller, as new media technologies have advanced, the 'boundaries between news, entertainment, public relations and advertising, always fluid historically, are now becoming almost invisible' (cited in McNair, 2006: 11). When faced with a newspaper's website, for example, it is not only the news story that we see: there are advertisements (often in the form of 'pop ups'), links to internal and external websites, forums, opinion polls and spaces to 'blog' comments about the story. For McNair, journalism is at the centre of media hybridity, where, dissolving too, are 'boundaries between journalism and not-journalism, between information and entertainment, objectivity and subjectivity, truth and lies' (ibid.). On the one hand, the digitalization of journalism brings with it a whole host of possibilities that develop the form from something standard to something special. Harrower believes that 'it'll become increasingly difficult to compete against the allure of digital media, where editors can combine text, photo, audio, videos, animated graphics, interactive chat and much more' (2007: 154). In this way, journalism becomes much more than it has traditionally been; it becomes interactive, user-friendly and user-reliant. On the other hand, the digitalization of journalism could be seen predominantly as a way of boosting a newspaper's revenue. Although Internet sites 'reach new audiences and bring a world-wide readership to British papers', thus raising their profile, 'we are beginning to see [them] introduce new advertising revenues that suggest sites will soon turn a profit' (Fletcher, 2005: 179). Although the pursuit of profit should not always be seen as something negative, it does raise interesting questions about the kind of journalism on offer and its root purpose; if advertisers are willing to spend, then how is the newspaper supporting them?

Those questions aside, newspaper websites can be seen as viable, perhaps better, alternatives to their print counterparts. As McNair states: 'innovators such as *BBC Online* and *Guardian Unlimited* were more than merely cyber versions of broadcast and print news; rather they became autonomous entities providing increasing qualities of web-only content, much of it free of charge' (2006: 120). Therefore, newspaper websites have the potential to reach new, fresh audiences, and because most of their content is provided free of charge, offer a greater sense of accessibility. Such developments have also brought with them increased opportunities for working in journalism, with more people working on a greater amount of content. For example, 'the full range of online skills for writers includes preparing headlines, single paragraph summaries, longer stories, and cross-heads. There are also picture captions to write and interactive boxes to prepare' (Hudson and Rowlands, 2007: 159).

What we must not lose sight of, however, is that although the medium of delivery may be very different, the message and its creation is not: 'journalism is gathering, writing and publishing factual information. How that information is published – in print or electronically – changes with the times. But there's no sign in the modern media landscape that there will be any less demand for professional journalists' (ibid.: 4). Quite simply, the technology of storytelling should not be confused with the art of storytelling (ibid.: 5); a hard or soft news story still has the same premise (to inform the people of a truth) and the same purpose (to capture emotionally that truth). In fact, according to Wilkinson *et al.*, there are at least five principles essential to journalism that have not changed with digital convergence: 'accuracy; attention to detail; compelling information; solid attribution; and proper grammar, word usage, spelling, and punctuation' (2009: 109).

Broadcast journalism

The main technological shift with regards to broadcast news is that much of it can now be accessed 'on-demand'. Unlike traditional television and radio broadcasts, which are scheduled months in advance and often as part of a continuous pattern, on-demand news means that we can choose when we watch or listen; furthermore, we can choose what we watch or listen to. For example, BBC iPlayer, the online 'catch-up' platform, allows us to choose from a range of television and radio news bulletins that we have missed over the past week. Not only that, once a programme has been selected, we have the power to pause, fast-forward and rewind at our leisure. Similarly, the ITV Local website streams regional news bulletins to the user's computer at the click of a button, again with the possibility of pausing, fast-forwarding and rewinding. McNair characterizes such a technological advent as an 'ideologically realigned, hyper-adversarial, decentralized and demand-driven media environment' (2006: vi), suggesting that the 'power' of media companies has somewhat shifted and is now in the hands of us, the consumers.

As well as television news bulletins 'going online', fragmented versions of news bulletins are able to be streamed via websites throughout the day. In other words, specific online news stories will use video footage, either produced by the broadcaster or donated by the consumer, to support the written text. This footage may go on to be used as part of the traditional news bulletin later in the day, but at the time of being uploaded it is a text in itself that is used solely for online purposes. For Morgan, this idea of immediate transmission and delivery of news items and events 'has brought about the "unbundling of news". This means it is no longer delivered only at specific times, and in bulletins, but continuously' (2008: 2). What this means for the journalist, then, is that for online environments written words are not always successful on their own. Rather, written news stories supported by supplementary visual forms may not only be more popular, they may be becoming 'the norm'.

Marketing communications

Recent changes in technology have opened up public relations markets to mass communications, and it is important that writers understand these changes and the impact these can have for the dissemination of written messages. The computer has gone beyond offering word processing and desktop publishing opportunities; technology has expanded the scope of both internal and external communications beyond that of traditional media. The most important component of these new technologies is the ability to be interactive, thereby enabling two-way symmetrical communications. Organizations can now offer added-value by providing an interactive forum for their consumers' voices, listening to those voices and acting upon them. The role of traditional media such as the news release, the newsletter and the corporate magazine has been expanded by the ability to make these once static delivery systems of information mobile and cooperative.

In addition, social media is another medium which, although initially designed to keep friends in touch, has been embraced by those working in public relations and advertising. Networks such as MySpace, Facebook and Twitter are no longer merely restricted to updating users of their friends' movements and holiday pictures: they are used by organizations (and individuals) directly to sell products and indirectly build brands. MySpace, for example, has become well known for promoting the work of musicians because of its ability to stream music and video and create forums in which others can make comments about what they see and hear. Facebook's technology allows organizations to target their advertisements at specific users, all because the user's 'profile' matches the organization's desired demographic: a single young male who may be interested in joining a dating website, for example. Even Twitter, specifically designed to keep friends up to date with each others' movements, now sees organizations using its 'micro-blogging' feature in order to keep their publics aware of what they are doing. Like RSS (Really Simple Syndication, or Rich Site Summary), 'news bites' are available to subscribers (followers) to let them know about any ongoing developments: news releases, job vacancies, special offers, etc. The key consideration here, we would argue, is that the message sent must be newsworthy. If not, the subscriber will slowly become irritated by messages which have no real meaning, and, in PR terms, this could be detrimental to the brand.

Screenwriting

Writing for the screen is probably the form of media writing that, to date, has been least affected by advances in digital technology. By this, we specifically mean the *writing* of a screenplay, not the consumption. Although there have been major changes in how films and television dramas are made and distributed, from small-scale independent filmmaking to large-scale online distribution (such as YouTube), their writing has not significantly changed at all. Strong narratives with engaging characters have always and probably will always be the backbone of a good screenplay, whether that screenplay is produced for a major Hollywood studio or a local community television station. In fact, as Batty and Waldeback highlight, easy-access technology such as mini-DV cameras and laptop editing software 'can result in "point-and-shoot" filmmaking, where record buttons are pressed with little thought for creative preparation [and] the quality of storytelling, structure and pace can be poor' (2008: 169). Therefore, traditional principles of screenwriting should always be fully embraced and only, when necessary, *appropriated* for a digitally led project.

There are, however, two areas of film and television writing that could be deemed as requiring reconsideration. Firstly, advances in digital technology make it possible to utilize the visual medium to the maximum. In other words, screen stories can be set anywhere and use a variety of special effects to enhance their storytelling. For example, if the story world of a film is somewhere in the distant future, the writer does not need to worry about how this will be realized; much can be achieved by computer software (CGI), both during and after the film has been made. Furthermore, special effects pending, visual-specific characters or objects can be created at the click of a button, making it possible to create the unimaginable. Therefore, writers are able to abandon any constraints about how they will tell their stories, perhaps opening up fresh, innovative styles of story-telling. Secondly, instant audience participation generated through websites and mobile phones can allow writers to create narrative 'options' which an audience will dictate the result of. For example, there are opportunities where a script can be written with alternative endings, where the ending will be chosen by the audience. A television drama, for example, may be split into two parts, where after part one the audience votes for which ending they would prefer to see. Later the drama will return with that chosen ending. This, however, may be seen as merely a gimmick because not only will specific endings have been written in the first place (a choice within a constrained framework), such endings are likely to lead eventually to the same place, where future episodes may have already been scripted and made.

In a similar way, interactive narratives for computer games and the Web allow users to explore variations of the same story. Unlike simulation games, such as those allowing a player to fly an aircraft, interactive narratives empower players into finding their own ways around a story; they are given a world that they are allowed to explore how they wish. However, this world is in fact limited, as Garrand explains: 'there is nothing unplanned in an interactive narrative. Someone who plays the program long enough will eventually see all the material the writer created. An interactive narrative essentially allows each player to discover the story in a different way' (2001: 212). Thus we are presented with narratives that are not limitless in terms of content, but limitless in terms of their exploration of content.

When writing such narratives, however, we must be aware that players usually like to have something to do: they like to be set a challenge. If the world is completely open and reliant upon the initiation of users themselves, as it is in the space of Second Life, then there is actually no reason to do anything. Of more concern here is the fact that there is no actual writing. Instead, interactive narratives rely upon writers to create stories that players can 'narrate' in their own way. As a general rule, 'the secret to the narrative success of games lies in their ability to exploit the most fundamental of the forces that move a plot forward: the solving of problems' (Ryan,

2004: 349). In other words, even though the player may be meandering through the world of an interactive computer game, he or she is in actual fact undertaking a series of challenges not too dissimilar to those found in a platform game. Thus, for screenwriters working in the field of computer games, it is essential to consider what a player can, or should, be doing at any one time. Players should not be left wandering around aimlessly in segments of non-story, because ultimately boredom will creep in and the game will be abandoned:

> Finding this balance – giving the player some control over the narrative, while allowing the writer to perform the necessary functions of the classical storyteller, including establishing characters and an engaging story structure – is the key challenge for the writer of interactive narrative. (Garrand, 2001: 219)

Task C.1

Play an interactive narrative computer game and consider how the story has been set up for the player. How much freedom do you really have within the game? What storyline are you actually following?

Task C.2

Using the game played for the exercise above, plan out how you might turn the narrative into a film. Who would be the protagonist? Who would be the antagonist? What would the underlying theme be? How would the film be structured?

As a final thought, consider this: in what format are you reading this book? Is it in its traditional paperback format, or are you reading it online or via a handheld device? If the former, how do you think the book would differ if read electronically? If the latter, how do you think the book would differ if read on paper? The answer is simple: although the *experience* of reading the book may differ, its *content* would not differ at all. Whether reading the book on the bus or in the university library, the book is still a book; it is still a continuous narrative that focuses upon explaining to readers the necessary skills of writing for the media. If the book took on an extra dimension, such as an interactive text with tasks that automatically popped up at the end of each section, then it would not be a book; it would be a game.

As such, the concluding message that we want to leave you with is that writing for the media can be a very exciting and rewarding career path for those who have a passion to write and can master the craft. It is not enough to be an average writer but a brilliant programmer or web designer; the written word will always outweigh its presentation. As outlined in the Introduction, all forms of media writing have at their core a universal range of components: story, purpose, shape, plot, address, persuasion and conviction. Therefore, although advances in digital technology may be paving the way for innovative platforms of delivery, the fundamental heart to all media writing is, simply, the writing.

Further reading

Garrand, T. (2001) *Writing for Multimedia and the Web*, 2nd edn, Boston, MA: Focal Press.

Hammerich, I. and Harrison, C. (2001) *Developing Online Content: The Principles of Writing and Editing for the Web*, Chichester: Wiley & Sons.

Harrower, T. (2007) *Inside Reporting: A Practical Guide to the Craft of Journalism*, New York: McGraw-Hill.

Holtz, S. (1999) *Writing for the Wired World: The Communicator's Guide to Effective Online Content*, California: IABC.

Hudson, G. and Rowlands, S. (2007) *The Broadcast Journalism Handbook*, Harlow: Pearson Longman.

Kelleher, T. (2006) *Public Relations Online: Lasting Concepts for Changing Media*, Thousand Oaks, CA: Sage.

Mill, D. (2005) *Content Is King: Writing and Editing Online*, Oxford: Elsevier Butterworth-Heinemann.

Phillips, D. and Young, P. (2009) *Online Public Relations: A Practical Guide to Developing an Online Strategy in the World of Social Media*, London: Kogan Page.

Ryan, M. (2004) *Narrative Across Media: The Languages of Storytelling*, Lincoln: University of Nebraska Press.

Vorvoreanu, M. (2008) *Website Public Relations: How Corporations Build and Maintain Relationships Online*, New York: Cambria Press.

Wilkinson, J.S., Grant, A.E. and Fisher, D.J. (2009) *Principles of Convergent Journalism*, New York: Oxford University Press.

Bibliography

Ali, M. (1997) *Copywriting*, Oxford: Butterworth-Heinemann.

Anderson, A. (1997) *Media, Culture and the Environment*, London: Routledge.

Anon (2000) *The Advertising Slogan Hall of Fame – The Best in Branding*, available at http://www.adslogans.co.uk/hof/mediacover.html (accessed 24 February).

Aristotle (1982) *Poetics*, tr. James Hutton, New York: W. W Norton & Co.

Aronson, L. (2001) *Screenwriting Updated: New (and Conventional) Ways of Writing for the Screen*, California: Silman-James.

Baker, D. (1995) *How to Write Stories for Magazines: A Practical Guide*, 3rd edn, London: Alison & Busby.

Bartram, P. (1999) *Writing a Press Release*, 3rd edn, Oxford: How To Books.

Bartram, P. (2006) *How To Write the Perfect Press Release*, Brighton: New Venture Publishing.

Batty, C. and Waldeback, Z. (2008) *Writing for the Screen: Creative and Critical Approaches*, Basingstoke: Palgrave Macmillan.

Bell, A. (1991) *The Language of News Media*, Oxford: Blackwell.

Benoit, W.L. and Benoit, P. (2008) *Persuasive Messages: The Process of Influence*, Oxford: Blackwell.

Berger, A.A. (1998) *Media Research Techniques*, 2nd edn, Thousand Oaks, CA: Sage Publications.

Bernard, S.C. (2007) *Documentary Storytelling: Making Stronger and More Dramatic Nonfiction Films*, 2nd edn, Oxford: Focal Press.

Bernays, E. (2004) *Crystallizing Public Opinion*, Whitefish, MT: Kessinger Publishing.

Bivins, T. (2005) *Public Relations Writing: The Essentials of Style and Format*, 5th edn, New York: McGraw-Hill.

Bivins, T.H. (2008) *Public Relations Writing, The Essentials of Style and Format*, 6th edn, New York: McGraw-Hill.

Blake, G. and Bly, R. (1997) *The Elements of Copywriting: The Essential Guide to Creating Copy That Gets the Results You Want*, New York: Macmillan.

Boyd, A., Stewart, P. and Alexander, R. (2008) *Broadcast Journalism: Techniques of Radio & Television News*, 6th edn, Oxford: Focal Press.

Bromley, B. (1994) *Teach Yourself Journalism*, London: Hodder & Stoughton.

Bugeja, M. (1998) *Guide to Writing Magazine Non-Fiction*, Boston, MA: Allyn & Bacon.

Burns, S.L. (2002) *Understanding Journalism*, London: Sage Publications.

Cain, S. (2009) *Key Concepts in Public Relations*, Basingstoke: Palgrave Macmillan.

Camp, L. (2007) *Can I Change Your Mind? The Craft and Art of Persuasive Writing*, London: A & C Black.

Campbell, J. (1993) *The Hero with a Thousand Faces*, London: Fontana.

Cialdini, R. (2007) *Influence: The Psychology of Persuasion*, New York: Harper-Collins.

Clayton, J. (2000) *Journalism for Beginners: How to Get into Print and Get Paid for it*, 2nd edn, London: Piatkus.

Cohen, A.A. (1987) *The Television News Interview*, Thousand Oaks, CA: Sage Publications.

Cook, J.S. (1996) *The Elements of Speechwriting and Public Speaking*, Harlow: Longman.

Crone, T. (2002) *Law and the Media*, Oxford: Focal Press.

Croton, G. (1986) *From Script to Screen: Documentaries*, Borehamwood: BBC Television Training.

Crystal, D. (2001) *Language and the Internet*, Cambridge: Cambridge University Press.

Cutts, M. (1999) *The Quick Reference Plain English Guide*, Oxford: Oxford University Press.

Dancyger, K. and Rush, J. (2007) *Alternative Scriptwriting: Successfully Breaking the Rules*, 4th edn, Oxford: Focal Press.

Davis, A. (1995) *Magazine Journalism Today*, Oxford: Focal Press.

Dick, J. (1996) *Writing for Magazines*, 2nd edn, London: A & C Black.

DiZazzo, R. (2004) *Corporate Media Production*, 4th edn, Oxford: Focal Press.

Essinger, J. (1999) *Writing Marketing Copy to Get Results*, London: Thomson Learning.

Festinger, L. (1970) *Theory of Cognitive Dissonance*, Stanford, CA: Stanford University Press.

Field, S. (2003) *The Definitive Guide to Screenwriting*, London: Ebury Press.

Fletcher, K. (2005) *The Journalist's Handbook: An Insider's Guide to Being a Great Journalist*, London: Macmillan.

Foster, J.L. (2005) *Effective Writing Skills for Public Relations*, London: Kogan Page.

Franklin, B. (1997) *Newszak and News Media*, London: Arnold.

Friedlander, E. and Lee, J. (2008) *Feature Writing for Newspapers and Magazines: The Pursuit of Excellence*, 6th edn, Boston, MA: Pearson Education.

Fulton, H., Huisman R., Murphet, J. and Dunn, A. (2005) *Narrative and Media*, Cambridge: Cambridge University Press.

Gabay, J. (2000) *Teach Yourself Copywriting*, 2nd edn, London: Hodder & Stoughton.

Galtung, J. and Ruge, M. Holmboe (1965) 'The Structure of Foreign News: The Presentation of the Congo, Cuba and Cyprus Crises in Four Norwegian Newspapers', *Journal of Peace Research*, 2, 64–91.

Garrand, T. (2001) *Writing for Multimedia and the Web*, 2nd edn, Boston, MA: Focal Press.

Gettins, D. (2006) *How to Write Great Copy: Learn the Unwritten Rules of Copywriting*, 2nd edn, London: Kogan Page.

Goddard, A. (2002) *The Language of Advertising: Written Texts*, London: Routledge.

Gorton, K. (2006) 'A Sentimental Journey: Television, Meaning and Emotion' in *Journal of British Cinema and Television*, 3(1), 72–81.

Gray, B. (1998) 'The Intimate Moment: The Art of Interviewing' in Michael Tobias (ed.) *The Search for Reality: The Art of Documentary Filmmaking*, California: Michael Wiese, pp. 87–95.

Green, A. (1999) *Creativity in Public Relations*, London: Kogan Page.

Gregory, A. (2000) *Planning and Managing a Public Relations Campaign: A Step-By-Step Guide*, London: Kogan Page.

Grodal, T. (1997) *Moving Pictures: A New Theory of Film Genres, Feelings, and Cognition*, Oxford: Oxford University Press.

Grunig, J. and Hunt, T. (1984) *Managing Public Relations*, Toronto: Holt, Rinehart & Winston.

Gulino, P.J. (2004) *Screenwriting: The Sequence Approach*, New York: Continuum.

Hall, C. (1999) *Writing Features and Interviews*, 2nd edn, Oxford: How To Books.

Hamilton, N. (2005) *Uncovering the Secrets of Magazine Writing: A Step by Step Guide to Writing to Writing Creative Non-Fiction for Print*, Boston, MA: Allyn & Bacon.

Hammerich, I. and Harrison, C. (2001) *Developing Online Content: The Principles of Writing and Editing for the Web*, Chichester: Wiley & Sons.

Hampe, B. (1997) *Making Documentary Films and Reality Videos: A Practical Guide to Planning, Filming and Editing Documentaries of Real Events*, New York: Henry Holt & Company.

Harris, G. and Sparks, D. (1997) *Practical Newspaper Writing*, 3rd edn, Oxford: Focal Press.

Harrower, T. (2007) *Inside Reporting: A Practical Guide to the Craft of Journalism*, New York: McGraw-Hill.

Hay, V. (1990) *The Essential Feature: Writing for Magazines and Newspapers*, Columbia: Columbia University Press.

Hennessy, B. (2006) *Writing Feature Articles*, 4th edn, Oxford: Focal Press.

Hiltunen, Ari (2002) *Aristotle in Hollywood: The Anatomy of Successful Storytelling*, Bristol: Intellect.

Hockley, L. (2007) *Frames of Mind: A Post-Jungian Look at Cinema, Television and Technology*, Bristol: Intellect.

Holtz, S. (1999) *Writing for the Wired World: The Communicator's Guide to Effective Online Content*, California: IABC.

Horton, J.L. (2001) *Online Public Relations: A Handbook for Practitioners*, New York: Quorum Books.

Howard, D. (2004) *How To Build a Great Screenplay*, London: Souvenir Press.

Hudson, G. and Rowlands, S. (2007) *The Broadcast Journalism Handbook*, Harlow: Pearson Longman.

Indick, W. (2004) *Psychology for Screenwriters: Building Conflict in Your Script*, California: Michael Wiese.

Jarl, S. (1998) 'A Manifest on the Subject of Documentaries' in Michael Tobias (ed.) *The Search for Reality: The Art of Documentary Filmmaking*, California: Michael Wiese, pp. 149–154.

Keeble, R. (1994) *The Newspapers Handbook*, London: Routledge.

Kelleher, T. (2006) *Public Relations Online: Lasting Concepts for Changing Media*, Thousand Oaks, CA: Sage Publications.

Kilborn, R. and Izod, J. (1997) *An Introduction to Television Documentary: Confronting Reality*, Manchester: Manchester University Press.

Kilian, C. (1999) *Writing for the Web*, Bellingham, WA: Self-Counsel Press.

Kochberg, S. (ed.) *Introduction to Documentary Production: A Guide for Media Students*, London: Wallflower.

Kopple, B. (2005) 'Foreword' in Megan Cunningham (ed.) *The Art of the Documentary*, California: New Rides, pp. viii–ix.

Kriwaczek, P. (1997) *Documentary for the Small Screen*, Oxford: Focal Press.

Langer, J. (1998) *Tabloid Television: Popular Journalism and the 'Other News'*, London: Routledge.

Maras, S. (2008) *Screenwriting: History, Theory and Practice*, London: Wallflower.

Marsen, S. (2006) *Communication Studies*, Basingstoke: Palgrave Macmillan.

McCombs, M. (1998) 'News Influence on our Pictures of the World' in Roger Dickinson, Ramaswami Harindranath and Olga Linneé (eds.) *Approaches to Audiences: A Reader*, London: Arnold, pp. 25–35.

McKane, A. (2006) *News Writing*, London: Sage Publications.

McKay, J. (2006) *The Magazines Handbook*, 2nd edn, London: Routledge.

McKee, R. (1999) *Story: Substance, Structure, Style, and the Principles of Screenwriting*, London: Methuen.

McLoughlin, L. (2000) *The Language of Magazines*, London: Routledge.

McNair, B. (2006) *Cultural Chaos: Journalism, News and Power in a Globalised World*, London: Routledge.

Meeske, M. (2003) *Copywriting for the Electronic Media: A Practical Guide*, 4th edn, London: Thomson Wadsworth.

Mill, D. (2005) *Content Is King: Writing and Editing Online*, Oxford: Elsevier Butterworth-Heinemann.

Miller, G.R. (1989) 'Persuasion and Public Relations: Two "Ps" in a Pod' in Carl H. Botan and Vincent Hazleton Jr. (eds) *Public Relations Theory*, Hillsdale, NJ: Lawrence Erlbaum, pp. 45–66.

Morgan, V. (2008) *Practising Videojournalism*, London: Routledge.

Moritz, C. (2001) *Scriptwriting for the Screen*, London: Routledge.

Neale, D. (2006) 'Writing What You Come to Know' in Linda Anderson (ed.) *Creative Writing: A Workbook with Readings*, London: Routledge, pp. 56–68.

Pape, S. and Featherstone, S. (2005) *Newspaper Journalism: A Practical Introduction*, London: Sage Publications.

Pape, S. and Featherstone, S. (2006) *Feature Writing: A Practical Introduction*, London: Sage Publications.

Phillips, D. (2002) *Online Public Relations: A Handbook for Practitioners*, London: Kogan Page.

Phillips, D. and Young, P. (2009) *Online Public Relations: A Practical Guide to Developing an Online Strategy in the World of Social Media*, London: Kogan Page.

Rabiger, M. (2004) *Directing the Documentary*, 4th edn, Oxford: Focal Press.

Ramet, A. (2007) *Writing for Magazines: How to Get your Work Published in Local Newspapers and Magazines*, Oxford: How To Books.

Randall, D. (2000) *The Universal Journalist*, 2nd edn, London: Pluto.

Rosen, E. (2000) *Net Words: Creating High-Impact Online Copy*, London: McGraw-Hill.

Rosenthal, A. (1996) *Writing, Directing, and Producing Documentary Films and Videos*, revised edn, Illinois: Southern Illinois University Press.

Roshco, B. (1999) 'Newsmaking' in Howard Tumber (ed.) *News: A Reader*, Oxford: Oxford University Press, pp. 32–36.

Ruberg, M. (2005) *Writer's Digest Handbook of Magazine Article Writing*, 2nd edn, London: Writer's Digest Books.

Ryan, M. (2004) *Narrative Across Media: The Languages of Storytelling*, Lincoln: University of Nebraska Press.

Schultz, B. (2002) *Sports Broadcasting*, Boston, MA: Focal Press.

Seger, L. (1994) *Making a Good Script Great*, 2nd edn, California: Samuel French.

Semenik, R. (2002) *Promotion and Integrated Marketing*, London: South-Western.

Shannon, C. and Weaver, W. (1949) *The Mathematical Theory of Communication*, Urbana: University of Illinois Press.

Smith, M. (1995) *Engaging Characters: Fiction, Emotion, and the Cinema*, Oxford: Oxford University Press.

Smith, R.D. (2008) *Becoming a Public Relations Writer: A Writing Process Workbook for the Profession*, 3rd edn, London: Routledge.

Sparks, C. (1999) 'The Press' in Jane Stokes and Reading (eds) *The Media in Britain: Current Debates and Developments*, Basingstoke: Macmillan, pp. 41–60.

Strunk, W. and White, E.B. (1999) *The Elements of Style*, 4th edn, Harlow: Longman.

Tobias, M. (ed.) *The Search for Reality: The Art of Documentary Filmmaking*, California: Michael Wiese.

Treadwell, D. and Treadwell J.B. (2005) *Public Relations Writing: Principles in Practice*, 2nd edn, Thousand Oaks, CA: Sage Publications.

Truby, J. (2007) *The Anatomy of Story: 22 Steps to Becoming a Master Storyteller*, New York: Faber & Faber.

Veloso, M. (2004) *Web Copy That Sells: The Revolutionary Formula For Creating Killer Copy Every Time*, New York: Amacom.

Vogler, C. (1999) *The Writer's Journey: Mythic Structure for Storytellers and Screenwriters*, 2nd edn, London: Pan Books.

Vorvoreanu, M. (2008) *Website Public Relations: How Corporations Build and Maintain Relationships Online*, New York: Cambria Press.

Waldeback, Z. (2006) 'The Purpose of Structure' in *ScriptWriter Magazine*, 29, pp. 20–25.

Watson, J. (1998) *Media Communication: An Introduction to Theory and Process*, Basingstoke: Macmillan.

Watson, J. and Hill, A. (2007) *Dictionary of Media and Communication Studies*, 7th edn, London: Hodder Arnold.

Welsh, T., Greenwood, W., and Banks, D., (2005) *McNae's Essential Law for Journalists*, Oxford: Oxford University Press.

White, H. (1994) *How to Produce Effective TV Commercials*, 3rd edn, New York: McGraw-Hill.

Wilcox, D. (2005) *Public Relations Writing and Media Techniques,* 5th edn, Boston, MA: Pearson Education.

Wilkinson, J.S., Grant, A.E. and Fisher, D.J. (2009) *Principles of Convergent Journalism*, New York: Oxford University Press.

Wolper, P.L. (1998) 'The Documentary: Entertain and Inform, Not Just Inform' in Michael Tobias (ed.) *The Search for Reality: The Art of Documentary Filmmaking*, Studio City, CA: pp. 285–287.

Young, J. (2002) 'Structure and Script' in Searle Kochberg (ed.) *Introduction to Documentary Production: A Guide for Media Students*, London: Wallflower, pp. 5–27.

Index

Note: **bold type** denotes extended discussion or a term highlighted in the text.